Identity, Neoliberalism

In recent years there has been growing concern over the pervasive disparities in academic achievement that are highly influenced by ethnicity, class and gender. Specifically, within the neoliberal policy rhetoric, there has been concern over underachievement of working-class young males, specifically white working-class boys in the United Kingdom. The historic persistence of this pattern, and the ominous implication of these trends on the long-term life chances of white working-class boys, has led to a growing chorus that something must be done to intervene.

This book provides an in-depth sociological study exploring the subjectivities within the neoliberal ideology of the school environment, in order to expand our understanding of white working-class disengagement with education. The chapters discuss how white working-class boys in three educational sites enact social and learner identities, focusing on the practices of 'meaning-making' and 'identity work' that the boys experienced, and the disjunctures and commonalities between them. The book presents an analysis of the varying tensions influencing the identity of each boy and the consequences of these pressures on their engagement with education.

Drawing on Bourdieu's theoretical tools and a model of egalitarian habitus, *Identity, Neoliberalism and Aspiration: Educating white working-class boys* will be of interest to academics, researchers and postgraduate students in the field of sociology of education, and those from related disciplines studying class and gender.

Garth Stahl is Lecturer in Literacy Education and Sociology in the School of Education, University of South Australia, Australia.

Routledge Research in Educational Equality and Diversity

Identity, Neoliberalism and Aspiration

Educating white working-class boys

Garth Stahl

Routledge
Taylor & Francis Group

LONDON AND NEW YORK

First published 2015
by Routledge
2 Park Square, Milton Park, Abingdon, Oxfordshire OX14 4RN

and by Routledge
711 Third Avenue, New York, NY 10017

First issued in paperback 2016

Routledge is an imprint of the Taylor & Francis Group, an informa business

British Library Cataloguing in Publication Data
A catalogue record for this book is available from the British Library

Library of Congress Cataloging-in-Publication Data
Stahl, Garth.
Identity, neoliberalism and aspiration : educating white working-class boys / Garth Stahl. — (Routledge research in educational equality and diversity)
Includes bibliographical references and index.
1. Boys—Education. 2. Children with social disabilities—Education.
3. Working class whites—Education. 4. Academic achievement.
5. Educational sociology. I. Title.
LC1390.S78 2015
371.8211—dc23
2014029395

ISBN 13: 978-1-138-29432-5 (pbk)
ISBN 13: 978-1-138-02587-5 (hbk)

Typeset in Galliard
by FiSH Books Ltd, Enfield

To my parents and grandparents for their support.

Contents

Figures and tables

Figures

Tables

Acknowledgements

My first debt of gratitude is to Diane Reay. As a mentor, she has provided constant (and reassuring) encouragement for the project with much patience and enthusiasm.

The collegial atmosphere at the University of Cambridge, Faculty of Education, has been a source of much intellectual encouragement. There I would like to thank (in no particular order): Sophie Wee, Niki Sol, Derron Wallace, Madeleine Brens, Alka Sehgal-Cuthbert, Nathanael Arnott-Davies, Chrysogonus Siddha Malilang and Quinton Lampkin.

I also thank those who have helped with specific enquiries or advice during my research: Hilary Cremin, Pamela Burnard, Madeleine Arnot, Jo-Ann Dillabough, Andrew Wilkins (Roehampton), Michael Reece (Indiana University), Marcus Weaver Hightower (University of North Dakota), Michael Ward (University of Cardiff), Steph Dimond (University of Cambridge), Nicola Ingram (University of Bath), Rosie Burt-Perkins (University of Cambridge), Allyson Eamer (University of Ontario), Cynthia Miller-Idriss (New York University), Marcel Suarez-Orozco (New York University), Bev Skeggs (Goldsmiths), Sadia Habib (Goldsmiths) Laura Plummer (Indiana University), Laura Stachowski (Indiana University), Prudence Carter (Stanford University), Sam Baars (University of Manchester), Joseph Nelson (New York University), Pere Ayling (University Campus Suffolk) and Andrew Peterson (University of South Australia).

Many friends have at different times provided invaluable support and encouragement: Anna Semmens, Amber Hitchman, Ben Hodges, Carol Williams, Miriam McKillop, Paul Brown, Shafia Choudury, Paul Ashton, Stephanie Dimond, Tamara Hayford, Maria Hegstad, Adam McWilliams, Dan Burns, Maxine Gordon, Hazeley Pascoe, Jason Gugliotti, Jessica Magnotta, Josephine Molyneux, Justin Hulbert, Kimberly Davis, Lynn Wood, Donato Esposito, Louis De Jager, Stefan Caddy-Retalic, Todd Catford and Margaret Sweet-Hoffman.

Julius Milo Kelly has been a constant and faithful supporter throughout. I can never fully express my gratitude for his boundless support, belief (and cooking).

Finally, a special thanks, also, to the school sites and – most importantly – the boys themselves who gave up their time voluntarily over the course of many months.

Introduction

When I first began working professionally in England in November 2002, two key experiences defined my introduction to the white working-class: first, teaching English at a failing school in Essex with a low level of teaching and learning; second, my weekly volunteer work with 'at risk' children through the Borough of Barking and Dagenham, which provided stability in the evenings for excluded students. These two experiences with the 'roughs and toughs' (Reay, 2004) taught me important first-hand lessons about disengagement, cultural deprivation and the role of education in British society. As an educator and mentor, I experienced competing demands, particularly when teaching boys whom I found were challenging to motivate. Throughout my professional and academic experience, I have been fortunate enough to approach white working-class boys in a variety of different roles and contexts either as a volunteer, a teacher, an administrator, a friend or a resource; each role has increased my understanding of their identity construction and relationship to education.

White working-class boys engage with learner identities, specific conceptualisations the children have of themselves as learners, which are regulated by the many overlapping and competing fields. Within the formal curriculum, the participants of the study experienced a variety of discursive regimes where 'pedagogy was constituting not only subject positions in some abstract sense but deeply felt subjectivities' (Whelen, 2011: 9). This research explores identity within a complex interplay between the fields of the school, the family, and the community. In the investigation of experiences, identities and aspirations, close attention was paid to the multifaceted nature of youth narrations (Dillabough and Kennelly, 2010) and how identity is enacted 'when learners' culturally inherited ways of knowing do not match those privileged in school curriculum' (Zipin, 2009: 317). Identity is always residual, refracted, emergent and contested.

The academic engagement and learner identities of the boys are interrelated and mutually constituted during a time of high-stakes education, where the rhetoric of 'learning equals earning' is pervasive (Brown, 2013: 685). How working-class boys construct and express their masculine, ethnic and classed identities in relation to conceptions of hegemonic masculinity, their schooling experience and the perceived 'successful' learner was a key focus (Mac an Ghaill, 1994, 2000; Renold, 2004; Connell, 2005; Francis, 2006). Drawing upon unequal 'repertoires of social and cultural resources' (Wexler, 1992: 7) it has become increasingly difficult for these young males to establish a so-called 'good life' within an era of high neoliberalism (Stahl, 2012). As potent sites of identity construction, schools and communities are spaces of contestation. Furthermore, the current neoliberal discourse, which prioritises a view of aspirations that is competitive, economic and status-based, shapes the subjectivities of these young males. The research shows how 'young people negotiate their own meanings, lives and futures, in the context of specific sociocultural, political and economic circumstances' (Hattam and Smyth, 2003: 381) and also how these contexts are often reductive, misguided and counterproductive.

Today's urban youth construct their identities in 'local/global contexts' (McLeod, 2009) and the participants of this study are 'working out their "place" and "legitimacy" within urban arrangements that are, at their best, residual spaces of surplus meaning pointing to previous forms of intense working-class resilience' (Dillabough and Kennelly, 2010: 105). The data collection for this study occurred immediately following the financial crisis of 2007–2008 and during the July 2011 riots in London, Manchester and Birmingham. Both events shaped discourses around economic austerity, gangs, benefit culture and anti-social behaviour in regards to young males who exist in urban spaces and are continually pathologised as '"unfit" and undesirable' (Archer et al., 2010) or 'rubbish' and 'shit' (Lucey and Reay, 2002). Therefore, the intermeshings of 'place', 'legitimacy' and 'respectability' are considered to be crucial components of both social and learner identity construction.

This study sought to access the complexities surrounding 'identity work' (Wexler, 1992). The term 'identity work', first introduced by Snow and Anderson (1987) and adopted later by Wexler (1992), is where the concept of identity is understood to be a 'conceptual bridge' (p. 1338) that links the individual with society. Identity is a complex value-laden process in which young people are 'working on, generating, and maintaining a sense of meaning and self-worth at an interface between their inner life and the social context in which they live. Identity is the manifestation of this dynamic, never-ending negotiation' (Hattam and Smyth, 2003: 382).

With this investigation of white working-class boys we see the tangled 'relationship between school structures and practises, students' biographical identities, and educational inequalities' (Youdell, 2004: 409). Similar to other recent work on youth, class and educational experience (Nayak, 2003; Archer et al., 2010), this research worked with the concept of social class as (re)formed through identities and historic cultural practices rather than a simple reflection of economic capital and occupations. Therefore, the primary purpose was to research the processes regarding how white working-class boys are 'socially positioned and discursively constituted subjects within educational sites' (Burke, 2007: 412). Simultaneously, this work considers the influence of different modalities of youth self-representation(s) within the wider pathologisation of white working-class culture (Reay, 2009). Beyond the schooling environment, working-class boys are exposed to and influenced by the social processes surrounding production and consumption of cultural capital (Bourdieu, 2004), and the research synthesises macro and micro approaches to enhance our understanding of the shifting nature of identities (Reay, 2010: 279).

Researching aspiration and identity

The process of 'aspiring' (and performing aspirations) is a 'relational, felt, embodied process, replete with classed desires and fantasies, defences and aversions, feelings of fear, shame and guilt, excitement and desire' (Allen, 2013b). Aspiration is highly influenced by dominant neoliberal ideologies which shapes schools as discourse communities where aspiration is rendered an 'unequivocal good' (Allen, 2013a: 2). Ball and Olmedo (2012: 88) argue:

> The apparatuses of neoliberalism are seductive, enthralling, and overbearingly necessary. It is a 'new' moral system that subverts and re-orients us to its truths and ends. It makes us responsible for our performance and for the performance of others. We are burdened with the responsibility to perform, and if we do not we are in danger of being seen as irresponsible.

As these neoliberal institutions shape and reshape learner identities, it is essential to address how working-class – or working-poor – students construct value within constraints and wider societal depictions and expectations (Stahl, 2012, 2014). Existing within this new moral system, subjectivities are in a 'process of becoming', where competing and contrasting definitions are resisted, contested, strategised, adopted and subverted.

Adopting a culturalist approach to examine identity composition, the research shows how the subjectivities of white working-class boys in South London are deeply relational and how their 'phenomenologies of meaning' are influenced daily by a complex dialectic of various milieus (Dillabough and Kennelly, 2010: 42–43). Therefore, 'low aspiration' and 'dis-engagement' are interconnected with a range of factors, including social, structural and economic. Through a culturalist approach, aspirations are theorised as 'subjective and intersubjective' processes 'constituted by multiple social-cultural resources, including policy and populist ideologics but also family and community histories and the lived-cultural agency of people in the present' (Zipin et al., 2013: 1–2). Within these neoliberal times, Brown (2013:

687) argues there is a shift toward an 'ideology of performocracy' where performativity is 'based on a market ideology where it is a winning performance that counts' and the daily goal is to '"achieve" a competitive advantage ... in the competition for credentials, jobs or income'. Therefore, the research presented here seeks to explore how neo-liberal processes fostered in the school dynamics (Davies and Bansel, 2007; Wilkins, 2011), and wider societal discourses, influence subjectivities of white working-class boys. The white working-class boys in this study negotiate various competing fields in a 'balancing act' that can render their social or learner identities as either 'fixed'[1] or 'fluid'.

The research intends to develop a nuanced view of white working-class male identity and problematises some of the barriers that are commonly (and crudely) associated with white working-class culture in educational contexts, such as lack of aspiration, parental attitudes toward school, insufficient work ethic and poor attendance (Evans, 2006; Demie and Lewis, 2010). We must consider how high levels of so-called 'disaffection' towards education in white working-class communities actually represent certain struggles to negotiate a 'care of the self' (Ball and Olmedo, 2012), out of limited repertoires of social and cultural resources within these institutions. How white working-class boys make sense of the resounding aspiration rhetoric in their school contexts and how it shapes their subjectivities (Gillborn and Kirton, 2000; McLeod, 2009) is a central focus in this research agenda. Such identity negotiations may result either in them 'finding' or 'losing' certain traditional working-class identities (Reay, 2001; Skeggs, 2004; Archer and Hutchings, 2010). Wexler (1992: 7) argues that the process of 'becoming somebody' is engrained within the daily schooling practices, where students 'wanted to be somebody, a real and presentable self, and one anchored in the verifying eyes of the friends whom they came to school to meet'. For a significant segment of white working-class boys, it is arguably the fragile and elusive successful learner identity that may remain their greatest barrier to learning and academic achievement.

The importance of context in understanding the white working-class boy phenomenon

Despite a plethora of policy rhetoric aimed to address inequality, the UK remains low in the international rankings of social mobility when compared to other advanced nations (Blanden and Machin, 2007). Given this disparity, England has one of the 'highest associations of social class with education performance in the OECD' (Cassen and Kingdon, 2007: 1). The reasons for social immobility in the UK are primarily economic. While the second half of the twentieth century saw a rise of middle-class employment culminating with a boom in the Thatcher years, since then the growth in middle-class occupations has stalled considerably. According to the Trades Union Congress

(TUC), in 2001 low-paid service sector work made up 42 per cent of labour-market occupations, while 'high skill' white-collar work made up less than 40 per cent, and that percentage is set to fall in the wake of severe austerity measures in the public sector (Blanchflower, 2012). The data from the Office for National Statistics (2012) show there is no longer precious room for all those who aspire to professional and managerial jobs, despite policy documents that falsely state 'the demand for skilled workers is currently outstripping supply, which suggests that there is "room at the top" for highly qualified graduates from all backgrounds' (Cabinet Office, 2011: 11).

The lack of social mobility is ironic in the light of the Michael Gove-era mantra of education proclaimed as a 'cure-all' to undesirable conditions. While policies of 'raising aspiration' are prevalent, they often 'increase rather than attenuate obstacles by operating ideologically to simplify the complexities and mute the severities of historic conditions in which young people in underclass and working-middle-class positions struggle to imagine and pursue futures' (Zipin *et al.*, 2013: 2). In the discourse of contemporary UK politics, 'Social mobility has a totemic role in UK society not just figuring powerfully in the strategic policies of our political elites but also capturing the popular imaginary' (Reay, 2013: 664). Within policy it is commonly pontificated that low rates of post-16 participation in education or training, particularly for working-class and some minority ethnic young people, is the result of a 'poverty of aspirations'. However, recent policy initiatives, such as the Coalition government's *Opening Doors, Breaking Barriers: A Strategy for Social Mobility* (Cabinet Office, 2011), which was devised to increase mobility, actually cut financial support to families from poorer backgrounds and trebled university tuition fees.

The rhetoric of aspiration continues to be the priority on both sides of the political divide. In November 2010, Secretary of State for Education Michael Gove declared that he wanted the UK to become an 'aspiration nation' (Richardson, 2010). Andy Burnham, shadow education secretary at the time, reflected this desire at the other end of the political spectrum by addressing the Labour Party conference with a plea for 'aspiration, aspiration, aspiration' (Vasagar, 2011). In terms of education, aspiration remains a clear focus of the Coalition government's approach and, increasingly, it has become the responsibility of the school to raise aspiration in order to 'challenge low aspirations and expectations, dispelling the myth that those from poorer backgrounds cannot aim for top universities and professional careers' (Cabinet Office, 2011: 35). Michael Gove aimed to create schools that were 'engines of social mobility providing every child with the knowledge, skills and aspirations they need to fulfil their potential' (Cabinet Office, 2011: 36). In fact, a recent White Paper entitled *The Importance of Teaching* (Department of Education, 2010: 29) asserts, 'Good teachers instil an ethos where aspiration is the best reason for children to avoid harmful behaviour', equating aspiration with a simple antidote to complex problems. Within these policy documents, low achievement and anti-social behaviour is often considered a natural link to what is widely considered a lack of 'aspirations' among working-class males.

Furthermore, Brown (2013: 683) argues, 'The lack of capacity within the economy to deliver on the opportunity bargain has led to labour-market crowding, along with wider congestion problems, as people seek to use the education system to "stand out from the crowd"'. The result is what Brown calls 'social congestion', where the main consequence is an 'opportunity trap' where upper-class and upper-middle-class families enact similar strategies to ensure a positional advantage over others because labour-market opportunities have failed to keep pace not only with increased participation in education but also with the implications of an expanded middle class. As everyone adopts the same strategies to get ahead, there is often a contribution 'to the very congestion people are trying to avoid' and subsequently schools, universities and employers all raise entry requirements within intensified positional competition (cf. Brown, 2013, for a more detailed analysis). In the severe competition for qualifications, the main consequence of such 'massification' of education is it generates too many individuals 'with educational credentials for jobs which become correspondingly more competitive and difficult to secure, including high-level knowledge economy jobs that are redistributing globally to labor markets with lower wage expectations' (Zipin et al., 2013: 9).

White working-class boys exist in a larger field of white working-class disengagement with education (Gillborn and Kirton, 2000; Evans, 2006, 2007), including highly polarised white British attainment at GCSE (General Certificate of Secondary Education) and lack of participation in post-compulsory education (Cassen and Kinddon, 2007; Platt, 2007; Strand, 2008, 2014). While the white working-class underachievement remains a cause for concern, it must be noted that across the UK 'nearly half of young people still do not achieve five good GCSEs at school. More still do not reach that standard in English and mathematics. And one in twenty leaves without a single GCSE pass' (Department for Education and Skills, 2003: 6). It has been widely documented that the reasons for this appalling high level of persistent disparity are incredibly complex and symptomatic of entrenched wider issues in the UK education sector (cf. MacBeath, 2009; Francis and Wong, 2013).

On the school level, the current A–C exam economy confounds social justice initiatives and increases 'difference' (Raphael Reed, 1998). Furthermore, it results in what Gillborn and Youdell (2000) have termed bureaucratic, institutional and classroom 'educational triage', with some students being saved while many students are written off from the moment they enter the school building.[2] Within an era of neoliberalism, schools have found it easier and advantageous to separate out students who struggle with learning and who are poorly equipped to combine an identity of academic success with a solid, respectable, white working-class identity (cf. Ball and Reay, 1998; Reay, 1998b, 2010; Reay and Wiliam, 1999; Boaler *et al.*, 2000; Gillborn and Kirton, 2000). The majority of white working-class boys learn in inadequate environments that 'ration education' and thus shape what is possible (Gillborn and Youdell, 2000). These boys, and their classmates, were clearly often subject to the 'soft bigotry of low expectations' (Dumenden, 2013).

Structure and organisation

The book is organised into two main sections. The first section, Part I, sets out the current educational policy debates in relation to white working-class boys, providing an overview of the relevant theoretical literature. Chapter 1 discusses white working-class boys as a historic phenomenon and also a problematic construct. The historical account is discussed alongside the 'boys in crisis' debates and how the current educational contexts are a contributing factor, before highlighting the major theoretical frameworks concerning class, gender and ethnic identity construction in sociology of education. Chapter 2 establishes a Bourdieusian framework, drawing upon the main theoretical tools before accounting for how these tools are applied to an exploration of aspiration and identity. There exists no singular reading of Bourdieu but rather a plethora of methods for employing his 'theory into action', which result in gaps, overlaps, divisions and, of course, disputes. Chapter 3 sets forth an argument for an egalitarian habitus as a counter-habitus to the neoliberal rhetoric in schooling. Egalitarianism allows for an analysis of positional suffering, including the affective dimensions of class (envy/deference, contempt/pity, shame/pride), and serves as a theoretical lens to analyse the empirical data in Part II.

The second section, Part II, is a detailed examination of the identity issues and tensions white working-class boys encounter in their schooling and how egalitarian habitus functions as a process of amelioration. Chapter 4 focuses on how the boys define social class and their own social class identifications, where the boys draw upon an egalitarian habitus in order to dodge labels, judgements and distinctions. Chapter 5 examines how the boys' reflexive knowledge of social class contributes to their engagement with their education and also how their aspirations are constituted. Chapter 6 shows the nuanced identity work of boys in the social field, specifically in regards to how they reaffirm and reconstitute their sense of selves through processes of 'othering' boys who exhibit behaviour they consider to be non-normative and inauthentic. Chapter 7 discusses the boys' aspirations and their ambivalence toward certain career trajectories and how their conceptions of power become a determining factor in how their aspirations are shaped. In conclusion, Chapter 8 examines the implications for policy and practice and sets forth recommendations for future research.

Notes

1   While I appreciate that is contentious to consider identity as 'fixed', I believe certain identities can become fixed in certain fields and that education is a field saturated with labels that render certain identities as fixed.

2   Young (1971: 40) discusses courses in '"low status" knowledge areas, and restricting their availability to those who have already "failed in terms of academic definitions of knowledge"' and that these failures are perceived as 'individual failures, either of motivation, ability or circumstances, and not failures of the academic system itself'. Furthermore, within education some courses 'deny pupils access to the kinds of knowledge associated with rewards, prestige and power in our society' (Young, 1971: 40).

References

Allen, K. (2013a) 'Blair's children': Young women as 'aspirational subjects' in the psychic landscape of class. *Sociological Review*, 61(4), 1–20.

Allen, K. (2013b) Coalition policy and 'aspiration raising' in a psychic landscape of class. *Journal of Youth Studies Conference*. Glasgow University.

Archer, L. and Hutchings, M. (2010) 'Bettering yourself'? Discourse of risk, cost and benefit in ethnically diverse, young, working-class, non-participants' constructions of higher education. *British Journal of Sociology of Education*, 21(4), 555–574.

Archer, L., Hollingworth, S. and Mendick, H. (2010) *Urban youth and schooling: The experiences and identities of educationally 'at risk' young people*. Berkshire: Open University Press.

Ball, S. J. and Olmedo, A. (2012) Care of the self, resistance, and subjectivity under neoliberal governmentalities. *Critical Studies in Education*, 54(1), 85–96.

Ball, S. J. and Reay, D. (1998) 'Making their minds up': Family dynamics and school choice. *British Educational Research Journal*, 24(4), 431–448.

Blanchflower, D. (2012) Let's call up Vince to get us out of this mess. *The Independent*, 30 July, 45.

Blanden, J. and Machin, S. (2007) *Recent changes in intergenerational mobility in Britain*. London: Centre for Economic Performance at LSE.

Boaler, J., Wiliam, D. and Brown, M. (2000) Students' experiences of ability grouping: Disaffection, polarisation, and the construction of failure. *British Educational Research Journal*, 26(5), 631–648.

Bourdieu, P. (2004) The forms of capital. In S. Ball (ed.), *The RoutledgeFalmer reader in sociology of education* (pp. 46–58). London: RoutledgeFalmer.

Brown, P. (2013) Education, opportunity, and the prospects for social mobility. *British Journal of Sociology of Education*, 34(5–6), 678–700.

Burke, P. (2007) Men accessing education: Masculinities, identifications and widening participation. *British Journal of Sociology of Education*, 28(4), 411–424.

Cabinet Office (2011) *Opening doors, breaking barriers: A strategy for social mobility*. London: The Cabinet Office, Her Majesty's Government.

Cassen, R. and Kingdon, G. (2007) *Tackling low educational achievement*. York: Joseph Rowntree Foundation.

Connell, R. W. (2005) *Masculinities*. Cambridge: Polity.

Davies, B. and Bansel, P. (2007) Neoliberalism and education. *International Journal of Qualitative Studies in Education*, 20(3), 247–256.

Demie, F. and Lewis, K. (2010) White working class achievement: An ethnographic study of barriers to learning in schools. *Educational Studies*, 33(2), 1–20.

Department for Education (2010) *The importance of teaching: The schools white paper 2010.* London: Author, 24 November.

Department for Education and Skills (2003) *14–19: Opportunity and excellence.* London: Author.

Dillabough, J.A. and Kennelly, J. (2010) *Lost youth in a global city: Class, culture and the urban imaginary.* New York: Routledge.

Dumenden, I. (2013) The soft bigotry of low expectations: The refugee student and mainstream schooling. (Doctoral Dissertation). La Trobe University, Melbourne. Retrieved from http://hdl.handle.net/1959.9/200217

Evans, G. (2006) *Educational failure and working class white children in Britain.* Palgrave: Macmillan.

Evans, G. (2007) *White Working Class Education Failure.* Book Launch: White Working Class Education Failure, London Metropolitan University.

Francis, B. (2006) Heroes or zeroes? The discursive positioning of 'underachieving boys' in English neo-liberal education policy. *Journal of Education Policy*, 21(2), 187–200.

Francis, B. and Wong, B. (2013) *What is preventing social mobility? A review of the evidence.* Leicester: Association of School and College Leaders.

Gillborn, D. and Kirton, A. (2000) White heat: Racism, under-achievement, and white working-class boys. *Inclusion and Special Educational Needs*, 4(4), 271–288.

Gillborn, D. and Youdell, D. (2000) *Rationing education: Policy, practice, reform and equity.* Buckingham: Open University Press.

Hattam, R. and Smyth, J. (2003) 'Not everyone has a perfect life': Becoming somebody without school. *Pedagogy, Culture and Society*, 11(3), 379–398.

Lucey, H. and Reay, D. (2002) Carrying the beacon of excellence: Social class differentiation and anxiety at a time of transition. *Journal of Education Policy*, 17(3), 321–336.

Mac an Ghaill, M. (1994) *The making of men: Masculinities, sexualities and schooling.* Buckingham: Open University Press.

Mac an Ghaill, M. (2000) The cultural production of English masculinities in late modernity. *Canadian Journal of Education*, 25(2), 88–101.

MacBeath, J. (2009) Border crossings. *Improving Schools*, 12(1), 81–92.

McLeod, J. (2009) Youth studies, comparative inquiry, and the local/global problematic. *Review of Education, Pedagogy, and Cultural Studies*, 31(4), 270–292.

Nayak, A. (2003) 'Boyz to Men': Masculinities, schooling, and labour transitions in de-industrial times. *Educational Review*, 55(2), 147–159.

Office for National Statistics (2012) *Graduates in the Labour Market 2012.* London: Office for National Statistics.

Platt, L. (2007) Making education count: The effects of ethnicity and qualifications on intergenerational social class mobility. *The Sociological Review*, 55(3), 485–508.

Raphael Reed, L. (1998) 'Zero tolerance': Gender performance and school failure. In D. Epstein, J. Elwood, V. Hey and J. Maw (eds), *Failing boys? Issues in gender and achievement* (pp. 56–76). Buckingham: University Press.

Reay, D. (1998a) *Class work: Mothers' involvement in their children's primary schooling.* London: UCL Press, Taylor and Francis Group.

Reay, D. (1998b) Setting the agenda: The growing impact of market forces on pupil grouping in British secondary schooling. *Curriculum Studies*, 30(5), 545–558.

Reay, D. (2001) Finding or losing yourself? Working-class relationships to education. *Journal of Education Policy*, 16(4), 333–346.

Reay, D. (2002) Shaun's story: Troubling discourses on white working-class masculinities. *Gender and Education*, 14(3), 221–234.

Reay, D. (2004) 'Mostly roughs and toughs': Social class, race, and representation in inner city schooling. *Sociology*, 38(5), 1005–1023.

Reay, D. (2009) Making sense of white working class educational underachievement. In K. P. Sveinsson (ed.), *Who cares about the white working class?* (pp. 22–28). London: Runnymede Perspectives.

Reay, D. (2010) Identity-making in schools and classrooms. In M. Wetherall and C. Talpade Mohanty (eds.), *The Sage handbook of identities* (pp. 277–294). Los Angeles: Sage Publications.

Reay, D. (2013) Social mobility, a panacea for austere times: Tales of emperors, frogs, and tadpoles. *British Journal of Sociology of Education*, 34(5–6), 660–677.

Reay, D. and Wiliam, D. (1999) 'I'll be a nothing': Structure, agency, and construction of identity through assessment [1]. *British Educational Research Journal*, 25(3), 343–354.

Renold, E. (2004) 'Other' boys: Negotiating non-hegemonic masculinities in the primary school. *Gender and Education*, 16(2), 247–265.

Richardson, H. (2010) Gove puts focus on traditional school values. *BBC News*, 24 November. Online at: www.bbc.com/news/education-11822208

Skeggs, B. (2004) *Class, self, culture*. London: Routledge.

Snow, D. and Anderson, L. (1987) Identity work among the homeless: The verbal construction and avowel of personal identities. *American Journal of Sociology*, 92(6), 1336–1371.

Stahl, G. (2012) Aspiration and a good life among white working-class boys in London. *Journal of Qualitative and Ethnographic Research*, 7(8–9), 8–19.

Stahl, G. (2014) The affront of the aspiration agenda: White working-class male narratives of 'ordinariness' in neoliberal times. *Masculinities and Social Change*, 3(2): 88–118.

Strand, S. (2008) Educational aspirations in inner city schools. *Educational Studies*, 34(4), 249–267.

Strand, S. (2014) Ethnicity, gender, social class, and achievement gaps at age 16: Intersectionality and 'getting it' for the white working class. *Research Papers in Education*, 29(2), 131–171.

Vasagar, J. (2011) Andy Burnham calls for Ucas-style applications system for apprenticeships. *The Guardian*, 28 September. Online at: www.theguardian.com/politics/2011/sep/28/andy-burnham-ucas-apprenticeships

Wexler, P. (1992) *Becoming somebody: Toward a social psychology of school*. London: The Falmer Press.

Whelen, J. (2011) *Boys and their schooling: The experience of becoming someone else*. New York: Routledge.

Wilkins, A. (2011) Push and pull in the classroom: Competition, gender, and the neoliberal subject. *Gender and Education*, 24(7), 1–17.

Youdell, D. (2004) Engineering school markets, constituting schools, and subjectivating students: The bureaucratic, institutional and classroom dimensions of educational triage. *Journal of Education Policy*, 19(4), 407–431.

Young, M. F. D. (1971) An approach to the study of curricula as socially organized knowledge. In M. F. D. Young (ed.), *Knowledge and control* (pp. 19–46). London: Collier Macmillan.

Zipin, L. (2009) Dark funds of knowledge, deep funds of pedagogy: Exploring boundaries between lifeworlds and schools. *Discourse: Studies in the Cultural Politics of Education*, 30(3), 317–331.

Zipin, L., Sellar, S., Brennan, M. and Gale, T. (2013) Educating for futures in marginalized regions: A sociological framework for rethinking and researching aspirations. *Educational Philosophy and Theory*, 45, 1–20.

Part I

Chapter 1

Working-class student educational experience

An amalgamation of factors

Social well-being depends upon cohesion and solidarity. It implies the existence, not merely of opportunities to ascend, but of a high level of general culture, and a strong sense of common interests, and a diffusion throughout society of a conviction that civilization is not the business of an elite alone, but a common enterprise which is the concern of all. And individual happiness does not only require that men [*sic*] should be free to rise to new positions of comfort and distinction; it also requires that they should be able to lead a life of dignity and culture, whether they rise or not.

(Tawney, 1964: 108)

Considering the extreme disadvantages many students start with, education remains a place where the working-class often feel 'powerlessness and educational worthlessness' (Reay, 2009: 25). Consequently, a significant percentage, mainly boys, 'perceive troublesome, oppositional and resistant behaviour within school as a social good' (Reay, 2009: 27), a necessary exercise in identity construction, and an outlet that elevates their status in their all-powerful peer group. Gilbert and Gilbert (1998: 21) argue 'schools are forced to spend considerable time, energy and resources on managing "bad boys", and on developing programmes and strategies to handle disruptive behaviour – especially for working-class boys'.[1] We must consider how behaviour is 'implicated (promoted, legitimated, recursively generated, etc.) through the structure and dynamics of school practices themselves, with their emphasis on competition and individualism' (Wilkins, 2011: 8). The interplay between social and learner identities, which can become fixed and fluid depending on field and capitals, requires the foundation of group affirmation. Boys' social constructions of masculinity remain extremely fragile and in constant flux (Martino and Pallotta-Chiarolli, 2003).

The interconnectedness between behaviour, identity and attainment starts very early in a child's schooling (Renold, 2001), as does the reductive educational (and deeply classed) processes of categorisation and labelling. From the moment a boy, specifically a working-class boy, enters a school, he is shaped according to his gender, as many 'teachers consistently rate girls higher than boys in deportment, and much of their contact with boys tends to be negative and disciplinary' (Entwisle *et al.*, 2007: 115). More specifically, primary school boys, 'are up to eight times more likely to be identified as having special educational needs than their female classmates' (Bleach, 2000: 5–6). Prior to schooling, research has shown that parents also treat elementary school children of the two sexes differently and expect them to behave differently in school (Entwisle *et al.*, 2007: 115). Childrearing is a process heavily influenced by class (Lareau, 2003) and gender (Nichols *et al.*, 2009; Siraj-Blatchford, 2010). White working-class boys, who exist in a complex web of constraints and hierarchies within schools, acquire working-class behaviours in their primary socialisation (Evans, 2006) that greatly impacts upon the learner and social identities they negotiate in the primary classroom (Hey *et al.*, 1998; Renold, 2001; Swain, 2004, 2006). Their initial socialisation within the family structure can position some working-class boys for failure, as when they enter school they often encounter middle-class teachers[2] who consider their behaviour to be problematic (Lareau, 2003). This can often lead to underperformance, and working-class boys have been documented to show signs of 'disaffection' as early as the age of seven (Noble, 2000). Finn (1989: 131) asserts, 'It is essential that non-participation be recognized in the earliest grade possible and that some form of institutional engagement be provided'. Unfortunately, current educational institutions are largely staffed by teachers and administrators untrained in sociology and psychology (Reay, 2006: 302). Educators today may falsely 'confuse working-class powerlessness with apathy' (Anyon, 2008: 206) in the quest for all-powerful exam results, which leads to pedagogic practices that may fix certain behaviours and identities.

Statistically, white working-class boys continue to under-perform academically and, in terms of aspiration, it has been documented that 'white young people have lower educational aspirations than most other ethnic groups. Similarly, the educational attainment of white boys is failing to improve at the rates of most other ethnic groups' (Communities and Local Government/Department for Children, 2008: 8). Poor whites are the UK's lowest educational underachiever with 31% of white British children entitled to free school meals gaining 'five good GCSEs in 2012, fewer than poor children from any other ethnic group' (*Economist*, 2014, para. 6). As evidenced by the Parliamentary hearing on the *Underperformance of White Working Class Children* in February 2014 (Select Committee on Education, 2014), the phenomenon continues to be a subject of concern and controversial debate. White working-class underachievement was also noted widely in the Office for Standards in Education [OFSTED], Children's Services and Skills (OFSTED, 2014) annual report for the 2012–2013 academic year, where a poverty of low expectations was linked to 'stubbornly low outcomes that show little sign of improvement' (p. 1). Within discussions of white working-class boys, working-class families are often pathologised and blamed for their 'failure' to act responsibly in regards to their education, but such discussions conceal massive structural inequalities and barriers (see Gewirtz, 2001).[3] Rachel Brooks (2002) argues that, since the late 1990s, although widening participation remains a central plank in the UK government's higher education policy,[4] its impact to date in terms of equity appears negligible. Or, as Brown (2013: 682) asserts, 'The result is a "fallacy of fairness" as policies to increase educational standards, including the student premium, or widened access to higher education, have little impact on "relative" mobility'.

The 'crisis of masculinity' debate, post-industrialisation and neoliberalism

In the late twentieth and early twenty-first centuries, many scholars (Fine *et al.*, 1997; Mac an Ghaill, 1994, 1996, 2000; Nayak, 2003a, 2003c, 2006; Weis, 2004) cited the massive societal shifts in economic and gender relations that have resulted in fragmented rites of passage (employment, marriage). Such fragmentation has placed the working-class male in a position of confusion commonly called the 'crisis of masculinity' (Faludi, 1999).[5] Evolving from the moral panic concerning boys' 'underachievement' (Griffin, 2000; Smith, 2003) and, more specifically, underachieving working-class males (Epstein, 1998), debate over 'failing boys' has focused on the complexities associated with the so-called 'crisis of masculinity' (Faludi, 1999) and boys 'underachievement' in schooling (cf. Pittman, 1993; Raphael Reed, 1998). A highly charged context of backlash politics has shaped a particular gender agenda, and in this miscellany we see arguments concerning boys (as a homogenised group) portrayed as victims of discrimination both in schooling and in wider society (Weaver-Hightower, 2003).

As the so-called 'crisis of masculinity' (Faludi, 1999) occurs beyond the classroom, there have also been major pedagogic shifts inside the classroom; school processes have become increasingly neoliberal (league tables, exam boards, a rise in accountability), which exacerbates differences and influences how the learner identities are formed (Francis, 2006; Wilkins 2011). In his analysis of the 'boy turn' in education, Weaver-Hightower (2003) argues that there have been four main strands to the ongoing debate on boys' education: popular-rhetorical, theoretically oriented, practice oriented, and the feminist and pro-feminist. Weaver-Hightower contend that a significant prompt for the 'boy turn' has been 'increasing neoliberal education reforms and the rise of the New Right – the conservative restoration since the 1980s', which is particularly true in England, where neoliberal reforms 'produced an educational choice structure in which schools compete with one another for students' (p. 476). Epstein *et al.* (1999) identified separate discourses used in the popular and academic press to explain boys' educational underperformance: 'poor boys', 'boys will be boys', 'at-risk boys' and 'problem boys'.

While these discourses have framed key debates in gender theory concerning boys, the neoliberal policy drivers ensure that working-class boys are individualised and held accountable for their failure (Francis, 2006: 191). Furthermore, such neoliberal discourses, while denying the existence of any real class distinctions, limit the discursive space in which various forms of working-class masculinity are acceptable.

Griffin (2000: 170) argues that the 'language of crisis, alarm and urgency' is typically followed by a list of school-based remedies that have been posed by policy-makers to counteract male 'underachievement' (for critiques see Skelton, 2003; Weaver-Hightower, 2008).[6] There have been a plethora of policy responses to this perceived 'crisis' but very few take into account the 'very significant ways in which the social construction of gender impacts significantly on curriculum, pedagogical practices and relations with and between students in schools' (Lingard et al., 2009: 9–10). In the policy discourses surrounding boys and schooling, there are 'constant slippages' that reaffirm what are 'natural predispositions or learning behaviours and orientations for both boys and girls' [emphasis in original] (Mills et al., 2007: 15). Drawing on biological essentialist notions and Gardner's multiple intelligences, certain common tropes such as kinaesthetic learning, devaluing inter/intrapersonal skills, preferring explicit/relevant teaching and requiring male role models to learn often tend to dominate. Such strategies fail to acknowledge the culture of masculinity as well as environments and discourses from which boys draw their identity. These initiatives risk homogenising working-class boys into one cohesive group when we must recognise their heterogeneity and diversity in values, attitudes and behaviour and how each are influenced heavily by their school and social contexts.

Our current generation of white working-class boys are poorly equipped with their 'parochial' social perspectives (Nayak, 2006: 82) to cope with the reality of post-industrialism with its new shifting geographies of power, wherein they themselves are arguably becoming an anachronism. In Britain, 'the importance of work, of a job, and a wage are well-known features of working-class masculinity' (Arnot, 1985: 44), and this foundation is endangered in austere times. Winlow (2001: 38), reminiscing on Sunderland, UK, during a time of economic stability and plentiful jobs, writes:

> Men not only expressed their maleness in a form of 'shop floor masculinity' … involving strength, skill autonomy, camaraderie and the ability to provide for his family, but also incorporated other working-class male traits. A lack of respect towards authority and having a 'laff' … existed alongside the desire to be released from the bonds of responsibility.

Undeniably, the historic infrastructures of respectable employment that have been the traditional bases of white male power 'have eroded rapidly' (Weis,

1990: 6). As traditional social structures have disappeared, young men, particularly those from lower and working-class backgrounds, have to negotiate their identity work around rapidly changing discourses of aspiration and power. In place of traditional, respectable, working-class employment we have seen the steady rise of service-level positions that require working-class men to 'learn to serve' (McDowell, 2003) or 'learn to loaf' (Marks, 2003: 87). If white working-class boys are drawing upon employment as part of their identity construction, they are now more likely to draw upon the 'McJob' (Bottero, 2009: 9). These subordinate positions remind us that 'to be dominated by another, or to let an affront go, was and is a process that can strip many working-class males of their image of themselves, and change their image in the eyes of others' (Winlow, 2001: 44). Bourdieu and Wacquant (1992: 82) write:

> For example, to oppose the school system, … is to exclude oneself from the school and increasingly, to lock oneself into one's condition of dominated. On the contrary, to accept assimilation by adopting school culture amounts to being coopted by the institution. The dominated are very often condemned to such dilemmas, to choices between two solutions which, each from a certain standpoint, are equally bad ones …

The 'crisis of masculinity' is arguably felt more harshly by the working-class male: the so-called 'macho lad', whose 'reproduction of working-class masculinity has been ruptured' (Kenway and Kraack, 2004: 107), and who, perhaps, finds it more difficult to adapt, becoming fixed. Today, working-class youth have to contend with a rise in credentialisation alongside a hazy economic future where stable employment is less common (Brown, 2013). The impact of post-industrialism on white working-class masculine identity, specifically how masculinity is constructed in relation to education and the labour market, is framed by efforts to preserve tradition, uncertainty, survivalist mentality, unrealistic expectations and new searches for 'respectability' and 'authenticity' (McDowell, 2003; Nayak, 2003b; Dolby and Dimitriadis, 2004). Considering identity as culturally constructed and deeply contextual, 'class remains an ever-present arbiter – if unacknowledged signifier – structuring young lives' (Nayak, 2006: 825).

As a result of post-industrialisation, working-class males draw on certain historically validated dispositions, such as social cohesion and social solidarity (through a legacy of union action and community involvement) to confirm their gendered, classed and ethnic subjectivities inside and outside of schooling (Mac an Ghaill, 1994: Pye *et al.*, 1996; Stenning, 2005). Social solidarity is often rendered through farouche 'laddish' or 'loutish' behaviours (cf. Francis, 1999) that can be socially empowering but also transgress boundaries of what is considered acceptable in a school context. Laddish behaviour is always a form of social validation and tied to self worth (Jackson,

2002, 2003). For example, Warrington *et al.*'s (2000: 405) study shows that 'individually, or in small groups, boys could see that [laddish] behaviour was not in their long-term interest; in the classroom, situation, however, they often found it difficult to deviate from an accepted group norm'. These practices can conjure labels that work to render certain identities as fixed.

The historical phenomenon of studying white working-class boys

To understand white working-class boys' educational experience, we must consider research that has approached the white working-class boy under-performance phenomenon from a variety of perspectives.[7] Bourdieu (1988) cautions against any division between history and sociology in an ethnographer's hermeneutic practice. Working-class culture cannot be understood 'without reference to the history of the state and to the history of those institutions which function to maintain and reproduce the social relations of capital' (Skeggs, 1992: 185). Due to the relevancy of history, a brief recapitulation of the main historic trends and critical analysis of the theoretical underpinnings will show the long-standing struggles of the working-class in education.

McCulloch's (1998) careful analysis in *Failing the Ordinary Child?* depicts social class and education as interconnected from the inception of mass education. Mass education was not a result of 'liberal' and 'collective ideals' but borne out of a need for social and 'class control' which furthered capitalism (Humphries, 1981: 2). Supporting this assertion, there is very little doubt that the universal education system of segregated social classes was unequal and under-funded with the working-class receiving a poor standard, as can be seen in the Newcastle Commission of 1956 and the Bryce Report of 1895 (McCulloch, 1998). A severe lack of social justice persisted through the 1920s and 1930s, with the Hadow Report (1924) and John Lewis Patton's appeal to sort 'mentals' from 'manuals' at the age of 11, despite politicians like Tawny arguing for a more egalitarian system in which all British citizens had access to gaining a 'synoptic mind' and full societal participation (McCulloch, 1998). Shockingly, when the tripartite education system was modified in 1944, it identified three 'types of intellect and character, ranging from those capable of "abstract thought" to those who could not progress beyond "concrete thought"' (Humphries, 1981: 16). Given this perspective, acts of resistance and rule breaking committed by working-class youth have tended to be viewed as an 'expression of psychological and intellectual deficiency' (Humphries, 1981: 19), rather than being analysed as responses to structural barriers. As a consequence of this systemic disparity, the white working-class educational experience has always historically been an experience of social differentiation, shaped by doubts as to working-class capabilities and the appropriateness of formal education (Brown, 1987).

Since the mid-1970s, social reproduction in schooling has been a vibrant area in the sociology of education with a long-standing fascination with the nihilistic, 'laddish' behaviours deployed by working-class males (Pascoe, 2005; Smith, 2007). Young working-class males, or 'anomalous beasts' (Delamont, 2000: 96) who enact anti-school and anti-social masculinities, have often been portrayed by 'celebratory' accounts of their strength and defiance (Skeggs, 1992). Such studies have used a variety of different theoretical frameworks and approaches. While the socio-psychological perspective has played a significant role in advancing the field (Frosh *et al.*, 2002; Jackson, 2003) alongside geography (McDowell, 2003, 2007), a sociological approach has the capacity to account for gender, ethnicity and class. Within the field of sociology, theorists have used the theoretical frameworks of Bourdieu (Reay 2001, 2002, 2004d; Archer *et al.*, 2007), Bernstein (Aggleton, 1987) and Foucault (Mac an Ghaill, 1994, 1996; Martino, 1999, 2000) to reveal and dissect learner identities in schooling. In analysing identity, we must be aware of the shifting overlaps between learner and social identities as classroom life is a 'cacophony of classed, gendered and raced voices' (Reay, 2010: 281) where students negotiate both their learner and social positioning (Pollard and Filer, 2007).

Historically, Marxism, with its attention to proletariat suffering, was a common structuralist theoretical framework for exploring resistant and rebellious working-class males. Marxist theory arguably serves as an example of producing common theoretical errors. The use of Marxism as a theoretical tool has faced criticisms for neglecting the complexity of lived youth identities (Dillabough and Kennelly, 2010: 32) and equally complex educational experience(s) (McLaren and Scatamburlo-D'Annibale, 2004: 47). In studying identity, Marxist theory has been widely noted to be economist and reductionist (Hall, 1996), accounting very little for agency. The overemphasis on Marxism in the canonical literature on white working-class boys and their education is a product of common theoretical practice in the 1960s and 1970s, which Bourdieu refers to as 'division into theoretical denominations', where much is 'lost in such sterile visions and in the false quarrels they elicit and sustain' (Bourdieu, 1988: 779). The use of these isolated schools of thought, strongly associated with the founding fathers of sociology, should always be considered sceptically when accounting for the individual.

In the debates focused on the relationship between white working-class masculinity, subcultures and educational experience, Willis's (1977) landmark study, *Learning to Labour*, furthered understanding of disaffection as a gendered, classed and ethnic process. The ethnography's central thesis is that it is primarily the working-class 'lad' culture that causes educational failure. Confirmed through the lad culture, the social aspects of physicality/practicality, toughness, collectivism, territoriality/exclusion, hedonism and opposition to authority are the primary influences in the young men's 'meaning-making', as well as their 'positions' and 'relationships' (Willis,

2004: 170). Willis concluded that it was the culture of the lads, and the promise of joining their fathers on the shopfloor, that led to their disaffection from their schooling; education, in their eyes, served no point. Willis (2004: 173) persuasively argues that:

> Through the mediations of the counterschool culture, 'the lads' of *Learning to Labour*, for instance, *penetrate* the individualism and meritocracy of the school with a group logic that shows that certification and testing will never shift the whole working-class, only inflate the currency of qualifications and legitimize middle-class privilege.

Willis remains very critical of the formal education and school processes the 'lads' experience, but that is not his central focus. Whilst the ethnography has had an extensive influence on subsequent research concerning white working-class boys and wider school ethnographies (Arnot, 2004) and arguably gave 'dignity back to the working-class responses to education' (Skeggs, 1992: 181), many critiques of Willis's work exist (McRobbie, 1980; Dolby and Dimitriadis, 2004; McLaren and Scatamburlo-D'Annibale, 2004).

In addition to Marxism, theorists, typically those from a criminology background such as Corrigan (1979), have attempted to use deviance and subcultural theories to understand why working-class males 'buy in' or 'buy out' of education. The key problem of deviancy and subculture theory is that it remains focused on value(s), specifically the subsequent tension between subculture values and mainstream values. As Corrigan (1979) discovered, his participants did not behave in accordance with the values they espoused. Rather, they 'played truant, acted as if they hated education, generally mucked about in school; they did all this in spite of the fact that they, like everyone else in society, felt that education was doing them good' (Corrigan, 1979: 19). While Corrigan feels the study of values is innately problematic, the study of values (and value judgements) and morality, in relation to class, has been well justified and continues to be of utmost important (see Skeggs 2002, 2004a; Sayer, 2005). What is particularly fascinating about Corrigan's work is how his initial focus on values, which imply fixity, changed so dramatically. Corrigan (1979: 46) argued:

> There seemed to be no real acceptance of school values by a lot of the boys at any time. In fact, the whole emphasis on "values" as a guide for action seemed to be wrong. The boys' actions were not created by such consistent things as "values".

While deviance, subculture theory and values, as well as the interplay between them, are intriguing, we cannot deny that larger culture and identity-shifts may be more salient in understanding why boys may (dis)engage with education.

Humphries (1981), primarily following the Marxist hermeneutic and focused on the years 1889 to 1939, examined the question of how closely 'pupil resistance may be related to the nature of deeply rooted class structures and relationships' (p. 31). His work sought to personalise the often 'depersonalizing imagery' of the working-class when impoverished lifestyle, classroom behaviour, 'larking about', family cohesion, street gangs and reformatories are all depicted as 'recalcitrant' actions (Willis, 2004: 176). Such depictions are linked to an often romanticised resistance/rebellion against class control.[8] Through various forms of social control, such as policing, schooling, reformatories, Humphries (1981: 239) emphasises, 'The more general ideological assault upon working-class youth culture that sought to reproduce and reinvigorate capitalist society by instilling habits of regularity and conformity and by inculcating attitudes of dependence on, and deference towards, middle-class adults'. It can be argued that both *Learning to Labour* (1977) and Humphries's *Hooligans or Rebels?* (1981) present a slightly idealised, heroic and anti-intellectual vision of the masculine working-class struggle against education. Both highlight the creative and agentic, if essentially futile, role that the rebellious 'lads' play within the wider social, political and economic structures that order their lives.

Critiquing Willis, who arguably creates a 'bi-polar' depiction of white working-class boys with extreme macho and 'laddish' behaviour set against 'ear'oles', Brown's (1987) *Schooling Ordinary Kids* sets out a framework in which the working-class students who are not 'lads' or 'ear'oles' fall into three frames of reference (FORs): 'getting in', 'getting out' or 'getting on', and at this point Brown's research highlights the heterogeneity of the working-class educational experience. While Willis's (1977: 21) lads loudly reject school by 'simply conforming to a script learnt during childhood in a particular type of working-class family', Brown (1987) enquires after the working-class boys who make an effort, and recognises that not all working-class pupils fail academically, and some do not partake in the development of an 'anti-school subculture yet still fail' (p. 25). For Brown, the majority of ordinary working-class pupils neither simply accept nor reject the school, but comply with it in an effort to 'get on', as they are aware of rising unemployment and job uncertainty. Brown's working-class boys are not trying particularly to break class boundaries to elevate their social position or reaffirm class boundaries and preserve the status quo; rather they are focused on moving forward.

While Marxism has informed a major part of the literature on working-class disadvantage, focusing narrowly on 'hooligans' and 'rebels', recent feminist scholarship has exposed a wider heterogeneity to working-class male identity formation (Connell, 1989; Epstein *et al.*, 1999; Archer *et al.*, 2001, 2007; Ingram, 2011). Many boys today certainly do still engage and find empowerment in the practice of 'laddish' behaviour, what Connell (2005) and Martino (1999) refer to as 'protest masculinity', especially in contexts where boys have very little power. However, we must examine identity through a multi-faceted approach that accounts for an under-emphasis on boys who actually engage with learning or boys who foster approaches to learning, despite social and identity barriers.

Frameworks of inequality: gender, class and ethnicity in the schooling context

Construction(s) of classed identities through schooling

Statistically, current research indicates that in Britain 'it is possible to combine socio-economic classification of the household with the children's overall developmental score at age of 22 months to accurately predict educational qualifications at the age of 26 years' (Evans, 2006: 3). Class is undeniably the largest determinant of how students engage with education. However, Reay (2004d: 151) has argued class is 'a complicated mixture of the material, the discursive, psychological predispositions, and sociological dispositions', where class identities are not fixed but rather social identities are re/produced through relational structures and processes that are contested (cf. Skeggs, 2004a). Current working-class students function in educational policies of 'exclusion and exclusivity' (Reay, 2004b: 1019) that establish paradoxes where the ethos is 'nominally about raising working-class achievement although its practices generate the exact opposite, ensuring that educational failure remains firmly located within the working-class' (Reay, 2001: 341).

For 'the majority of the working-classes, education has remained something to be got through rather than go into' (Reay, 2001: 353). Withdrawal from education is withdrawal from a system that has arguably lost its capacity to compensate for socio-economic deprivation. Whilst class is vital to understanding the identity work that (white) working-class boys undergo, class itself shapes educational processes in a myriad of ways, often fixing the boys into certain positions within the classroom. Debates concerning disaffection/disengagement often centre on schools imposing middle-class and neoliberal values (Davies and Bansel, 2007), and there is little doubt that the education system rewards and even valorises middle-class capitals rather than working-class capitals (Bourdieu and Accadro, 1993). As proficient neoliberal subjects, the middle classes are dealt better cards in the high-stakes game, but they have also internalised the knowledge of how to compete through economic and cultural advantages, of when and how best to play those cards to secure an advantageous position (Bathmaker et al., 2013). In regards to persistent white working-class underachievement and lack of qualifications, perhaps the most obvious reason for this occurrence is that many working-class students go to 'failing' schools as they lack the 'economic, cultural, and social capitals' to manipulate the neoliberal market system (Reay, 2004c: 541).

In understanding the role social class plays in identity formation, it is important to note identities are 'a form of cultural capital that are worked and ... inhabited' as well as being a kind of 'reflective and interpretative agency' (Skeggs, 2004a: 29), which, when activated, allows individuals easier movement between various social spaces. For a substantial number of white working-class boys, attending school is entering an entirely different 'social space' dominated by middle-class values. Therefore, the rejection of schooling for many working-class boys is a (gendered and classed) performance; for the most part their 'resistance' and 'disaffection' is a process of excluding themselves from what they are already excluded from (Bourdieu and Accadro, 1993).[9]

Construction(s) of masculine identities through schooling

Socially constructed and deeply contextual, there are multiple patterns of masculinity that have been analysed through Foucauldian, post-structural, postmodern and discursive psychology perspectives (cf. Kimmel, 2010, for critique). Connell (1989) asserts that masculine identities are actively constructed and accomplished in everyday actions within institutions such as families, sports, armies, schools and corporations and she believes 'masculinity shapes education, as well as education forming masculinity' (p. 298). The influence of Connell and Messerschmidt's (2005) distinctly modernist theoretical framing shows the power of the peer group and the hegemonic in shaping masculine identities. Gilbert and Gilbert (1998: 46) assert that:

> Becoming a man is a matter of constructing oneself in and being constructed by the available ways of being male in a particular society. It is a matter of negotiating the various discourses of femininity and masculinity available in our culture, those powerful sets of meaning and practices which we must draw on to participate in our culture and to establish who we are.

For Connell (2005) and many other theorists, gender is a performance, a 'process' or a project toward understanding one's identity, individually and in relation to other's identities as 'social practice'. Clearly, masculinity is constructed contextually within the school environment, or 'formally' and 'informally' (O'Donnell and Sharpe, 2000).

Despite the large volume of different perspectives and theoretical frameworks on masculinity, each perspective holds social power as significant to the study of a masculine identity. For working-class males, their social interaction and peer group is often a generative space for producing behaviours counterproductive to schooling. Since Connell's work, researchers now widely accept that the process of masculinity formation is contextual and bounded by history. Masculinity is not a fixed thing; instead masculinity is constantly in flux (being formed and reformed) and constantly being impacted upon. In this plural model of power relations, gender intersects with other forms of power and is constituted out of interaction between structure and agents. According to her three-fold model of masculine identity, consisting of power (e.g. subordination of women), production (e.g. division of labour) and cathexis (e.g. emotional attachments), Connell and Messerschmidt argue that gender intersects with race and class and that white masculinities are constructed in relation to all Others, whether it be white women, black men, Asian women, etc. (Connell and Messerschmidt, 2005).

Stuart Hall (1996: 4–5) reminds us that it is 'the Other, the relation to what it is not, to precisely what it lacks', which becomes an essential ingredient to how identity is constructed. For boys, Othering is a process of achieving status and preserving hegemonic masculinity (Renold, 2004: 253). Since Willis's 'lads', there have been nearly 40 years of economic and racial recomposition alongside the advancement of women. This rapid change has altered the way (white) working-class males form their identity, and, as a result, masculinity research must be integrated with more general analyses of social change (cf. Weis, 1990; Fine et al., 1997; Connell and Messerschmidt, 2005).[10] In her study of the white American working-class, Weis (1990) asserts that racism and sexism, though arguably eroded in society, are powerful forms of legitimate capital for white working-class men and part of how they render their identities. While this analysis runs the risk of pathologising working-class males as an angry mob, identity construction against 'the Other' is well documented as a process of identity composition (Mac an Ghaill, 1994: 90; Skeggs, 2002; Hollingworth and Williams, 2009).

Construction(s) of an ethnic identity through schooling

Hall (2002: 453) defines race as 'a discursive system, which has "real" social, economic, and political conditions of existence and "real" material and symbolic effects'. Fine (1997: 58) writes, 'Schools and work, for example, do not merely manage race; they create and enforce racial meanings'. Race and ethnicity are difficult to research, especially with the opaqueness of investigating whiteness, yet they are tremendously important. However, young people, especially white British, find it difficult to talk about what being white means to them (Phoenix, 1997). Racial identity, as a social construction that is diasporic, incoherent and conflicted, is 'process-oriented and relational' (Nayak, 2006: 825), where:

> Race is constructed in and through space, just as space is often constructed through race. As a geographical project the co-production of race and space is never uncontested, and thus the spatiality of race often needs ordering and policing. Such policing manifests itself in all manner of quite ordinary – and sometimes extraordinary – ways.
>
> (Mitchell, 2000: 230)

Gilroy's (2004) concept of melancholia de-historicises white working-class disadvantage and shows how white working-class identities are formed in opposition to migrants. Social and cultural geographers, such as Nayak (2009), have addressed how the English working class has been perceived both as 'white' and 'not-white' – shifting in and out of whiteness – depending upon historical and contemporary contexts, and due as well as to cultural and social discourses (p. 3). Preston (2009: 5) argues whiteness is 'far from a homogeneous category being contested, determined and re-classified over time as part of an ongoing process of white racialisation', where whiteness is constantly in formation and not all groups benefit from whiteness equally. While masculinity is clearly a marked aspect of identity, in the UK, Anglo-whiteness as an ethnic construct remains largely an unmarked aspect of identity, 'invisible' yet dominant (Luke and Carrington, 2000; Moore, 2013). In her analysis of white Eastern European migrants, Moore (2013) shows how whiteness becomes a performative act where whiteness is continually made and remade, 'all the while remaining invisible to white people, eluding scrutiny and detection through their apparent normalcy', while within different '"shades" of white', other points of distinction such as 'language, physical appearance, perceived "traits" or "qualities", and poverty' rise to the surface as racialised boundaries are constructed (pp. 5–6).

At this point it is worth considering the term 'chav'[11] as racially charged (Tyler, 2008), where it can reference the whole of the white working-class or segments of the underclass (Preston, 2009: 35). Chav in popular discourse involves a group of young people (usually white), clad predominantly in cheap sports apparel and clunky jewellery. As a specific section of the white working class, 'chavs' have in the past often been represented in the media as embodying dishonesty, hypersexuality, laziness, fecundity and rudeness (Skeggs, 2004a; Hayward and Yar, 2006). Chavs, as part of the underclass, were not 'only represented, but also shaped by disparate discourses of familial disorder and dysfunction', (Skeggs, 2004a: 87). In several deep ethnographic works, Skeggs (1991, 2002, 2005, 2009) has shown white working-class women contend, negotiate and subvert pejorative and demeaning social constructions surrounding class, gender and ethnicity in order to establish themselves as respectable.

Given that official statistics reveal that most groups experiencing poverty achieve relatively poor results regardless of ethnic background (Gillborn, 2009: 18), it is interesting to consider how white students are constructed within education and how they construct themselves. Demie and Lewis (2010) found specific barriers with the white working-class as an ethnic group, specifically lack of community and school engagement, low levels of parental engagement and lack of targeted support. Where there is extensive literature discussing whiteness as it equates to power and entitlement, in the schooling context of this study whiteness was often socially created as undesirable and equated with low-aspirational, stagnant and anti-educational stances. Equally disadvantaged and in need of special support, the white working-class consistently do not have access to special programmes aimed at raising their achievement and thus are constructed as new race victims (Keddie, 2013a, 2013b). Furthermore, Gillborn and Kirton (2000), as well as Fine *et al.* (2008), have documented how white working-class boys were aware of class and ethnic disadvantages. They describe how the white working-class were aware that they were not eligible to receive the same level of help as the EAL (English as an additional language) students and therefore 'the students' experience of education connects with powerful racist myths that are current in the wider community' (Gillborn and Kirton 2000: 281).

The study of identity in neoliberal and globalised times

Class, gender and ethnicity, while contested areas, all play a role in the constitution of identity as 'the self' is not fixed. Identities are not distinct from discourses but instead produced by and through them. As collections of meaning imbued with symbolic connotations, discourses define objects and set parameters on what we can think, feel and be (MacLure, 2003), where we may 'make ourselves but not in conditions of our own choosing' (Archer *et al.*, 2010). Neoliberalism, as an extension of human capital theory that suggests that individuals and society derive economic benefits from investments in people (Sweetland, 1996: 341), was a step toward eliminating 'class as a central economic concept' (Bowles and Gintis, 1975: 74). Current iterations of neoliberalism function as a political, economic and ideological system that gives considerable credence to the market as the best, most efficient platform for distributing public resources. This macro-level structural framework attributes greater consideration of individual duty than government responsibility (Gillborn and Youdell, 2000; Reay *et al.*, 2005; Weis and Fine, 2012; Zipin *et al.*, 2013).

Archer and Francis (2007: 19) write that in the neoliberal reading 'there are no foundational aspects of selfhood such as "race" or gender that preclude an individual from taking up the opportunities available to them – failure to do so simply reflects an individual lack of enterprise'. Within a neoliberal discourse, it is argued that the self is malleable, constantly made and remade adaptive to one's circumstances. Neoliberal ideology privileges the reflexive modernisation thesis where historic conventions of femininity and masculinity can arguably be reinscribed in new ways (cf. Adkins, 2000; Kenway and Kelly, 2000) and where historic and gender-based inequalities exist simultaneously with evidence of changed expectations (Adkins, 1999, 2000). In our neoliberal times, Davies and Bansel (2007: 252) claim:

> The so-called 'passive' citizen of the welfare state becomes the autonomous 'active' citizen with rights, duties, obligations, and expectations – the citizen as active entrepreneur of the self; the citizen as

morally superior. This is not simply a reactivation of liberal values of self-reliance, autonomy and independence as the necessary conditions for self-respect, self-esteem, self-worth, and self-advancement but rather an emphasis on enterprise and the capitalization of existence itself through calculated acts and investments combined with the shrugging off of collective responsibility for the vulnerable and marginalized.

The neo-liberal rhetoric, where context is ignored for the sake of the entre-preneurial self, has the ability to create conditions of heightened fixity, especially if one lacks certain capitals. Within neoliberalism, risk is always pervasive where today young people often seek to manage the riskiness of transitions from school to work through a range of strategies including culti-vating certain identities. Saturated in labels of success/failure and active/stagnant, education today is infused with the neoliberal prerogative that increasingly fixes identities within rhetoric is risk.

The neoliberal policy that permeates classroom discourses becomes a powerful mediating force in the identity construction of all students (Phoenix, 2004). Neoliberalism, with its promotion of 'efficiency', 'productivity', 'targets' and 'choice', enables competition and market-driven results without strategic consideration to the gross economic inequalities it creates, particularly for marginalised communities (Ball, 2009, 2012). In the UK, white working-class boys both present learner identities and have learner identities imposed upon them within a highly pressurised and stratified educa-tional environment where 'tropes of *excellence* and *standards* pepper policy documents and the speeches of education ministers, and a culture of 'rigor-ous' surveillance and testing prevails' (Francis, 2006: 190). As pedagogic processes become influenced by neoliberal logic, there are overt and subtle consequences for gender identities. The presence of a competitive 'perfor-mance-oriented culture generates anxiety, especially among boys whose gender identity needs to be based on achieving power, status, and superiority' (Arnot, 2004: 35). In terms of gender, we must consider the sublimation of certain elements of the self as particularly potent for working-class boys who construct their masculinity around traditional models of 'breadwinners' in economies where their employment 'choices' are increasingly limited and where the label of 'Not in Education, Employment or Training' (or NEET) is particularly prevalent (McDowell, 2003). In contrast, femininity seems to be less impacted by neoliberal logics as young women have been documented as ideal, flexible, neoliberal subjects (Walkerdine, 2003; McRobbie, 2008).

In considering the identity work of students, the concept of 'positioning' raises the question of possible selves that are contradictory both to other selves and to internal selves (Davies, 1989: 229). The production of the self, our subjectivity, involves learning inclusive and exclusive practices and posi-tioning oneself in relation to these practices to establish a sense of belonging (Davies and Harre, 1990). Further, it is argued that human beings 'are characterized both by continuous personal identity and by discontinuous personal diversity', where selfhood is the product of discursive practices and these processes lead to a multiplicity of selves (Davies and Harre, 1990: 46). As a result, individuals are active agents who position themselves ('reflexive positioning') and are positioned by others through social interaction ('interactive positioning') as gendered, classed and ethnic individuals (Davies and Harre, 1990). Therefore, identity work involves grappling with both subjective constraints and the constraints of accepted discursive practices (Renold, 2004), often within powerful neoliberal discourses (Francis, 2000; Archer and Francis, 2007).

The study of the multiple and taxing identities working-class boys enact daily is well documented (Pye *et al.*, 1996; Gilbert and Gilbert, 1998; Francis, 1999; Martino, 1999; Jackson, 2002; Connell, 2005; Kane, 2006). The self, according to subjectivity theorists, is always an interactive, discursive process, fragile and 'vulnerable to the discourses through which it is spoken and speaks itself into existence' (Whelen, 2011: 16). Education has always been:

> about changing people and this is why it is potentially such a strong emotional experience. Once they have gone through school young people are different – they are constructed and they are expected to construct themselves both objectively and subjectively in ways made available through school.
>
> (Furlong, 1991: 298)

When considering an analysis of learner identities with engagement/disaffection, the emotional power of education is in the creation of the self. In schooling, the self is increasingly sublimated through neoliberal agendas, where 'it is the duty of the individual to be sufficiently flexible to maximize the opportunities available to her/him, and any failure resides in the individual rather than in the socio-economic structures' (Francis, 2006: 191). When considering identity as negotiated through school contexts, it is essential to consider the 'web' of numerous and complex factors that contribute to disaffection toward school (Stevenson and Ellsworth, 1991). Therefore, school failure/success is bound up with the process of students doing 'identity work', where young people's engagement with schooling 'depends in part on the sense they make of themselves, their community, and their future and in part on "the adaptive strategies" they use to accept, modify, or resist the institutional identities made available' (Smyth, 2006: 290). Within or beyond the classroom, identity is positioned through conceptions of the collective and the individual and in a constant form of negotiation as it is constructively articulated, debated and problematised.

According to the 'crisis of masculinity' debate, as traditional social structures and rites of passage disappear, young men, particularly those from lower and working-class backgrounds, have to negotiate their identity work around rapidly changing discourses of aspiration and power. Furthermore, influences upon their masculine identities come from new directions (media, the internet, social networking). Archer and Yamashita's (2003: 120) study of inner-city masculinities shows how boys' dialogues:

> combined globalized and localized discourses that cross-cut ethnic and national groupings … [where] identity constructions combine traces of various social, historical, geographical, and cultural elements, and indicate the shifting nature of masculinities, which are created and recreated across time and context.

Contemporary youth research is conducted in an era of increased cultural, social and economic globalisation (Jeffrey and McDowell, 2004; MacLeod, 2009), with uneven and unpredictable effects where local communities mediate global processes (Nayak, 2003b, 2006). Youth researchers must reflexively pay close attention to both embodied and local habits and cultures and also to global flows in order to establish nuanced analyses (cf. Nayak, 2003b; Kenway et al., 2006). In the use of the term 'culture', we must be cautious of using it like shorthand; culture should be conceptualised 'as shifting, complex and continuously shaped (and reshaped) by relations of power' (Archer et al., 2010: 44). Zipin (2009: 324) writes, 'Cultures are dynamic: not primarily thing-like products but living processes wherein socially interactive and communicative people (re)create things and practices, and invest them with sense and meaning'. Compared to early ethnographies on white working-class boys such as Willis (1977) and Humphries (1981), today's working-class male social identities are increasingly fragmented and complex where there is uncertainty surrounding sense-making practices (Jeffery and McDowell, 2004; McDowell, 2012). However, what remains persistent, despite or because of the onslaught of neoliberal discourses of global change, is the peer group as the primary site for identity construction and where a certain hegemonic masculinity may be established (Clarke et al., 1975; Hall, 1975; Kehily and Nayak, 1997; Frosh et al., 2002; Connell, 2005; Lingard et al., 2009).

In the analysis of learner identities, 'academic "success" is closely connected to ideological projects of identity construction' (McGregor, 2009: 347), and these processes are always embedded in overlapping contexts. In the neoliberal social order, if the subject behaves in ways that are taken to be 'excessive, unhealthy, irresponsible, or undisciplined' then they are rendered moral failures (Griffin et al., 2009). Furthermore, depictions of urban working-class youth, as 'publicly immoral', proliferate in the media (Skeggs, 2002, 2005) and contribute to an ongoing moral panic that has implications when considering the concepts of fixity and social identities. Therefore, morally ambiguous symbolic renderings, which are embedded in everyday life and spatial landscapes, play a significant role in identity construction (Tyler and Bennett, 2010). These renderings, which construct the working-class as 'lacking', influence how 'the self' is constructed (Skeggs, 2004a, 2004b, 2004c). In the negotiation around making and re-making 'the self', there is also a degree of choice albeit small and highly influenced by class:

> As people and places are drawn seemingly closer together, local cultures are no longer immune from international cross-fertilization. Mass communication systems and changing patterns of consumption – including the development of youth, niche and lifestyle markets – have broadened a range of youth identities available in the global market.
>
> (Nayak, 2003c: 106)

The urban imaginaries and subjectivities of youth remain areas of contention within youth subcultural theory and, indeed, post-subcultural practice where questions and debates remain around 'choice' and 'fluidity' (Dillabough and Kennelly, 2010: 40). Through both Skeggs' and Nayak's work we see the forces that shape either fluidity or fixity of identity.

 ## Summary

This chapter has discussed approaches to the study of working-class male educational experience through a critique of historic trends. Identity work, particularly for working-class boys today, is increasingly a complex negotiation and often requires social validation in order to overcome significant structural barriers. In the examination of different frameworks of inequality, each framework is relational, influenced by power, defined by constraints, and process-oriented. Careful attention to class, gender and ethnicity allows for a more nuanced exploration of social dynamics that contribute to inequality and multiple axes of disadvantage. There are dangers when focusing solely on the individual level of identity, where it 'becomes all too easy to ascribe educational inequities to perceived characteristics and (in)abilities of marginalized individuals or groups, rather than the economic, social, and political practices that perpetuate these inequities' (Núñez, 2014: 88).

There also exists tremendous overlap and cross-pollination between these frameworks. In the analysis of identity construction, class, gender and ethnicity, all form an interlocking relationship in how boys engage with their learning and, furthermore, how their engagement is socially validated. How masculine and classed identities are constructed in context can be seen in Archer and Francis' (2005) research with Chinese boys who were born outside the UK and who were less likely to adopt 'laddism', or take laddish behaviour to an extreme. The capital of laddish behaviour was operationalised in their social identity, but it did not infringe on their socially mobile learner identities, which supports the argument that certain identity processes can be fluid.

Also, research has documented how white and black boys negotiate/ contest/resist schooling in different ways (Archer *et al.*, 2001). Kuriloff and Reichert's (2003) study of African-American and white working-class males at an elite boarding school found African-American boys were able to develop a set of strategies that tapped into discourses of class and ultimately propelled their engagement. In contrast, white working-class boys lacked the class critique, absorbed the meritocratic ethos of the school, and saw their deficiencies as personal failings. Whilst not researching at a prestigious school, MacLeod (2009) found a similar ethnic learner identity dynamic in relation to aspiration and engagement. For MacLeod, his African-American 'brothers' failures result in the inability to see that meritocracy is a myth and they simply blame themselves when they do not achieve. This contrasts the (mostly) white 'Hallway Hangers' in his study, who locate their failure in the complex amalgam of agency and unequal societal structures. To be clear, boys have historically disaffected from education, but this research seeks to explore the gendered, classed and ethnic identity work surrounding (dis)engagement with education in recent neoliberal times, with reference to how these young men 'negotiate and are formed in the intersection of local and global contexts' (MacLeod, 2009: 270).

In an exploration of learner identities, there also exists an emphasis toward social solidarity when boys feel vulnerable or fragile in educational contexts that espouse the neoliberal rhetoric of individualisation. In Renold's (2004) study of primary school boys who invested in non-hegemonic masculinities, she shows how they draw on resources available to them to create certain capitals; through renouncing the hegemonic, they use humour and parody to establish support and solidarity. Within schools, Mac an Ghaill (1994) argues that the peer group's hyper-masculine attention to 'fighting, fuckin', and football' served as a safety net against anxiety and fear in educational contexts. Clearly, in the case of Mac an Ghaill's work, this 'safety net' furthers 'anti-educational' stances in the creation of legitimate masculinities.

Neoliberal school contexts often trap working-class boys in a binary between either action, which fixes boys as 'arrogant' and 'loutish', or the alternatively passive lack of action, which fixes them as 'non-workers', 'apathetic' and 'lazy'. The 'bad boy' masculine identity, which typically rejects school (Delamont, 2000; Frosh *et al.*, 2002; MacLeod, 2009), continues to be a substantial force in the lives of many boys where masculine honour is a privilege and a trap (Bourdieu, 2001). However, 'bad boy' masculinities, though potent, are not the only identity discourse boys draw upon, as boys' subjectivities were 'in process, multi-placed and shifting' (Martino and Pallotta-Chiarolli, 2003: 9). Qualitative research suggests that a more detailed treatment of 'youthscapes' (Nayak, 2003c) that is influenced by 'push' and 'pull' factors is needed (Ingram, 2011). Within these discourses and frameworks of inequality, we see subjectivities interpellate, where competing and contrasting definitions are resisted, contested, subverted and strategised.

Notes

1   In considering boys behaviour and the cost to the school, it is: '"commonly reported 80% of administrators' and teachers' time which is devoted to managing boys' behaviour is time lost to curriculum leadership, organizing supportive school environments, community liaison and parent support" (Matinez 1994)' (Gilbert and Gilbert, 2001: 5–6).
2   Entwisle *et al.* (2007: 117) explore both the capital working-class boys have when entering the classroom and the consequent labels they acquire within the hierarchy: 'Yet because most teachers are middle class, they may find the behaviour of middle-SES [socio-economic status] boys to be more compatible with their standards than the behaviour of low-SES boys'.
3   Archer *et al.* (2010: 24) argue while 'cultural factors' can be 'part of the explanation for the persistence of poverty ..., this understanding of poverty fails to take into account structural factors ... It fundamentally rests on the notion of meritocracy, assuming there is equality of opportunity, which by inference places the onus of responsibility on individuals while failing to recognise how people live within conditions of inequality'.
4   Government initiatives like *Aiming High*, among many other resources and projects, have been concerned with elevating young people's aspirations with a specific focus on them accessing university.
5   The central feature in the crisis of masculinity rhetoric is 'loss of essential male' and many theorists, specifically Gilbert, have expressed concern that people are using this 'loss' to justify, rather than to explain, behaviour.
6   These schemes include male mentoring schemes, boy-friendly curriculum, recruitment of black and Latino male teachers, recruitment of male teachers at the primary level and national policies to promote boy-friendly pedagogy. These efforts, which are typically sex-role theory-based, have been effectively delineated and criticised (cf. Weaver-Hightower, 2008; Whelen, 2011).
7   Connell (2005: 40) asserts, 'A weakness of much academic research is the product of two forms of occupational blindness – the inability of sociologists to recognise the complexities of the person and the unwillingness of psychologists to recognise the dimension of social power'. Connell (2005) also writes that gender both 'intersects' and 'interacts' with race and class.
8   Humphries' work shows that the working-class 'rebel' or 'hooligan' is not a new embodiment. More likely it was concealed from society in reformatories. In his vivid description of a compromised working-class identity, Humphries (1981: 215) writes: 'The reformatory, then, was an institution of class control, in which all daily activities were part of an overall plan to liquidate the inmate's former personality and reshape it into a conformist mold. In this context, resistance, even though it was severely punished, was essential if the inmate was to maintain a personal, as opposed to an institutional, identity'.
9   Whereas past studies have interpreted through a Marxist ideology, Bourdieu arguably 'leaves no room for notions such as resistance' as his world is far more: 'reproductive than transformative' (Mills, 2008: 79).
10   At this point, Connell (2005) cites Jung's two theories of masculinity. According to Jung, masculinity is self-constructed in transaction with the social environment (persona) and additionally constructed through the unconscious formed through the repressed elements. Jung was interested in the balance between masculine persona and feminine anima (Connell, 2005: 12).
11   According to Tyler (2008: 20–21), 'Chav, and its various synonyms and regional variations (including Pikey, Townie, Charver, Chavette, Chavster, Dumbo, Gazza, Hatchy, Hood Rat, Kev, Knacker, Ned, Ratboy, Scally, Scumbag, Shazza,

Skanger), have become ubiquitous terms of abuse for the white poor within contemporary British culture'.

References

Adkins, L. (1999) Community and economy: A retraditionalization of gender? *Theory Culture Society*, 16(1), 119–139.

Adkins, L. (2000) Objects of innovation: Post-occupational reflexivity and re-traditionalisations of gender. In S. Ahmed, J. Kilby, C. Lury, M. McNeil and B. Skeggs (eds), *Transformations: Thinking through feminism* (p. 331). London: Routledge.

Aggleton, P. (1987) *Rebels without a cause? Middle class youth and the transition from school to work*. London: The Falmer Press.

Anyon, J. (2008) Social class and school knowledge. In L. Weis (ed.), *The way class works* (pp. 189–209). New York: Routledge.

Archer, L. and Francis, B. (2005) 'They never go off the rails like other ethnic groups': teachers' constructions of British Chinese pupils' gender identities and approaches to learning. *British Journal of Sociology of Education*, 26(2): 165–182.

Archer, L. and Francis, B. (2007) *Understanding minority ethnic achievement*. Oxon: Routledge.

Archer, L. and Yamashita, H. (2003) Theorising inner-city masculinities: 'Race', class, gender, and education. *Gender and Education*, 15(2), 115–132.

Archer, L., Pratt, S. D. and Phillips, D. (2001) Working-class men's constructions of masculinity and negotiations of (non) participation in higher education. *Gender and Education*, 13(4), 431–449.

Archer, L., Halsall, A. and Hollingworth, S. (2007) Class, gender, (hetero) sexuality and schooling: Paradoxes within working-class girls' engagement with education and post-16 aspirations. *British Journal of Sociology of Education*, 28(2), 165–180.

Archer, L., Hollingworth, S. and Mendick, H. (2010) *Urban youth and schooling: The experiences and identities of educationally 'at risk' young people*. Berkshire: Open University Press.

Archer, L., DeWitt, J. and Willis, B. (2013) Adolescent boys' science aspirations: Masculinity, capital, and power. *Journal of Research in Science Teaching*, 1–30.

Arnot, M. (1985) How shall we educate our sons? In R. Deem (ed.), *Co-Education reconsidered* (pp. 37–57). Milton Keynes: Open University Press.

Arnot, M. (2004) Male working-class identities and social justice: A reconsideration of Paul Willis's *Learning to Labor* in light of contemporary research. In N. Dolby, G. Dimitriadis and P. Willis (eds), *Learning to Labor in new times* (p. 231). New York: Routledge.

Atkinson, K. (2004) Opportunities and despair: It's all in there. *Sociology*, 38(3), 437–455.

Ball, S. J. (2009) Academies in context: Politics, business and philanthropy and heterarchical governance. *Management in Education*, 23(3), 100–103.

Ball, S. J. (2012) *Global Education Inc.: New policy networks and the neo-liberal imaginary*. London: Routledge.

Bathmaker, A. M., Ingram, N. and Waller, R. (2013) Higher education, social class, and the mobilisation of capitals: Recognising and playing the game. *British Journal of Sociology of Education*, 34(5–6), 723–243.

Bleach, K. (ed.) (2000) *Raising boys' achievement in schools*. London: Trentham Books.

Bottero, W. (2009) Class in the 21st Century. In K. P. Sveinsson (ed.), *Who cares about the white working class?* (pp. 7–15). London: Runnymede Perspectives.

Bourdieu, P. (1988) Vive la crise! For heterodoxy in social science. *Theory and Society*, 17(5), 773–787.

Bourdieu, P. (2001) *Masculine Domination*. Oxford: Blackwell Publishers Ltd.

Bourdieu P. and Accadro, A. (1993) *The weight of the world: Social suffering in contemporary society*. Stanford University Press.

Bourdieu, P. and Wacquant, L. (1992) *An invitation to reflexive sociology*. Cambridge: Polity Press.

Bowles, S. and Gintis, H. (1975) The problem with human capital theory – A Marxist critique. *The American Economic Review*, 65(2), 74–82.

Brooks, R. (2002) 'My mum would be as pleased as punch if I actually went, but my dad seems a bit more particular about it': Paternal involvement in young people's higher education choices. *British Educational Research Journal*, 30(4), 495–514.

Brown, P. (1987) *Schooling ordinary kids: Inequality, unemployment and the new vocationalism*. New York: Travistock Publication.

Brown, P. (2013) Education, opportunity, and the prospects for social mobility. *British Journal of Sociology of Education*, 34(5–6), 678–700.

Clarke, J., Hall, S., Jefferson, T. and Roberts, B. (1975) Subcultures, cultures, and class. In S. Hall and T. Jefferson (eds), *Resistance through rituals* (pp. 1–79). London: Hutchinson & Co.

Communities and Local Government/Department for Children, Schools and Families (2008) *Aspiration and Attainment amongst young people in deprived communities*. London, Cabinet Office, 1–63.

Connell, R. W. (1989) Cool guys, swots and wimps: The interplay of masculinity and education. *Oxford Review of Education*, 15(3), 291–303.

Connell, R. W. (2005) *Masculinities*. Cambridge: Polity.

Connell, R. W. and Messerschmidt, J. W. (2005) Hegemonic masculinity: Rethinking the concept. *Gender and Society*, 19(6), 829–859.

Corrigan, P. (1979) *Schooling the Smash Street Kids*. London: Macmillan Press Ltd.

Davies, B. (1989) The discursive production of the male/female dualism in school settings. *The Oxford Review of Education*, 15(3), 229–241.

Davies, B. and Bansel, P. (2007) Neoliberalism and education. *International Journal of Qualitative Studies in Education*, 20(3), 247–256.

Davies, B. and Harre, R. (1990) Positioning: The discursive production of selves. *Journal for the Theory of Social Behaviour*, 20(1), 44–63.

Delamont, S. (2000) The anomalous beasts: Hooligans and the sociology of education. *Sociology*, 34(1), 95–11.

Demie, F. and Lewis, K. (2010) White working class achievement: An ethnographic study of barriers to learning in schools. *Educational Studies*, 33(2), 1–20.

Dillabough, J. A. and Kennelly, J. (2010) *Lost youth in a global city: Class, culture and the urban imaginary*. New York: Routledge.

Dolby, N. and Dimitriadis, G. (2004) Learning to labor in new times: An introduction. In N. Dolby, G. Dimitriadis and P. Willis (eds), *Learning to Labor in new times* (p. 231). New York: RoutledgeFalmer.

Economist, The (2014) Island mentality. *The Economist*. 25 January. Online at: www.economist.com/news/britain/21594986-bad-schools-and-low-aspirations-used-be-inner-city-problems-not-any-more-island-mentality

Epstein, D. (1998) Real boys don't work: 'Underachievement', masculinity, and the harassment of 'sissies'. In D. Epstein, J. Elwood, V. Hey and J. Maw (eds), *Failing boys? Issues in gender and achievement* (pp. 96–108). Buckingham: Open University Press.

Epstein, D., Elwood, J., Hey, V. and Maw, J. (eds) (1999) *Failing boys? Issues in gender and achievement.* Buckingham: Open University Press.

Entwisle, D. R., Alexander, K. L. and Olson, L. S. (2007) Early schooling: The handicap of being poor and male. *Sociology of Education*, 80, 114–138.

Evans, G. (2006) *Educational failure and working class white children in Britain.* Palgrave: Macmillan.

Faludi, S. (1999) *Stiffed: The betrayal of the American man.* New York: Perennial.

Fine, M. (1997) Witnessing whiteness. In M. Fine, L. Weis, L. C. Powell and L. M. Wong (eds), *Off white: Readings on race, power, and society* (pp. 57–66). New York: Routledge.

Fine, M., Weis, L., Addelston, J. and Marusza, J. (1997) (In)Secure times: Constructing white working-class masculinities in the late 20th century. *Gender and Society*, 11(1), 52–68.

Fine, M., Burns, A., Torre, M. E. and Payne, Y. A. (2008) How class matters: the geography of educational desire and despair in schools and courts. In L. Weis (ed.), *The way class works: Readings on school, family, and the economy* (pp. 225–243). New York: Routledge.

Finn, J. D. (1989) Withdrawing from school. *Review of Educational Research Association*, 59(2), 117–142.

Francis, B. (1999) Lads, lasses, and (new) labour: 14–16-year-old students' responses to the 'laddish behaviour and boys' underachievement' debate. *British Journal of Sociology of Education*, 20(3), 355–371.

Francis, B. (2000) *Boys, girls and achievement: Addressing the classroom issues.* London: RoutledgeFalmer.

Francis, B. (2006) Heroes or zeroes? The discursive positioning of 'underachieving boys' in English neo-liberal education policy. *Journal of Education Policy*, 21(2), 187–200.

Frosh, S., Phoenix, A. and Pattman, R. (2002) *Young masculinities.* Hampshire: Palgrave.

Furlong, V. J. (1991) Disaffected pupils: Reconstructing the sociological perspective. *British Journal of Sociology of Education*, 12(3), 293–307.

Gewirtz, S. (2001) Cloning the Blairs: New Labour's programme for the re-socialization of working-class parents. *Journal of Education Policy*, 16(4), 365–378.

Gilbert, P. and Gilbert, R. (2001) Masculinity, inequality and post-school opportunities: Disrupting oppositional politics about boys' education. *International Journal of Inclusive Education*, 5(1), 1–13.

Gilbert, R. and Gilbert, P. (1998) *Masculinity goes to school.* London: Routledge.

Gillborn, D. (2009) Education: The numbers game and the construction of white racial victimhood. In K. P. Sveinsson (ed.), *Who cares about the white working class?* (pp. 15–22). London: Runnymede Perspectives.

Gillborn, D. and Kirton, A. (2000) White heat: Racism, under-achievement, and white working-class boys. *Inclusion and Special Educational Needs*, 4(4), 271–288.

Gillborn, D. and Youdell, D. (2000) *Rationing education: Policy, practice, reform and equity.* Buckingham: Open University Press.

Gilroy, P. (2004) *Melancholia and multiculture*. Online at: www.opendemocracy.net/arts-multiculturalism/article_2035.jsp

Griffin, C. (2000) Discourses of crisis and loss: Analysing the 'boys' underachievement' debate. *Journal of Youth Studies*, 3(2), 167-188.

Griffin, C., Bengry-Howell, A., Hackley, C., Mistral, W. and Szmigin, I. (2009) 'Every time I do it I absolutely annihilate myself': Loss of (self-)consciousness and loss of memory in young people's drinking narratives. *Sociology*, 43(3), 457–476.

Hadow Report (1931) *Board of Education report of the Consultative Committee on the primary school*. London: HM Stationery Office. Online at: www.educationengland.org.uk/documents/hadow1931/hadow1931.html

Hall, S. (1975) *Resistance through rituals*. Birmingham: Harper Collins.

Hall, S. (1996) Who needs 'identity'? In S. Hall and P. Du Gay (eds), *Questions of Cultural Identity* (pp. 1–18). London: Sage Publications.

Hall, S. (2002) Reflections on 'Race, articulations, and societies structured in dominance'. In P. Essed and D. T. Goldberg (eds), *Race critical theories: Text and context* (pp. 449–455). Oxford, UK: Blackwell.

Hayward, K. and Yar, M. (2006) The 'chav' phenomenon: Consumption, media and the construction of a new underclass. *Crime Media Culture*, 2(1), 9–28.

Hey, V., Leonard, D., Daniels, H. and Smith, M. (1998) Boys' underachievement, special needs practices and questions of equity. In D. Epstein, J. Elwood, V. Hey and J. Maw (eds), *Failing boys? Issues in gender and achievement* (pp. 128–144). Buckingham: Open University Press.

Hollingworth, S. and Williams, K. (2009) Constructions of the working-class 'Other' among urban, white, middle-class youth: 'Chavs', subculture and the valuing of education. *Journal of Youth Studies*, 12(5), 467–482.

Humphries, S. (1981) *Hooligans or rebels? An oral history of working-class childhood and youth 1889–1939*. Oxford: Basil Blackwell Publisher Limited.

Ingram, N. (2011) Within school and beyond the gate: The complexities of being educationally successful and working class. *Sociology*, 45(2), 287–302.

Jackson, C. (2002) 'Laddishness' as a self-worth protection strategy. *Gender and Education*, 14(1), 37–50.

Jackson, C. (2003) Motives for 'laddishness' at school: Fear of failure and fear of the 'feminine'. *British Educational Research Journal*, 29(4), 583–598.

Jeffrey, C. and L. McDowell (2004) Youth in a comparative perspective: Global change, local lives. *Youth and Society*, 36(2), 131–142.

Kane, J. (2006) School exclusions and masculine, working-class identities. *Gender and Education*, 18(6), 673–685.

Keddie, A. (2013a) 'There isn't kind of a White History Month or anything like that for them': Equity, schooling and the problematics of group identity politics. 30 August. *International Journal of Inclusive Education*, 1–14.

Keddie, A. (2013b) 'We haven't done enough for white working-class children': Issues of distributive justice and ethnic identity politics. December 16. *Race Ethnicity and Education*, 1–20.

Kehily, M. J. and Nayak, A. (1997) 'Lads and laughter': Humour and the production of heterosexual hierarchies. *Gender and Education*, 9(1), 69–88.

Kenway, J. and Kelly, P. (2000) Local/global labour markets and the restructuring of gender, schooling, and work. In N. Stromquist and K. Monkham (eds),

Globalisation and education: Integration and contestation across cultures (pp. 173–195). Lanham, MD: Rowman & Littlefield.

Kenway, J. and Kraack, A. (2004) Reordering work and destabilizing masculinity. In N. Dolby, G. Dimitriadis and P. Willis (eds), *Learning to Labor in new times* (p. 231). New York, London, RoutledgeFalmer.

Kenway, J., Kraack, A. and Hickey-Moody, A. (2006) *Masculinity beyond the metropolis*. London: Palgrave.

Kimmel, M. (2010) *Boys and school: A background paper on the 'boy crisis'*. Swedish Government Official Reports.

Kuriloff, P. and Reichert, M. (2003) Boys of class, boys of color: Negotiating the academic and social geography of an elite independent school. *Journal of Social Issues*, 59(4), 751–769.

Lareau, A. (2003) *Unequal childhoods*. Berkley: University of California Press.

Lingard, B., Martino, W. and Mills, M. (2009) *Boys and schooling: Beyond structural reform*. London: Palgrave.

Luke, C. and Carrington, V. (2000) Race matters. *Journal of Intercultural Studies*, 21(1), 5–24.

Mac an Ghaill, M. (1994) *The making of men: Masculinities, sexualities and schooling*. Buckingham: Open University Press.

Mac an Ghaill, M. (1996) Sociology of education, state schooling and social class: Beyond critiques of the new right hegemony. *British Journal of Sociology of Education*, 17(2), 163–176.

Mac an Ghaill, M. (2000) The cultural production of English masculinities in late modernity. *Canadian Journal of Education*, 25(2), 88–101.

MacBeath, J. (2009) Border crossings. *Improving Schools*, 12(1), 81–92.

McCulloch, G. (1998) *Failing the ordinary child?: The theory and practice of working-class secondary education*. Buckingham: Open University Press.

MacDonald, R., Shildrick, T., Webster, C. and Simpson, D. (2005) Growing up in poor neighbourhoods: The significance of class and place in the extended transitions of 'socially excluded' young adults. *Sociology*, 39(5), 873–891.

McDowell, L. (2003) *Redundant masculinities?: Employment change and white working class youth*. Malden, MA: Blackwell Pub.

McDowell, L. (2007) Respect, respectability, deference and place: What is the problem with/for working class boys? *Geoforum*, 38(2), 276–286.

McDowell, L. (2012) Post-crisis, post-Ford and post-gender? Youth identities in an era of austerity. *Journal of Youth Studies*, 15(5), 573–590.

McGregor, G. (2009) Educating for (whose) success? Schooling in an age of neo-liberalism. *British Journal of Sociology of Education*, 30(3), 345–358.

McLaren, P. and Scatamburlo-D'Annibale, V. (2004) Paul Willis, class consciousness and critical pedagogies. In N. Dolby, G. Dimitriadis and P. Willis (eds). *Learning to Labor in new times* (p. 231). New York: RoutledgeFalmer.

MacLeod, J. (2009) *Ain't no makin' it*. Boulder, CO: Westview Press.

MacLure, M. (2003) *Discourse in educational and social research*. Buckingham: Open University Press.

McRobbie, A. (1980) Settling accounts with subcultures: A feminist critique. *Screen Education*, 34(Spring), 1–18.

McRobbie, A. (2008) *The aftermath of feminism: Gender, culture and social change*. London: Sage Publications.

Marks, A. (2003) Welcome to the new ambivalence: Reflections on the historical and current cultural antagonism between the working class male and higher education. *British Journal of Sociology of Education*, 24(1), 83–93.

Martino, W. (1999) 'Cool boys', 'party animals', 'squids', and 'poofters': Interrogating the dynamics and politics of adolescent masculinities in school. *British Journal of Sociology of Education*, 20(2), 239–263.

Martino, W. (2000) Mucking around in class, giving crap, and acting cool: Adolescent boys enacting masculinities at school. *Canadian Journal of Education*, 25(2), 102–112.

Martino, W. and Pallotta-Chiarolli, M. (2003) *So what's a boy?*. Maidenhead: Open University Press.

Mills, C. (2008) Reproduction and transformation of inequalities in schooling: the transformative potential of the theoretical constructs of Bourdieu. *British Journal of Sociology of Education*, 29(1), 79–89.

Mitchell, D. (2000) *Cultural geography: A critical introduction*. Oxford: Blackwell.

Moore, H. (2013) Shades of whiteness? English villagers, Eastern European migrants, and the intersection of race and class in rural England. *Critical Race and Whiteness Studies*, 9(1), 1–19.

Nayak, A. (2003a) 'Boyz to Men': Masculinities, schooling and labour transitions in de-industrial times. *Educational Review*, 55(2), 147–159.

Nayak, A. (2003b) 'Ivory Lives': Economic restructuring and the making of whiteness in a post-industrial youth community. *European Journal of Cultural Studies*, 6(3), 305–325.

Nayak, A. (2003c) *Race, place and globalization: Youth cultures in a changing world*. Oxford: Berg.

Nayak, A. (2006) Displaced masculinities: Chavs, youth and class in the post-industrial city. *Sociology*, 40, 813–831.

Nayak, A. (2009) Beyond the pale: Chavs, youth, and social class. In K. P. Sveinsson (ed.), *Who cares about the white working class?* (pp. 28–35). London: Runnymede Perspectives.

Newcastle Commission [Royal Commission on the State of Popular Education in England] (1956) Parliamentary papers, 1861, XXI. pp. 293–328. In G. M. Young and W. D. Hancock (eds) *English historical documents, XII(1), 1833–1874* (pp. 891–897). New York: Oxford University Press.

Nichols, S., Rixon, H. and Roswell, J. (2009) The 'good' parent in relation to early childhood literacy: Symbolic terrain and lived practice. *Literacy*, 43(2), 65–74.

Noble, C. (2000) Helping boys do better in their primary schools. In K. Bleach (ed.), *Raising boys' achievement in schools* (pp. 21–37). London: Trentham Books.

Núñez, A.-M. (2014) Employing multilevel intersectionality in educational research: Latino identities, contexts, and college access. *Educational Researcher*, 43(2), 85–92.

O'Donnell, M. and Sharpe, S. (2000) *Uncertain masculinities*. London: Routledge.

OFSTED (Office for Standards in Education, Children's Services and Skills) (2014) *Early years annual report 2012/13*. Online at: www.ofsted.gov.uk/earlyyearsannualreport1213

Pascoe, C. J. (2005) 'Dude, you're a fag': Adolescent masculinity and the fag discourse. *Sexualities*, 8(3), 329–346.

Phoenix, A. (1997) 'I'm white! So what?' The construction of whiteness for young Londoners. In M. Fine, L. Weis, L. C. Powell and L. M. Wong (eds), *Off white:*

Readings on race, power, and society (pp. 187–197). New York: Routledge.

Phoenix, A. (2004) Neoliberalism and masculinity: Racialization and the contradictions of schooling for 11-to-14-year-olds. *Youth Society*, 36(2), 227–246.

Pittman, F. (1993) *Man enough: Fathers, sons, and the search for masculinity*. New York: The Berkley Publishing Group.

Pollard, A. and Filer, A. (2007) Learning, differentiation and strategic action in secondary education: Analyses from the *Identity and Learning Programme*. *British Journal of Sociology of Education*, 28(4), 441–458.

Preston, J. (2009) *Whiteness and class in education*. Dordrecht: Springer.

Pye, D., Haywood, C. and Mac an Ghaill, M. (1996) The training state, De-industrialisation and the production of white working-class trainee identities. *International Studies in Sociology of Education*, 6(2), 133–146.

Raphael Reed, L. (1998) 'Zero Tolerance': Gender performance and school failure. In D. Epstein, J. Elwood, V. Hey and J. Maw (eds), *Failing boys? Issues in gender and achievement* (pp. 56–76). Buckingham: Open University Press.

Reay, D. (2001) Finding or losing yourself? Working-class relationships to education. *Journal of Education Policy*, 16(4), 333–346.

Reay, D. (2002) Shaun's story: Troubling discourses on white working-class masculinities. *Gender and Education*, 14(3), 221–234.

Reay, D. (2004a) 'It's all becoming habitus': Beyond the habitual use of habitus in educational research. *British Journal of Sociology of Education*, 25(4), 431–444.

Reay, D. (2004b) 'Mostly roughs and toughs': Social class, race, and representation in inner city schooling. *Sociology*, 38(5), 1005–1023.

Reay, D. (2004c) Exclusivity, exclusion, and social class in urban education markets in the United Kingdom. *Urban Education*, 39(5), 537–560.

Reay, D. (2004d) Rethinking social class: Qualitative perspectives on class and gender. In S. Hesse-Biber and M. C. Yaiser (eds), *Feminist perspectives on social research* (pp. 140–154). Oxford: Oxford University Press.

Reay, D. (2006) 'I'm not seen as one of the clever children': Consulting primary school pupils about the social conditions of learning. *Educational Review*, 58(2), 171–181.

Reay, D. (2009) Making sense of white working class educational underachievement. In K. P. Sveinsson (ed.), *Who cares about the white working class?* (pp. 22–28). London: Runnymede Perspectives.

Reay, D. (2010) Identity-making in schools and classrooms. In M. Wetherall and C. Talpade Mohanty (eds), *The Sage handbook of identities* (pp. 277–294). Los Angeles: Sage Publications.

Reay, D., David, M. E. and Ball, S. (2005) *Degrees of choice: Social class, race and gender in higher education*. London: Institute of Education.

Renold, E. (2001) Learning the 'hard' way: Boys, hegemonic masculinity, and the negotiation of learner identities in the primary school. *British Journal of Sociology of Education*, 22(3), 369–385.

Renold, E. (2004) 'Other' boys: Negotiating non-hegemonic masculinities in the primary school. *Gender and Education*, 16(2), 247–265.

Sayer, A. (2005) *The moral significance of class*. Cambridge: Cambridge University Press).

Select Committee on Education. (2014) *Underachievement in Education by White Working Class Children*. 1st Report. Session 2013–2014. London: UK Parliament, House of Commons.

Skeggs, B. (1991) Challenging masculinity and using sexuality. *British Journal of Sociology of Education*, 12(2), 127–139.

Skeggs, B. (1992) Paul Willis, learning to Labour. In M. Barker and A. Beezer (eds), *Reading into Cultural Studies* (pp. 181–193). Abingdon: Routledge.

Skeggs, B. (2002) *Formations of class and gender*. Nottingham: Sage Publications.

Skeggs, B. (2004a) *Class, self, culture*. London: Routledge.

Skeggs, B. (2004b) Exchange, value and affect: Bourdieu and 'the self'. *Sociological Review*, 75–95.

Skeggs, B. (2004c) Shame in the habitus. *Theory Culture Society*, 20(6), 19–33.

Skeggs, B. (2005) The making of class and gender through visualizing moral subject formation. *Sociology*, 39(5), 965–982.

Skeggs, B. (2009) Haunted by the spectre of judgement: Respectability, value and affect in class relations. In K. P. Sveinsson (ed.), *Who cares about the white working class?* (pp. 36–44). London: Runnymede Perspectives.

Skelton, C. (2003) Male primary teachers and perceptions of masculinity. *Educational Review*, 55(2), 195–209.

Siraj-Blatchford, I. (2010) Learning in the home and at school: How working class children 'succeed against the odds'. *British Educational Research Journal*, 36(3), 463–482.

Smith, E. (2003) Failing boys and moral panics: Perspectives on the underachievement debate. *British Journal of Educational Studies*, 51(3), 282–295.

Smith, J. (2007) 'Ye've got to 'ave balls to play this game sir!' Boys' peers and fears: The negative influence of school-based 'cultural accomplices' in constructing hegemonic masculinities. *Gender and Education*, 19(2), 179–198.

Smyth, J. (2006) 'When students have power': Student engagement, student voice, and the possibilities for school reform around 'dropping out' of school. *International Journal of Leadership in Education*, 9(4): 285–298.

Stenning, A. (2005) Where is the post-socialist working class?: Working-class lives in the spaces of (post-) socialism. *Sociology*, 39(5), 983–999.

Stevenson, R. B. and Ellsworth, J. (1991) Dropping out in a working class high school: Adolescent voices on the decision to leave. *British Journal of Sociology of Education*, 12(3), 277–291.

Swain, J. (2004) The resources and strategies that 10–11-year-old boys use to construct masculinities in the school setting. *British Educational Research Journal*, 30(1), 167–185.

Swain, J. (2006) Reflections on patterns of masculinity in school settings. *Men and Masculinities*, 8(3), 331–349.

Sweetland, S. R. (1996) Human capital theory: Foundations of a field of inquiry. *Review of Educational Research*, 66(3), 341–359.

Tawney, R. H. (1964) *Equality*. London: Unwin Books.

Tyler, I. (2008) Chav mum chav scum. *Feminist Media Studies*, 8(1), 17–34.

Tyler, I. and Bennett, B. (2010) 'Celebrity chav': Fame, femininity and social class. *European Journal of Cultural Studies*, 13(3): 375–393.

Walkerdine, V. (2003) Reclassifying upward mobility: Femininity and the neo-liberal subject. *Gender and Education*, 15(3), 237–248.

Warrington, M., Younger, M. and Williams, J. (2000) Student Attitudes, Image and the Gender Gap. *British Educational Research Journal*, 26(3), 393–407.

Weaver-Hightower, M. (2003) The 'boy turn' in research on gender and education.

Review of Educational Research, 73(4), 471–498.

Weaver-Hightower, M. (2008) *The politics of policy in boys' education*. New York: Plagrave Macmillan.

Weis, L. (1990) *Working class without work*. New York: Routledge.

Weis, L. (2004) Revisiting a 1980s 'moment of critique': Class, gender, and the new economy. In N. Dolby, G. Dimitriadis and P. Willis (eds), *Learning to Labor in new times* (p. 231). New York: RoutledgeFalmer.

Weis, L. and Fine, M. (2012) Critical bifocality and circuits of privilege: Expanding critical ethnographic theory and design. *Harvard Educational Review*, 82(2), 173–201.

Whelen, J. (2011) *Boys and their schooling: The experience of becoming someone else*. New York: Routledge.

Wilkins, A. (2011) Push and pull in the classroom: Competition, gender, and the neoliberal subject. *Gender and Education*, 24(7), 1–17.

Willis, P. (1977) *Learning to labour: How working class kids get working class jobs*. New York: Columbia University Press.

Willis, P. (2004) Twenty-five years on: Old book, New times. In N. Dolby, G. Dimitriadis and P. Willis (eds), *Learning to Labor in new times* (p. 231). New York: RoutledgeFalmer.

Winlow, S. (2001) *Badfellas: Crime, tradition and new masculinities*. Oxford: Berg.

Zipin, L. (2009) Dark funds of knowledge, deep funds of pedagogy: Exploring boundaries between lifeworlds and schools. *Discourse: Studies in the Cultural Politics of Education*, 30(3), 317–331.

Zipin, L., Sellar, S., Brennan, M. and Gale, T. (2013) Educating for futures in marginalized regions: A sociological framework for rethinking and researching aspirations. *Educational Philosophy and Theory*, 45, 1–20.

Chapter 2

Establishing a framework to explore identity

Education is not, as older social science pictured it, a mirror of economic or cultural inequalities. That is all too still an image. Education systems are busy institutions. They are vibrantly involved in the production of social hierarchies. They select and exclude their own clients; they expand credentialed labour markets; they produce and disseminate particular kinds of knowledge to particular users.

(Connell, 1993: 27)

Recently there has been a revival of interest in Bourdieu's work in educational research, specifically with feminist re-engagements (McLeod, 2005), where his theoretical tools have been used to undertake a more nuanced analysis of gender identities and aspirations (Connolly, 2006; Archer *et al.*, 2013). Through processes of capital mobilisation and acquisition, Bourdieu's framework has been used to show how students make sense of their capitals in an increasingly competitive educational environment (Archer and Francis, 2005; Fuller 2009; Threadgold and Nilan, 2009; Allen, 2013; Bathmaker *et al.*, 2013; Hart, 2013). Bourdieu's tools are contested and subject to extensive critiques (cf. Jenkins, 1992; Throop and Murphy, 2002; Mouzelis, 2007). There exists no singular reading of Bourdieu but rather many ways of putting his 'theory into action', which result in gaps, overlaps, divisions and, of course, disputes. This chapter defines Bourdieu's theoretical tools and demonstrates the merits of his theoretical framework when applied to educational contexts. How his tools are interlinked, how disjunctures between habitus and field are theorised, as well as gender and habitus, are addressed before setting out how Bourdieu's framework can provide insights into how aspirations are influenced. The chapter closes with a consideration of how the self is constituted in neoliberal times, highlighting fragility and the influence of discourses.

Bourdieu's theoretical framework

A central element of Bourdieu's work is his attempt to undermine the dualisms of objectivism and subjectivism, structure and agent, where habitus and field are intended to offer an 'alternative conceptualization of the individual as socially embedded' and shaped by one's location within social fields (Kenway and McLeod, 2004: 528). Bourdieu posits a circular relationship between structures and practices, in which 'objective structures tend to produce structured subjective dispositions that produce structured actions which, in turn, tend to reproduce objective structure' (MacLeod 2009: 15). As a cultural reproduction theorist who is often criticised for asserting class structures to be overly deterministic of life choices (Levinson and Holland, 1996: 7), Bourdieu argues that structural disadvantages are internalised through socialisation and they produce forms of behaviour that result in unequal educational attainment. Bourdieu refused to 'establish sharp demarcations between the external and internal, the conscious and the unconscious, the bodily and the discursive' (Bourdieu and Wacquant, 1992: 19), where his tools are instead designed to explore how 'not only is the body in the social world, but also the ways in which the social world is in the body' (Reay, 2004b: 432).

Bourdieu conceived of education as a 'mechanism for consolidating social separation' (Grenfell, 2008: 29) where education represents 'a central ideological and cultural site of socialization that … was often more likely to reproduce, rather than challenge, social inequality in the state' (Dillabough, 2004: 490). Rendered simply, Bourdieu argues that within educational contexts, the cultural capital of the middle and upper classes are rewarded, while the capitals of the lower classes are systematically devalued. Educational institutions ensure the profitability of the dominant classes' cultural capital where 'abilities measured by scholastic criteria often stem not from natural "gifts" but from the greater or lesser affinity between class cultural habits and the demands of the educational system' (Mills, 2008: 83). Therefore, in addressing the subjective experiences of class, especially (divided) working-class student experiences in schooling, Bourdieu's tools of class analysis provide a valuable framework for analysis.

As he sought to introduce new ways of thinking about social class, Bourdieu held to his principle belief that society cannot be analysed simply in terms of economic classes and ideologies. Bourdieu believed that, in order to gain a more accurate representation of social classes, we must understand the educational and cultural factors that foster subjectivities and establish capital(s). Bourdieu's theoretical tools show how social and cultural differences are 'inseparable and that, through time, the social, which is synonymous with natural or indigenous culture, is modified by degrees of initiation into artificial, acquired culture' (Robbins, 2005: 23). Within wider processes of meaning-making, 'social structures and cognitive structures are recursively and structurally linked, and the correspondence between them provides one of the most solid props of social domination' (Bourdieu and Wacquant, 1992: 14). Through a Bourdieusian lens, social structures:

are constituted by the same socially defining principles. It is therefore possible to analyse the way the same structural relations are actualized in both the social and individual through studying structures or organization, thought and practice, and the ways in which they mutually constitute each other.

(Grenfell, 2008: 46)

For Bourdieu, the link between social and cognitive structures is not mutually constituted; there is not meaning-making in the abstract as represented by post-structuralists, but more concrete (Dillabough, 2004: 497). The individual is not merely constructed through their experiences within the world but also through their reflexive relationship with their own subjectivities. The meanings ascribed to their behaviours are highly constrained by the meanings that they have internalised through the objective structures of their experiences in the world.

To understand Bourdieu's conceptual framework on class and reproduction, it is necessary to examine how he positions power and agency. The structures, according to Bourdieu, are a constraining framework in which meaning is derived by a social agent in order to form subjectivity, as opposed to meaning and subjectivity being determined by the internalisation of external structures. In her analysis of Bourdieu in relation to post-structuralism, Dillabough (2004: 498) writes:

> Some post-structuralists do not seize the opportunity to advance a theory of identity that might explain how it is that some individuals appear to assert greater levels of 'freedom' and 'agency' than others, and are therefore in a social position precisely to articulate and assert their 'freedoms'. Bourdieu's point, I believe, is that no one is ultimately free. Individuals are certainly bound by the conditions of their political, economic and cultural circumstances.

In order to understand a social phenomena and interactions between people, it is necessary, according to Bourdieu, to examine the social space and to locate the object within 'specific local and globalised contexts, while thinking in terms of relations between structures and the individual' (Grenfell, 2008: 67). Whilst culturalist and class-conscious explanations of resistance and disengagement may be waning in light of increased attention to individualisation, researchers must remain suspicious of an individualised 'makeover' of 'social and learner identities' (Reay, 2010: 281). A Bourdieusian analytical approach is cultural, relational and contextual and, therefore, opens up exciting analytical spaces when considering learner identities in the social space of a school.

Bourdieu's tools of capitals, field and habitus

Bourdieu's concepts of capitals, field and habitus, are highly interrelated and interdependent, particularly when theorising educational contexts. Bourdieu defines four forms of capital:

- economic: money and assets
- social: affiliations and networks; family, religious and cultural heritage
- symbolic: prestige, reputation, 'exchange value' between fields
- cultural: forms of knowledge; taste, language.

Symbolic capital, which he considers another name for distinction, is nothing other than capital rendered through symbolic hierarchies where it is legitimatised (Bourdieu, 1984: 731). Bourdieu argues that, whatever the form, capital provides resources that reflect power and reproduce inequality (Reay, 2002). The social position of an individual is influenced not simply by their economic capital but also by their 'portfolio of economic, cultural, symbolic and other forms of capital' and also the individual's ability to activate these capitals to their advantage within a given field (Hart, 2013: 52–53). Within the field of education, capitals are convertible resources developed and exchanged within schooling systems, home contexts and related social fields.

Cultural capital

Cultural capital encompasses a broad array of linguistic competences, manners, preferences and orientations, which are 'subtle modalities in the relationship to culture and language' that further social mobility beyond the economic means available to the individual (Bourdieu and Passeron, 1977: 82). Cultural capital is the familiarity with the dominant culture of society, especially the ability to understand and use 'educated' language (Sullivan, 2002). Superior knowledge, skills, dispositions and qualifications that compose cultural capital are believed to have exchange value where they can be converted to economic and symbolic capitals, thus granting privileged access to better jobs, income and status. Bourdieu identifies three primary variations of cultural capital that impact social status and class positions. The first is in the embodied state incorporated in mind and body, where the accumulation of cultural capital in its embodied form begins in early childhood. Second is the objectified state, in the form of cultural goods and artefacts that are owned and exchanged for profit. Third, cultural capital exists in the institutionalised state through institutionalised forms such as educational qualifications (Bourdieu, 1984).

Carrying the accumulated logic of economic capital, cultural capital 'operates as a historically materialised, deeply structuring, and covertly institutionalised logic' consisting of accruing 'something scarce that is vested with worth' (Zipin *et al.*, 2012: 179). Within educational contexts, Lareau and Weininger (2003) proposed that cultural capital becomes institutionalised high status cultural signals used for social and cultural exclusion. They argue:

> Cultural capital in school settings must identify the particular expectations – both formal and, especially, informal – by means of which school personnel appraise students. Secondly, as a result of their location in the stratification system, students and their parents enter the educational system with dispositional skills and knowledge that differentially facilitate or impede their ability to conform to institutionalized expectations.
>
> (Lareau and Weininger 2003: 488)

Therefore, schooling experiences are shaped by the possession of capitals and the ability to operationalise them in order to make the system work in their favour. Middle-class pupils whose parents have access to ample educational supplies (books and audio/visual aids), leisure activities (vacations, museum and theatre visits) and organised support (private tutors) are more likely than their working-class peers to develop and transfer a value system of specific knowledge, desires, tastes that will serve them advantageously in their formal education (Lareau, 2003; Laureau and Weininger, 2003). Cultural capital emphasises micro-interactional processes where 'individuals' strategic use of knowledge, skills and competence comes into contact with institutionalized standards of evaluation' (Lareau and Weininger 2003: 2). In addressing the transfer of capitals, MacLeod (2009: 14) writes:

> Hence, schools serve as the trading post where socially valued cultural capital is parlayed into superior academic performance. Academic performance is then turned back into economic capital by the acquisition of superior jobs. Schools reproduce social inequality, but by dealing in the currency of academic credentials, the educational system legitimates the entire process.

In reference to the reproduction of social inequality, students' identities play a significant role, as they are formed in relation to the individuals' perception of their own embodied cultural capital, the labelling, the understanding of the system and their ability to manipulate the system to their advantage. As Hart (2013) notes, the concept of cultural capital is particularly relevant to rethinking the position of young people from different backgrounds regarding their perspective on academic education and social mobility. If the capitals individuals possess do not fit with the system, then agents often look for spaces in which their capitals will be useful and elevate status. This research works with a broad understanding of cultural capital, one which emphasizes 'the affective aspects of inequality' (Skeggs, 2002: 10), and subjective aspects such as 'levels of confidence, certainty, and entitlement' (Reay et al., 2005: 20).

Fields

Fields designate 'bundles of relations' where there is often struggle over different types of capital, whether economic, social, cultural or symbolic (Bourdieu and Wacquant, 1992: 16). Fields, or social spaces, are particularly important in the study of youth cultures, as youth often collectively occupy more than one social field simultaneously and are exposed to competing and contrasting 'logics of practice'. Fields, as sites of endless change, are 'where agents and institutions constantly struggle according to the regularities and the rules constitutive of this space of play' and where there exists a set of 'logics' particular to that field (Bourdieu and Wacquant, 1992: 102). While participants possess capitals that can be operationalised in the field, capitals cannot always be operationalised with equal ease. The game that occurs in these fields, according to Bourdieu, is always competitive, where the accumulation of capitals and status is always at stake. Each field, whether it is economic, social or educational, has 'distinctions' that are symbolically valued. Distinction can become a key focus for symbolic struggles in which agents attempt to establish superiority; though it should be noted distinction differences and ultimately inequalities 'appear natural and thus both inevitable and just' (Grenfell, 2008: 96). Grenfell (2008: 73) writes that even though a field is profoundly hierarchised and characterised by struggle, 'dominant social agents and institutions having considerable power to determine what happens within it, there is still agency and change'. To maintain the equilibrium, the field mediates what social agents do in specific contexts, but within the dialectic of field/habitus, there is often tension.

Habitus

Bourdieu's use of habitus represents an attempt to overcome the dualism between agency and structure, and allow for the research of various practices and ways of using or operationalising cultural and social capital. Whilst habitus is valuable, it remains an abstract and contested sociological concept that took many shapes even in Bourdieu's own writing (Reay, 2004b). Habitus captures 'the intentionality without intention, the knowledge without cognitive intent, the pre-reflective, infra-conscious mastery that agents acquire in the social world' (Bourdieu and Wacquant, 1992: 19). In his investigation of the relationship between schooling and systems of thought, Bourdieu argues that the school is a central generative space for habitus, where the student is directly and indirectly imparted with patterns of thinking (Ingram, 2009). As socialised subjectivity, the habitus allows for structure and agency, as well as the individual and the collective, where there is a relational structure between habitus and fields (Grenfell, 2008: 53, 61). The field structures the habitus, but there is space for improvisation as the habitus is 'creative, inventive, but within the limits of its structures' (Bourdieu and Wacquant, 1992: 19). In an 1989 interview with Wacquant, Bourdieu claims:

> Social reality exists, so to speak, twice, in things and minds, in fields and in habitus, outside and inside agents. And when habitus encounters a social world of which it is the product, it finds itself 'as a fish in water', it does not feel the weight of the water and takes the world about itself for granted.
>
> (Grenfell and James, 1998: 14)

In the exploration of learner and social identities, habitus not only allows for agency and choice, but also recognises that choices are limited and restricted by positioning, which can predispose individuals towards certain behaviours.

Habitus, as the 'embodied accumulation and effects of dispositions' (McLeod, 2005: 14), places emphasis on the structuring forces of life experiences, and conceptualises dispositions as the internalisation of the schemes that these experiences produce. In his analysis of theoretical constructs of social mobility, Friedman (2013: 11) writes:

> Habitus is especially useful because it helps to conceptualise how the mobile person's past can shape their horizon of expectations in the present. More specifically, it illuminates how the embodied inscription of this history has an indelible impact. It explains how, even when the mobile person's conscious presentation of self may align with the subjectivities of those that mobility has brought them into contact with.

Habitus allows for a consideration of how white working-class boys are positioned within the field of the school and how field influences their learner identities. Through habitus, which has the utility to link the macro-structural relations in society with the micro level of the individual, Bourdieu composes a tool to show that the ways in which people see the world not only become naturalised, but also that the arbitrariness of the processes through which they are naturalised often becomes invisible. Moving in space and across/within fields, the habitus strengthens people's perceptions that things are as they are because of the natural order, rather than through the influence of culturally determined principles.

Not fully determined by structure, and incorporating agency, habitus represents a constant interaction between structure and agency. Agency and structure both reside within the habitus, mutually shaping one another. Agency is, therefore, not reducible to structures; it is not determined by experience, but it is constrained by it. These internalised structures may be viewed as more determined aspects of habitus that have left Bourdieu open to criticism, but habitus can only operate through an agent, and, as such, must incorporate an element of consciousness. Habitus is a method of working with data, rather than applying it to data (Reay, 2004b). In the interpretation of the specific and cultural practices that may produce certain ways of being, both inside and outside of school contexts, habitus 'cannot be directly observed in empirical research', it has to be apprehended interpretively (Reay *et al.*, 2005: 25).

The interaction between capitals, habitus and field

Habitus is where one's perceptions and conceptions are conditioned by the structures of the environment in which they are engendered; yet the habitus does not operate identically for all people and is deeply dependent on capitals and field. As a set of durable and transposable dispositions, the habitus is not 'set' but evolving as the field too is in constant flux. Being the product of previous experiences, habitus is never fixed, 'it may be changed by history, that is by new experiences, education, or training (which implies that aspects of what remains unconscious in habitus be made at least partially conscious and explicit)' (Bourdieu, 2002: 29). Habitus and field operate in two inter-related and overlapping ways:

> On one side, it is a relation of conditioning: the field structures the habitus, which is the product of the embodiment of the immanent necessity of a field (or of a set of intersecting fields, the extent of their intersection or discrepancy being at the root of the divided or even torn habitus). On the other side, it is a relation of knowledge or cognitive construction. Habitus contributes to constituting the field as a meaningful world, a world endowed with sense and value, in which it is worth investing one's energy.
>
> (Bourdieu and Wacquant, 1992: 127)

As a result of the internalisation of external structures, habitus reacts to the solicitations of the field by 'actions [that] are not purposeful but, rather, continuously adaptive' (Robbins, 2000: 29). The habitus is permeable and responsive where current circumstances are acted upon but also internalised. Therefore, habitus does not rule out strategic choice or deliberation, remaining a tool Bourdieu uses to reconcile dualisms, transcend dichotomies and encourage us to think relationally between habitus, capital and field.

Habitus disjunctures

When habitus accords with the logic of the field, 'it finds itself "as fish in water"; it does not feel the weight of the water and takes the world about itself for granted' (Bourdieu and Wacquant, 1992: 18). The dialectical confrontation between habitus and field – other than the field of origin – results in a degree of accommodation, where the habitus accepts the legitimacy of the new field's structure and is, in turn, structured by it, thus enabling a modified habitus. Bourdieu's framework also allows for analytical work in regard to when habitus and field do not accord and also when there are disjunctures and individuals feel like a 'fish out of water'. When the habitus encounters a new field, it is still constrained by the structuring forces of the field of origin. This internalisation of new experiences and schemes of perception can lead to the internalisation of conflicting dispositions.

Drawing upon Lahire (2011), Friedman (2013: 11) writes of a habitus clivé, where the habitus is 'out of sync with the field it inhabits'. When theorising habitus disjunctures, habitus clivé is a useful tool for understanding experiences of social mobility in contemporary times where conflicting dispositions struggle for pole position, and the individual can, at times, feel pulled in different directions; in other words where they both feel the weight of the water and an uncertainty in how best to swim. The tension between habitus and field is relevant to the study of learner identities and engagement with schooling. For many working-class students, their learning experiences are shaped by disjunctures that can generate not only change and transformation, but also ambivalence, insecurity, uncertainty and disengagement (Reay, 2005). Within a high-attaining grammar school in a deprived area, Ingram (2011) observed the habitus of white working-class boys undergoing forms of mediation and negotiation in relation to the habitus of the institution, i.e. the grammar school. Her cohort was able to carefully articulate the restructuring of their own habitus as it aligned with and against the tough-boy 'Smick'. Ingram (2011) illustrates the working-class boys' habitus tug, when pulled by forces of different fields simultaneously; destabilised habitus, when 'no one knows who you actually are'; and disjunctive habitus, when the divided habitus causes division. All of which were largely processes centring on legitimating simultaneously being both clever and working-class.

Gender and habitus

Bourdieu's theory of practice illustrates how individuals come to embody, albeit in diverse ways, everyday social practices or how hierarchies are differentiated and reproduced (Bourdieu, 1984; Bourdieu and Accardo, 1993), yet there is no clear line of inquiry into how gender is incorporated in the habitus. In his account of the role of gender, Bourdieu (2001) makes frequent references to common masculinity tropes such as physical virility, pursuit of glory and the rejection of tenderness to show that the 'social world constructs the body as a sexually defined reality and as the depository of sexually defining principles of vision and division' (pp. 10, 12). Bourdieu's *Masculine Domination* (2001) simply reproduced 'standard binaries of masculine domination and female subordination as if these structures are unitary, coherent and unchanged by and in contemporary social life' (McLeod, 2005: 53). As Mottier (2002: 350) notes, Bourdieu conceptualises gender primarily in terms of sexual difference, which is why it is so problematic. To counteract Bourdieu's inadequacies regarding gender, recent empirical work has attempted to articulate the role of gender within the habitus (cf. Adkins, 1999; McNay, 1999; Skeggs, 2004; Connolly, 2006; Coles, 2009). Recent feminist scholarship has sought to show the complexities when gendering Bourdieu's conceptual tools, specifically habitus (Adkins, 2003; Lawler, 2004; McNay, 2004; Reay, 2004a). Such theoretical work often combines Bourdieu's tools with other theoretical frameworks (e.g. Butler, Fraser), while reworking gender and status, gender and culture, and the importance of emotion.

Though Bourdieu's work largely implies that 'gender is a secondary characteristic to social class' (Dumais, 2002: 45), gender is a significant part of habitus and should not be discounted in understanding the construction of learner and social identities. Arguably, in her analysis of feminist rereading of Bourdieu, McLeod (2005: 12) argues that habitus and field 'lead us to reconceive the cultural and social practices of gender'. Gender can be theorised as sexually characterised habitus, where gender represents 'a particular kind of habitus that has force because it appears part of the natural order of things' (McLeod, 2005: 18). For McLeod, the relationship between gender and habitus tends to take two main forms. First, social fields 'are understood as differentiated by gender (and by class and race) and the habitus is formed in the midst of and structured by these differential relations of power and identity positions' (McLeod, 2005: 19). This structuring forms dispositions that operate within the habitus but are dependent on encounters with other fields; conventions of gender are secured through internalisation of particular structures. Secondly, 'subjective dispositions can be gendered' where gender is an '"inherited" and embodied way of being that is shaped in interaction with social fields, constituting a repertoire of orientations and dispositions' (McLeod, 2005: 19). McLeod shows how, when extending habitus and field to account for gender identities, the interplay between habitus and field must be accounted for.

Taking a slightly different viewpoint to McLeod, for Skeggs (2002, 2005), gender, class and race are social positions, knowledge positions and ways of understanding shaped by lived experience. For Skeggs (2002: 9) gender, class and race 'are not capitals as such, rather they provide the relations in which capitals come to be organized and valued'. Social class positions and different forms of capital are, therefore, mediated through local social power relations and through gender where masculinity and femininity are uninhabitable as complete, coherent identities (Skeggs, 1997: 102). Conceptions of masculinities and femininities are essential to understanding how gender is constituted in habitus. Much of the scholarship on gender and habitus operates on the assumption that the processes of constituting gender are not undergoing significant historical change in relation to globalisation and neoliberalism, where masculinities and femininities reflect the specific social and economic contexts in which they are located.

Adding to this complexity, McNay (1999, 2000) unsettles the key conceptual frameworks that have underpinned much past and current theoretical work on gender habitus. McNay (1999: 107) is critical of the 'overemphasis on the alignment that the habitus establishes between subjective dispositions and the objective structure of the field with regard to gender identity'. Where Bourdieu would argue for the stability of gender norms in the forming of subjectivities, McNay's approach includes attention to a greater instability in gender norms in an era of high modernity. McNay (1999: 103) writes: 'While gender identity is not an immutable or essential horizon, there are many pre-reflexive aspects of masculine and feminine behaviour – sexual desire, maternal feelings – that call into question the process of identity transformation highlighted by some theories of reflexivity'.

While pre-reflexive aspects of gender may exist, these aspects are (re)constituted in reference to the continually changing field and degree of reflexivity. Furthermore, McNay (1999: 106–107) writes that while habitus 'draws attention to the entrenched nature of gender identity, it is important to consider the extent to which its effects may be attenuated by the movement of individuals across fields'. In considering the identity work of white working-class boys, the influence of fields on gendered habitus is at play alongside the gendered processes that are pushed to the forefront, depending on different fields. Therefore, we must consider how gender, within the habitus, interacts with fields, when gender identity may come to the forefront, depending on the field.

While feminist theorists such as Adkins, Skeggs and McNay have sought to show the role of gender in the habitus, there also exists a radically different approach to theorising gender and habitus. In his innovative work, Coles (2009) contends that Bourdieu's tools can be combined with many of gender's conceptual tools, specifically hegemonic masculinity, to produce theoretical models that define 'relations of power that centre on capital and the tensions that exist between dominant and subordinate groups of men' (pp. 33–34). Placing an emphasis on the power of the field – a field of masculinity – Coles (2009: 36) contends there exists a 'struggle for legitimacy' between dominant and subordinated masculinities in the field of masculinity where, arguably certain forms become 'validated by habitus and the belief that one's own masculinity is "natural" and "true"'. For Coles, masculinity represents a special kind of field since it has the ability to transverse other social fields, allowing for individual differences between how men perform it. Fields, as sites of struggles, often 'form, socialize, reward, and punish those who pass through them – according to the logic of practice of the particular field – and offer the social conditions of existence for its "members"' (Grenfell, 2011: 31). The conceptual work of Coles (2009) attempts to question how men negotiate masculinity, especially in considering masculinity as an unconscious strategy within the habitus where masculinity forms 'part of the habitus of men that is both transposable and malleable to given situations to form practical dispositions and actions to everyday situations' (p. 39). Whilst habitus may enable us to understand how men negotiate their masculinity, we must recognise not all men use (or are able to use) masculinity as a resourceful strategy in their everyday lives (Coles, 2009: 38). Instead there exist many variations in how masculinity is deployed.

Applying Bourdieu's framework to aspiration and identity

In neoliberal times, learner identities and aspiration are bounded by multiple logics of capital: cultural, economic, human and social. Schools are expected to produce a neoliberal subject who espouses values of 'self-reliance, autonomy, and independence,' in order to gain 'self-respect, self-esteem, self-worth, and self-advancement' (Davies and Bansel, 2007: 252). As the neoliberal rhetoric divorces subjects from contexts, the 'value' of the learner becomes rooted in their acceptance of the social mobility rhetoric of the educational system. While aspiration may be regarded as a personal character trait in policy contexts (Spohrer, 2011: 58), the choices of young people have been 'strongly inflected, shaped, and constrained by identities and inequalities of gender, social class, 'race'/ethnicity' (Archer *et al.*, 2010: 80)

   Aspiration and social mobility have been explored through a variety of different theoretical frameworks from scholars such as Appadurai (2003, 2004), Boudon's social opportunity model (1974), Bauman (1998), Beck (1992), Goldthorpe (1998) and Giddens (1991), each with their strengths and weaknesses. Bourdieu's theory of practice shows how relations of privilege and domination are produced through the interaction of habitus, a matrix of dispositions that shape how the individual operates in the social world and capital that is, economic, cultural, social and symbolic; and field, i.e. social contexts. Forsaking the idea of 'rules' in favour of strategies, the social action of individuals is guided by a practical sense, by what Bourdieu calls a 'feel for the game' (Bourdieu 1988: 782). Game, as a provocative metaphor, helps us to understand the dialectical relationship between the 'nexus of habitus, capital and field' (Wacquant, 2011: 86). Through habitus, we invest ourselves in the game, where:

> We can picture each player as having in front of her a pile of tokens of different colors, each color corresponding to a given species of capital she holds, so that her relative force in the game, her position in the space of play, and also her strategic orientation toward the game [and] the

moves she makes, more or less risky or cautious, subversive or conservative, depend both on the total number of tokens and on the composition of the piles of tokens she retains, that is, on the volume and structure of her capital.

(Bourdieu and Wacquant, 1992: 99)

The strategies of the player always operate in relation to the volume and structure of his or her capital. Even when practice appears as rational action to an impartial observer who possesses all the necessary information to reconstruct it as such, rational choice is not its principle. The structure of strategies depends on: '(1) "their position in the field" (the volume and composition of capital); (2) "the perception that they have of the field" (habitus); and (3) "the state of the instruments of reproduction" (field)' (Yang, 2013: 7). Indeed, Bourdieu (1988: 782–783) writes that social action has very little to do with rational choice, 'except perhaps in very specific crisis situations when the routines of everyday life and the practical feel of cease to operate'. Rational action theory, according to Bourdieu, fails to recognise that action and intentional choice emanates from an actor who is himself economically and socially conditioned. In short, the theory ignores the dialectic between the range of options available, the range of options visible to us and our dispositions (habitus), the embodied experiences of our journey (Grenfell, 2008: 52).

Within what can only be called a 'meritocratic illusion' (Mills, 2008: 83), recent theorists have utilised Bourdieu's concepts of field, capital and habitus to further the analysis of working-class interaction with education (Reay, 2002; Archer and Francis 2005; Archer et al., 2007; Lareau and Horvat, 1999). Using a Bourdieusian lens, these studies explore learner and social identities in relation to conceptions of aspiration, hegemonic masculinity, parental engagement and working-class cultural ethos, in order to untangle explanations of class, aspiration, status and power in pedagogic contexts. In Reay's (2002: 222) case study Shaun's Story, she utilises Bourdieu's 'the duality of the self' to depict the fractured relationship of 'white working-class masculinities with educational success' and the 'heavy psychic costs' involved in embodying 'tough boy on the street versus good boy in the classroom'. This research explores the processes of identity work that burdens working-class boys where they contend with the 'habitus divided against itself' (Bourdieu, and Accadro, 1993: 511). White working-class boys are exposed to competing fields that impel them, to varying extents, to operationalise their capitals, as well as their unconscious 'feel for the game'. Habitus, therefore, allows for an exploration into how the boys reconcile competing life-worlds, deeply contextual social processes and the im/possible aspirations. Charlesworth (2000), in his deep ethnography of working-class Rotherham, illustrates how habitus is transmitted from one generation to the next, where class ethos becomes 'a specific embodied morality that operates

in a practical mode and it governs the nuances of honour between people'
(p. 30). Working-class habitus, in relation to neoliberal discourses, is an integral part of the puzzle as to why some working-class boys consistently reject
education or why education rejects them.

Bourdieu's habitus is helpful in revealing what he calls 'symbolic violence',
the 'violence which is exercised upon a social agent with his or her complic-
ity' where 'social agents are knowing agents who, even when they are
subjected to determinisms, contribute to producing the efficacy of that
which determines them insofar as they structure what determines them'
(Bourdieu and Wacquant, 1992: 167). Symbolic violence is the 'mode of
domination in which the oppressed contribute to their own subjugation
through processes of socialization and self-formation' (Giroux, 1981: 9).
The habitus becomes a site where individuals 'fit between determinants and
the categories of perception' as the effect of domination arises and takes hold
(Bourdieu and Wacquant, 1992: 167). Through symbolic violence, working-
class students do not aspire highly because, according to Bourdieu, they have
internalised and reconciled themselves to the 'limited opportunities that exist
for those without much cultural capital' (Swartz, 1997: 197). The level of
aspiration of individuals is 'essentially determined by the probability (judged
intuitively by means of previous successes or failures) of achieving the desired
goal' (Bourdieu and Passeron, 1977: 111). Young working-class males may
come to see the aspiration toward academic success as a symbolically legitimated form that not only falls largely beyond their grasp but also beyond
their desire.

For Bourdieu it is through discourse that certain beliefs and assumptions
circulate, which contributes to the establishment of common sense logics of
practice or doxa. Within the neoliberal discourse, symbolic violence is very
potent where often individuals 'buy in' to the common sense or doxic expectation that everyone can accumulate qualifications, and failure to do so lies
in the individual as opposed to wider societal structures. Consequently, low
socio-economic status (SES) students see themselves as deficient, when
unsuccessful in the pursuit of doxic goals. In rethinking aspiration according
to the concept of doxa, Zipin et al. (2013: 7) cite Bourdieu's concept of
symbolic violence to enhance their extension of Bourdieu's theoretical tools:

> When such verdicts take an individualist-psychological cast (as is
> typical), ignoring or underweighting social-structural barriers, this
> insinuates … a lack of inventive cleverness compared to those who
> succeed. This can further imply that they suffer deficiencies in
> intelligence, resilience and/or wholesome lifestyles … and [might need
> to] so adjust themselves to 'lower level' aspirations. Such simplistic
> judgments fail to read the complex, but not easily articulated,
> emotional labors at work beneath what may appear as unrealistically
> ambitious expressions of aspiration.

They then put forth a three-part conceptual framework for rethinking aspirations: a doxic logic for aspiring, founded upon populist-ideological mediations; a habituated logic for aspiring that draws upon biographic-historical conditions and is embodied as habitus among people in given social-structural positions; and emergent senses of possible futures grounded in lived social-cultural resources they call 'funds of aspiration' (Zipin *et al.*, 2013: 5). In each approach, aspiration, constructed in relation to discourses, form subjectivities where the dispositional structures of the habitus come to embody 'possibilities-within-limits of given social-structural positions' and where the habitus becomes 'self-limiting possibility' in terms of probable futures (Zipin *et al.*, 2013: 9).

In understanding how subjectivities are formed, Bourdieu's methodological concept of reflexivity is his most important contribution as 'many and perhaps most of our actions are co-determined by both our habitus and our reflexive deliberations' (Elder-Vass, 2007: 335). Reflexivity is central to understanding how agents compose identities in relation to structural inequalities. For Bourdieu reflexivity, the degree of awareness of gendered, classed and ethnic positioning, is formed in the habitus and that is unique to certain class factions. Reflexivity is not restricted to the middle classes, though 'young people are also not homogeneously reflexive, and those who are reflexive do not necessarily gain much advantage from this in their work or educational lives' (Farrugia, 2012: 686).

There exist different interpretations of reflexivity and contentious debate regarding how reflexivity contributes to mobility (Kenway and Mcleod, 2004; Threadgold and Nilan, 2009; Farrugia, 2012). Yet, most interpretations regarding reflexivity and reflexive subjectivity 'aim to describe and theorize the way in which people relate to themselves', where reflexivity operates according to an agent's understanding of their own context and their positionality within the context (Farrugia, 2013: 284). In his argument for reflexive modernity, Beck (1992) states that individuals respond differently to situations based on their own individualised reflexive understanding of that situation. The tenants of neoliberalism, competition and risk require people to advertise or perform their individuality and to become neoliberal subjects. Implicit in the discourse of risk, particularly neoliberal conceptualisations of risk, is the idea that individuals are rational and active choosers who, therefore, are capable of avoiding risk by exercising reflexivity. This assumes that reflexivity can be exercised in the same way for all individuals regardless of class. While fluidity and the ability to adopt multiple identities have been recognised as capital, mainly among the middle-class youth (Threadgold and Nilan, 2009; Skrbis *et al.*, 2013), this work will explore how working-class youth reaffirm and retraditionalize identities.

The creation of the self in neoliberal times

While Bourdieu used the concept of the self in his early writings, Bourdieu was mainly 'opposed to the concept of self, which he considers to be a bourgeois fabrication' in favour of habitus which 'decentralizes the self, making it opposite to conscious action and will-power' (Skeggs, 2004: 83).[1] While habitus is a valuable theoretical tool, the self is important to consider when accounting for powerful neoliberal discourses where 'education has been reinvented as an aspirational project for the self' (Reay, 2013: 665). While adopting Bourdieu as the primary framework of analysis, it is also important to acknowledge post-structural theorising where the self is constituted through increasingly pluralistic and diverse processes.

Shaped by the material and symbolic resources of history, language and culture required to sustain it, identity remains a challenging and contested area of research (Hall, 1996: 4). Post-structuralist theory explores gendered, classed and ethnic constructions of identities through the appropriation of available sets of meanings and practices, i.e. discourses, within various cultural settings such as home, school, community and peer groups. According to Davies (1982: 238), the self is 'exposed to competing discourses, so we are positioned in different ways and have the opportunity to see ourselves in different ways'. In a post-structuralist framework, discourses provide viable 'ways to be' (subjectivities), and the construction of pupil identities is seen as a process of 'struggle and of negotiation, rejection, acceptance, and ambivalence' (Pollard and Filer 2007: 448). This creates a 'fragility of self', requiring constant maintenance work (Davies, 1982: 238). Furthermore, individuals experience critical moments in the ongoing development of individual identity where there is the task of 'maintaining the preferred discursive practices which makes one's reality meaningful' (Davies, 1982: 238). In the production of our own sense of who we are, of our subjectivity, categories are multiple and fluid:

> We are always in some sense both and neither of the binary categories, the accomplishment of unequivocal membership of one and not the other, and the simultaneous accomplishment of the 'I' as this person and not any other, involves the expulsion of the other.
>
> (Davies, 2006: 73–74)

In considering the creation of the self, Davies' conceptions of category-maintenance work is part of what agents engage in to separate themselves out into the binary category to which they have been assigned, largely through social construction processes. The discursive, or fluid, approach to identity considers it to be a continual process, not necessarily determined by a sense of 'won or lost', 'sustained or abandoned' (Hall, 1996: 2).

Neoliberalism attempts to erase issues surrounding inequality and positions individual students as equal players where they falsely come to understand themselves as 'responsible for the production of a self' (Burke, 2007: 414). The rhetoric of neoliberalism disregards how the cultural resources for self-making are still very much constrained by class (Skeggs, 2004). Within the process of self-making, it should be noted there exists a long history in Britain 'in which the working-class have been (through representation) continually demonized, pathologized', and that most representations of working-class people contribute to 'devaluing and delegitimating their already meagre capitals, putting further blocks on tradability, denying any conversion into symbolic capital' (Skeggs, 2002: 10). Where Paul Willis' 'lads' were positive in the creation of their working-class identity with patriarchal support and a group collectiveness in their rejection of education, our current working-class boys face a ubiquitous social construction by the mass media that stigmatises them as 'yobs', sexual predators and members of an 'underclass' (cf. Peterson, 1992; Skeggs, 2002; McDowell, 2003; Yar and Hayward 2006).[2] Lacking in cultural resources, while being saturated with negative media representations (Archer *et al.*, 2007), significantly limits the working-class ability to constitute a self as having value (McDowell, 2003; Skeggs, 2005). Through this process, we see the potential for 'fixity' as agents who are deprived of capital are 'either physically or symbolically held at a distance from goods that are the rarest socially; they are forced to stock with the most undesirable and the least rare persons or goods. The lack of capital intensifies the experience of finitude: it chains one to a place' (Bourdieu and Accadro, 1993: 127). Within neoliberal times, it is increasingly difficult for those from less-privileged backgrounds to demonstrate the appropriate 'economy of experience' that involves translating everyday life into a narrative of employability (Brown and Hesketh, 2004). Today, the self, as a reflexive project, has to be 'worked at', molded and remolded upon a 'narrative of individual employability, often at the expense of intrinsic human experience' (Brown, 2013: 688).

Summary

Bourdieu's tools establish a framework to explore identity and aspiration where aspirations are influenced by a 'logic of practice' according to an ongoing series of processes and negotiations. The habitus is composed of both learner identities and social identities: learner identities that are primarily shaped by neoliberal ideology, and social identities that are primarily shaped by gender and class shifts. In the educational experience, social and learner identities are intertwined and mutually constitute one another. The nexus between learner and social identities influence how identities become fixed and fluid, how resistance and conformity is fostered, and how engagement and disengagement occur. However, social identities:

> cannot be transposed onto learner identities, there is not a neat fit but rather varying degrees of overlap and synergy in which the development of a sense of self as a learner is crucial to the shaping of a coherent and viable wider identity.
>
> (Reay, 2010: 279)

In studying white working-class boys' educational experience, the use of Bourdieu's habitus, field and capitals allow for analysis where disaffection is imbued with cultural resonances and where habitus becomes a site of mediation regarding objective possibilities.

Notes

1   For Skeggs (2004), habitus is a contradictory concept, it is not only 'the product of strategies objectively co-ordinated by mechanisms unknown to the individual' but also the 'future-projected, strategizing, accruing, exchange-value self' Habitus impacts 'upon the structures that shape it, with the potential to change the formation of the field from whence it came' (pp. 83, 85).
2   Skeggs (2002) notes that while men were historically allowed to feel working-class pride, working-class women have never been allowed that advantage, and when the working class label is applied to women, it carries demeaning implications.

References

Adkins, L. (1999) Community and economy: A retraditionalization of gender?. *Theory Culture Society*, 16(1), 119–139.

Adkins, L. (2003) Reflexivity: Freedom or habit of gender?. *Theory Culture Society*, 20(6), 21–42.

Allen, K. (2013) 'Blair's children': Young women as 'aspirational subjects' in the psychic landscape of class. *Sociological Review*, 61(4), 1–20.

Appadurai, A. (2003) Archive and aspiration. In J. Brouwer and A. Mulder (eds), *Information is alive* (pp. 14–25). Rotterdam: NAI.

Appadurai, A. (2004) The capacity to aspire: Culture and the terms of recognition. In V. Rao and M. Walton (eds), *Culture and public action* (pp. 59–84). Stanford, CA: Stanford University Press.

Archer, L. and Francis, B. (2005) Negotiating the dichotomy of Boffin and Triad: British-Chinese pupils' constructions of 'laddism'. *The Sociological Review*, 495–521.

Archer, L., Halsall, A. and Hollingworth, S. (2007) Class, gender, (hetero)sexuality and schooling: Paradoxes within working-class girls' engagement with education and post-16 aspirations. *British Journal of Sociology of Education*, 28(2), 165–180.

Archer, L., Hollingworth, S. and Mendick, H. (2010) *Urban youth and schooling: The experiences and identities of educationally 'at risk' young people*. Berkshire: Open University Press.

Archer, L., DeWitt, J. and Willis, B. (2013) Adolescent boys' science aspirations: Masculinity, capital, and power. *Journal of Research in Science Teaching*, 1–30.

Bathmaker, A.M., Ingram, N. and Waller, R. (2013) Higher education, social class, and the mobilisation of capitals: Recognising and playing the game. *British Journal of Sociology of Education*, 34(5–6), 723–243.

Bauman, Z. (1998) *Globalization: The human consequences*. New York: Columbia University Press.

Beck, U. (1992) *Risk society: Towards a new modernity*. London: Sage Publications.

Boudon, R. (1974) *Education, opportunity and social inequality: Changing prospects in Western society.* London: John Wiley.

Bourdieu, P. (1984) *Distinction: A Social critique of the judgement of taste.* Oxon: Routledge.

Bourdieu, P. (1988) Vive la crise! For heterodoxy in social science. *Theory and Society,* 17(5), 773–787.

Bourdieu, P. (2001) *Masculine domination.* Oxford: Blackwell Publishers Ltd.

Bourdieu, P. (2002) Habitus. In J. Hillier and E. Rooksby (eds), *Habitus: A sense of place* (pp. 27–34). Aldershot: Ashgate.

Bourdieu, P. and Accadro, A. (1993) *The weight of the world: Social suffering in contemporary society.* Stanford: Stanford University Press.

Bourdieu, P. and Passeron, J.C. (1977) *Reproduction in education, society, and culture.* London: Sage Publications.

Bourdieu, P. and Wacquant, L. (1992) *An invitation to reflexive sociology.* Cambridge: Polity Press.

Brown, P. (2013) Education, opportunity, and the prospects for social mobility. *British Journal of Sociology of Education,* 34(5–6), 678–700.

Brown, P. and Hesketh, A. (2004) *The Mismanagement of talent: Employability and jobs in the knowledge economy.* Oxford: Oxford University Press.

Burke, P. (2007) Men accessing education: Masculinities, identifications, and widening participation. *British Journal of Sociology of Education,* 28(4), 411–424.

Charlesworth, S. J. (2000) *The phenomenology of working class experience.* Cambridge: University Press.

Coles, T. (2009) Negotiating the field of masculinity: The production and reproduction of multiple dominant masculinities. *Men and Masculinities,* 12(1), 30–44.

Connell, R. W. (1993) *Schools and social justice.* Philadelphia: Temple University Press.

Connolly, P. (2006) The masculine habitus as 'distributed cognition': A case study of 5- to 6-year-old boys in an English inner-city, multi-ethnic primary school. *Children and Society,* 20(2), 140–152.

Davies, B. (1982) *Life in the classroom and playground.* London: Routledge and Kegan Paul.

Davies, B. (2006) Identity, abjection, and otherness. In M. Arnot and M. Mac an Ghaill (eds), *The Routledge reader in gender and education* (pp. 72–90). Oxon: Routledge.

Davies, B. and Bansel, P. (2007) Neoliberalism and education. *International Journal of Qualitative Studies in Education,* 20(3), 247–256.

Dillabough, J. A. (2004) Class, culture and the 'predicaments of masculine domination': Encountering Pierre Bourdieu. *British Journal of Sociology of Education,* 25(4), 489–506.

Dumais, S. A. (2002) Cultural capital, gender, and school success: The role of habitus. *Sociology of Education,* 75(1), 44–68.

Elder-Vass, D. (2007) Reconciling Archer and Bourdieu in an emergentist theory of action. *Sociological Theory,* 25(4), 325–345.

Farrugia, D. (2012) Young people and structural inequality: Beyond the middle ground. *Journal of Youth Studies,* 16(5), 679–693.

Farrugia, D. (2013) The reflexive subject: Towards a theory of reflexivity as practical intelligibility. *Current Sociology,* 61(3), 283–300.

Friedman, S. (2013) The price of the ticket: Rethinking the experience of social mobility. *Sociology*, 48(2): 1–17.

Fuller, C. (2009) *Sociology, gender, and educational aspirations: Girls and their ambitions*. London: Continnum.

Giddens, A. (1991) *Modernity and self-identity: Self and society in the late modern age*. Cambridge: Polity.

Giroux, H. (1981) Hegemony, resistance, and the paradox of educational reform. *Interchange*, 12(2–3), 3–26.

Goldthorpe, J. H. (1998) Rational action theory for sociology. *The British Journal of Sociology*, 49(2), 167–192.

Grenfell, M. (2008) *Pierre Bourdieu: Key concepts*. Durham: Acumen.

Grenfell, M. (2011) *Bourdieu, language and linguistics*. London; New York: Continuum International Publishing Group.

Grenfell, M. and James, D. (1998) *Bourdieu and education: Acts of practical theory*. Abingdon: RoutledgeFalmer.

Hall, S. (1996) Who needs 'identity'? In S. Hall and P. Du Gay (eds), *Questions of cultural identity* (pp. 1–18). London: Sage Publications.

Hart, C. S. (2013) *Aspirations, Education and Social Justice: Applying Sen and Bourdieu*. London, Bloomsbury.

Ingram, N. (2009) Working-class boys, educational success and the misrecognition of working-class culture. *British Journal of Sociology of Education*, 30(4), 421–434.

Ingram, N. (2011) Within school and beyond the gate: The complexities of being educationally successful and working class. *Sociology*, 45(2): 287–302.

Jenkins, R. (1992) *Pierre Bourdieu*. London: Routledge.

Kenway, J. and McLeod, J. (2004) Bourdieu's reflexive sociology and 'spaces of points of view': Whose reflexivity, which perspective?. *British Journal of Sociology of Education*, 25(4), 525–544.

Lahire, B. (2011) *The plural actor*. Cambridge: Polity.

Lareau, A. (2003) *Unequal childhoods*. Berkley: University of California Press.

Lareau, A. and Horvat, E. M. (1999) Moments of social inclusion and exclusion: Race, class and cultural capital in family–school relationships. *Sociology of Education*, 72(1), 37–53.

Lareau, A. and Weininger, E. B. (2003) Cultural capital in educational research: A critical assessment. *Theory and Society*, 32(5/6), 567–606.

Lawler, S. (2004) Rules of engagement: Habitus, power and resistance. *Theory Culture Society*, 20(6), 110–128.

Levinson, B. A. and Holland, D. C. (1996) The cultural production of the educated person: An introduction. In B. A. Levinson, D. E. Foley and D. C. Holland (eds), *The cultural production of the educated person* (pp. 1–56). New York: State University of New York Press.

McDowell, L. (2003) *Redundant masculinities?: Employment change and white working class youth*. Malden, MA: Blackwell Pub.

McLeod, J. (2005) Feminists re-reading Bourdieu: Old debates and new questions about gender habitus and gender change. *Theory and Research in Education*, 3(1), 11–30.

MacLeod, J. (2009) *Ain't no makin' it*. Boulder, CO: Westview Press.

McNay, L. (1999) Gender, habitus and the field: Pierre Bourdieu and the limits of reflexivity. *Theory, Culture, Society*, 16(1), 95–117.

McNay, I. (2000) *Gender and agency: Reconfiguring the subject in feminist and social theory.* Cambridge: Polity Press.

McNay, L. (2004) Agency and experience: Gender as a lived relation. *Theory Culture Society,* 20(6), 175–190.

Mills, C. (2008) Reproduction and transformation of inequalities in schooling: the transformative potential of the theoretical constructs of Bourdieu. *British Journal of Sociology of Education,* 29(1), 79–89.

Mottier, V. (2002) Masculine domination: Gender and power in Bourdieu's writings. *Feminist Theory,* 3(3), 345–359.

Mouzelis, N. (2007) Habitus and reflexivity: Restructuring Bourdieu's theory of practice. *Sociological Research Online,* 12(6). Online at: www.socresonline.org.uk/12/6/9.html

Peterson, P. E. (1992) The urban underclass and the poverty paradox. *Political Science Quarterly,* 106(4), 617–637.

Pollard, A. and Filer, A. (2007) Learning, differentiation and strategic action in secondary education: Analyses from the *Identity and Learning Programme. British Journal of Sociology of Education,* 28(4), 441–458.

Reay, D. (2002) Shaun's story: Troubling discourses on white working-class masculinities. *Gender and Education,* 14(3), 221–234.

Reay, D. (2004a) Gendering Bourdieu's concepts of capitals? Emotional capital, women and social class. *Theory Culture Society,* 20(6), 57–74.

Reay, D. (2004b) 'It's all becoming habitus': Beyond the habitual use of habitus in educational research. *British Journal of Sociology of Education,* 25(4), 431–444.

Reay, D. (2005) Beyond consciousness?: The psychic landscape of social class. *Sociology,* 39(5), 911–928.

Reay, D. (2010) Identity-making in schools and classrooms. In M. Wetherall and C. Talpade Mohanty (eds), *The Sage handbook of identities* (pp. 277–294). Los Angeles: Sage Publications.

Reay, D. (2013) Social mobility, a panacea for austere times: Tales of emperors, frogs, and tadpoles. *British Journal of Sociology of Education,* 34(5–6), 660–677.

Reay, D., David, M. E. and Ball, S. (2005) *Degrees of choice: Social class, race and gender in higher education.* London: Institute of Education.

Robbins, D. (2000) *Bourdieu and culture.* London: Sage Publications.

Robbins, D. (2005) The origins, early development and status of Bourdieu's concept of 'cultural capital'. *The British Journal of Sociology,* 56(1), 13–20.

Skeggs, B. (2002) *Formations of class and gender.* Nottingham: Sage Publications.

Skeggs, B. (2004) Exchange, value and affect: Bourdieu and 'the self'. *Sociological Review,* 75–95.

Skeggs, B. (2005) The making of class and gender through visualizing moral subject formation. *Sociology,* 39(5), 965–982.

Skrbis, Z., Woodward, I. and Bean, C. (2013) Seeds of cosmopolitan future? Young people and their aspirations for future mobility. *Journal of Youth Studies,* 1–12.

Spohrer, K. (2011) Deconstructing 'aspiration': UK policy debates and European policy trends. *European Educational Research Journal,* 10(1), 53–62.

Sullivan, A. (2002) Bourdieu and education: How useful is Bourdieu's theory for researchers?. *The Netherlands Journal of Social Sciences,* 38(2), 144–166.

Swartz, D. (1997) *Culture and power: The sociology of Pierre Bourdieu.* Chicago, IL: The Chicago Press.

Threadgold, S. and Nilan, P. (2009) Reflexivity of contemporary youth, risk and cultural capital. *Current Sociology*, 57(1), 47–68.

Throop, J. C. and Murphy, K. M. (2002) Bourdieu and phenomenology: A critical assessment. *Anthropological Theory*, 2(2), 185–207.

Wacquant, L. (2011) Habitus as topic and tool: Reflections on becoming a prize-fighter. *Qualitative Research in Psychology*, 8, 81–92.

Yang, Y. (2013) Bourdieu, practice, and change: Beyond the criticism of determinism. *Educational Philosophy and Theory*, 45, 1–19.

Yar, M. and Hayward, K. (2006) The 'chav' phenomenon: Consumption, media and the construction of a new underclass. *Crime Media Culture*, 2(1), 9–28.

Zipin, L., Sellar, S. and R. Hattam, R. (2012) Countering and exceeding 'capital': a 'Funds of knowledge' approach to re-imagining community. *Discourse: Studies in the Cultural Politics of Education*, 33(2), 179–192.

Zipin, L., Sellar, S., Brennan, M. and Gale, T. (2013) Educating for futures in marginalized regions: A sociological framework for rethinking and researching aspirations. *Educational Philosophy and Theory*, 45, 1–20.

Chapter 3

Egalitarianism in the habitus

'Class' could be something in the blood, in the very fibre of a man or woman, a way of growing, feeling, judging, taken out of the resources of generations gone before. Not something to be shuffled off with new possessions, new prospects, new surroundings; to be overlaid perhaps, or felt in new ways.

(Jackson and Marsden, 1966: 192)

The chapter addresses both the main findings of the research and how habitus will be used to theorise the ways in which boys construct their identities and aspirations surrounding their conceptions of success and failure. How dispositions are formed within the habitus requires attention to the dialectic of competing fields as well as the generative and creative capacity of the habitus. The habitus carries with it the seeds of new responses that allow it to contest, resist and possibly transcend social and economic conditions, but such contestations are restricted (Bourdieu and Accadro, 1993). Against the neoliberal rhetoric that perpetuates certain aspirational constructs, there is a process of sense-making within the habitus where there are disjunctures between habitus and field and individuals feel a 'fish out of water' (Bourdieu and Wacquant, 1992: 127). This is a process of both amelioration and compromise as the habitus seeks to constitute itself as valuable in moments of crisis.

Given its versatility, it should be noted that there are nuanced differences and different wordings in how habitus has been operationalized and used as a theoretical tool in empirical work on identity. Archer and Francis (2005, 2006) describe 'narratives', both personal and collective narratives that are historically constituted in the habitus, while Archer et al. (2007a, 2007b) analysed 'components', 'elements' and 'performances'. Skeggs' (2004) work addresses the generative capacity of the habitus and how it seeks to accrue value and also symbolic power, while Lareau (1987) and Lareau and Horvat (1999) examine the cultural capital and educational expectations that form part of the habitus. Reay's (1998a, 1998b, 2004) works use the terminology of 'dispositions', which accounts for the permeability of habitus, institutional habitus and the focus on individual subjectivities and social positioning.

An egalitarian counter-habitus to the neoliberal rhetoric

In using habitus, I consider powerful narratives structuring the disposition(s) of the boys and simultaneously the agentic capacity of the habitus to constitute a self of value. The main finding of the research is the boys centre their 'identity work' on what I call egalitarianism, defined as the internal process of reconciling dispositions, which allows them to constitute themselves as 'having value' in the hegemonic neoliberal discourses of 'best' and 'worst', where they are often devalued. Egalitarianism is defined through a disposition toward 'fitting in' and being 'loyal to oneself', where everyone has an 'equal say in the world' and where 'no one is better than anyone else' or 'above their station' (Lawler, 1999; Reay, 1999; Archer and Leathwood, 2003; MacDonald *et al.*, 2013). An egalitarian habitus has inflections of 'sameness' and 'ordinariness', a commitment to collective well-being that has been documented in other studies focusing on working-class identities (Skeggs, 2002; Reay, 2003). Egalitarianism is structured through the conflict between the school and the familial life where there is a lower degree of synergy between the boys' habitus and the institutional habitus. In holding both structure and agency in tension, the habitus of these white working-class boys is a form of 'mental and corporeal schemata of perception, appreciation, and action' (Bourdieu and Wacquant, 1992: 16). Dispositions toward historic, solidarist, working-class communal values also contribute to the formation of egalitarianism. Egalitarianism is also founded upon a serendipitist disposition towards 'what will be, will be', 'making do' or 'waiting and seeing', which became apparent in discussion with teachers and school administrators, who continually expressed frustration at what they perceived as apathy toward education among the white working-class students.

As a counter-habitus to the neoliberal ideology, egalitarianism is, of course, a falsehood that the boys buy into as they come to understand the cards they have been dealt. The habitus, which incorporates the immanent structures of the neoliberal field, is established in relation to dominant or privileged cultures yet, as the habitus is agentic, it does not simply accept the field. While Butler (1999) completely rejects the Bourdieusian project as rigid determinism, arguing the field/habitus relation as one where habitus encounters the field and submits due to the compelling authority of the field, the data show how the habitus is in constant negotiation with the field. For the habitus to submit to the field would mean that each field has the same authority and that the habitus is simultaneously submitted to multiple interlocking fields. Bourdieu's tools allow for a nuanced analysis of contradictory demands and the complex interweaving of categories available, the emotional meaning participants attach to these categories and the stories/narratives/myths through which they make sense of these discourses.

While class may be in our 'blood' and 'fibre' (Jackson and Marsden, 1966: 192), egalitarianism represents the creative and inventive capacity where the boys make an effort to contest/ignore/subvert inequalities in recognition and distribution, becoming a means of maximising their capacity to negotiate potential failure.

Habitus allows for an exploration of how young people are simultaneously both unique individuals with agency and also subjects who are produced by their structural locations, in the sense that their ways of thinking about and engaging with the world are strongly inflected by identities and inequalities of 'race', social class and gender (Archer *et al.*, 2010: 31). As opposed to treating white working-class boys as undifferentiated monoliths, habitus allows for analysis of individual and group praxes where habitus has the potential to generate a wide repertoire of possible actions, simultaneously enabling the individual to draw on transformative and constraining courses of action' (Reay *et al.*, 2005: 23). Egalitarianism also allows for an analysis of positional suffering where the affective dimensions of class (envy/deference, contempt/pity, shame/pride) are constructed and reconstructed in a milieu where the legitimisation of an authentic working-class identity is either endangered or non-existent. Egalitarianism becomes an axis, both the social and learner identities are shaped upon. This chapter will show how egalitarianism manifests itself in a variety of overlapping and mutually constituting ways.

Egalitarianism reinforces primary socialisation

When the habitus encounters a new field, it is still constrained by the structuring forces of the field of origin; therefore, it can be argued, the habitus feels most at ease when it can embody a field similar to the field of origin. An egalitarian habitus reinforces the boys' primary socialisation that is grounded in traditional working-class values. Many theorists have demonstrated that family socialisation practices reproduce social class differences across generations (Gillies, 2005; Evans 2006; Hartas 2010; Vincent *et al.*, 2013). Accounting for differences in primary socialisation, it has been documented that middle-class parents consistently describe their children as 'bright', fostering certain dispositions toward academic attainment (Reay *et al.*, 2007a, 2007b). Middle-class parents 'put a tremendous amount of effort into cultivating particular identities stacking the deck in their child's favor', which 'results in the normalization of these values and identities' (Weis and Cipallone, 2013: 710). Gillies (2005: 845) found that working-class parents' fundamental aspiration was for their 'children to gain a basic education, stay out of trouble, and survive the psychological injuries of school failure', whereas the middle-class prerogative is focused on academic performance.

The experience of childhood is influenced by the amount and forms of resources (capital) families both possess and are able to operationalise when 'they confront various institutional arrangements (field) in the social world'

(Lareau, 2003: 275). Lareau (2003) documents how middle-class parents engage in a process of 'concerted cultivation', where opportunities are seized in order to ensure that an advantageous position is maintained, whereas working-class parents facilitate the 'accomplishment of natural growth', which may offer intrinsic benefits but often plays out in schools in negative ways. Through the accomplishment of 'natural growth', in which working-class parents are supportive but not pressuring, we see egalitarian habitus, specifically 'what will be, will be' in regards to their children's educational attainment and future aspirations. Through my research, it was clear the family life of the participants were sites of the accomplishment of natural growth where there were expectations for behaviour in school and some pressure to gain the necessary grades, but not necessarily an insistence to achieve a position of university placement or high employment. How the boys perceived their parental attitudes toward education (familial habitus) informed the interplay between neoliberal aspiration rhetoric and the boys' counter-habitus of egalitarianism. Parenting styles lend considerable weight to how the habitus is constituted over the course of childhood and also the dispositions in the egalitarian habitus the boys are drawn toward. The egalitarian habitus is not about cultivating certain identities that would be conducive to upward mobility; instead it is grounded in a natural, less adaptive approach.

Egalitarianism as a process of symbolic violence

Within the neoliberal discourse, symbolic violence is extremely potent where individuals 'buy in' to the doxic expectation that everyone can accumulate qualifications and failure to do so lies in the individual, as opposed to wider societal structures. The inter-workings of the habitus, where dispositions struggle for dominance depending on field, are closely intertwined with symbolic violence, where culture is imposed upon groups or classes in such a way that they are experienced as legitimate. Students, according to Byrom and Lightfoot (2013: 818), 'get caught up in discourses that present education as an equal playing field where decisions, choices and outcomes are influenced by the individual', and where it becomes challenging to reconcile the impact of educational failure with their career aspirations. Young people come to falsely 'see themselves as individuals in a meritocratic society, not as classed or gendered members of an unequal society' (Ball et al., 2000: 4). The habitus is where class is internalised and individual aspiration is mediated alongside collective history and where power relationships are internalised in the habitus as 'categories of perceptions'. These processes of categorising become essential to how the boys see themselves as learners and aspirant individuals.

Moving in space and across/within fields, the habitus strengthens people's perceptions that things are as they are because of the natural order, rather than through cultural domination. Aspirations are based on the dispositional structures of habitus and 'embody the possibilities-within-limits of given social–structural positions' (Zipin *et al.*, 2013: 9). Operating within constraints and as both collective and individual trajectories/histories, the habitus mediates what is possible from a limited range of possibilities. For the boys in this study, egalitarianism in the habitus represents an internalisation of objective structures, but it is also shaped by the external forces/structures of their schooling. Reay *et al.* (2005: 24) write, 'Working class acquiescence, a propensity to accept exclusion or exclude oneself rather than attempt to achieve what is already denied, arises because the dispositions, which make up habitus, are the products of opportunities and constraints framing the individual's earlier life experiences'. As a consequence of this process, working-class students draw upon certain strategies in order to maintain value in light of exclusionary processes and opportunity denials (Abrahams and Ingram, 2013).

Egalitarianism guards against a potential habitus clivé

According to a Bourdieusian theoretical framework, an individual's position, in terms of social relations in the field, will be influenced by 'their ability to perform in appropriate ways in a given environment (field) by alignment with the recognized "tastes" and "preferences" associated with that social space' (Hart, 2013: 51). In their analysis of social mobility, Byrom and Lightfoot (2013) discuss a 'habitus in tension', where the trajectories of students differ substantially from that of their parents, where going back was not an option, and where going forward was fraught with challenges (p. 816). A working-class habitus requires transformation in order for an individual to fit into middle-class contexts. The process of social mobility and transformation results in an emerging secondary habitus, a 'cleft habitus' (Bourdieu, 1999) or habitus clivé, where a destabilised habitus enables students to accept the particular messages about education and upward mobility but simultaneously maintain their key dispositions in their habitus of origin. As Reay (2013: 667) reminds us:

> Social mobility is a wrenching process. It rips working-class young people out of communities that need to hold on to them, and it rips valuable aspects of self out of the socially mobile themselves as they are forced to discard qualities and dispositions that do not accord with the dominant middle-class culture that is increasingly characterized by selfish individualism and hyper-competition.

There is a complex negotiation that exists in the habitus where working-class students engage in an internalisation of possibilities, which becomes simultaneously a process of resistance and acceptance, ever evolving. Individuals who are not winners in the game of accumulating capital (economic, cultural and social) experience different degrees of inferiority that potentially have long-standing emotional effects. Such experiences of abjection influence aspirations 'which are structurally constrained in subtle ways that present significant difficulties for the less advantaged' (Zipin *et al.*, 2012: 187). A habitus divided against itself is in continual negotiation with itself and therefore, arguably, destined to a kind of duplication, to a double perception of the self, to enact multiple identities (Bourdieu, 1999: 511). The participants in this research hold on to their conception of egalitarianism, reflecting the field of origin, in an effort to contest a potential cleft habitus and maintain value in a field where they perceive a lack of capital to be successful.

Egalitarianism ameliorates neoliberal discourses of 'ability'

The egalitarian habitus, with a balance between individual agency and sensitivity to societal restraints, shapes how my participants desire to be perceived in their classroom and how they negotiate potential failure. The boys' attachment to the subjectivities of ordinariness, or average-ness, reveals another dimension of egalitarianism (cf. Stahl, 2014a, 2014b). The majority of the participants saw their aspirations as adequately fulfilled by a drive towards 'middling', and this aligns with the work of Savage *et al.* (2001: 887) where 'what seemed to matter more for our respondents was being ordinary'. According to Savage *et al.* (2001), who focused on social class identification and not learner identities, 'middling' could be 'a strategy to resist the dominance of cultural capital' whereby individuals distance themselves from what they do not possess. Through labelling themselves as 'ordinary, people claimed to be just themselves, and not socially fixed people who are not "real" individuals but rather social ciphers' where they are 'devoid of social distinction' (Savage, 2005: 889, 938). Savage suggests that such responses are an indirect way of 'refusing' class identity, a process of repudiating the discourse of inequality altogether (Savage, 2000: 35).

Through egalitarianism, my respondents internalised their own feelings of educational failure, where middling can be seen as a mediation between fear of success and fear of failure. As part of the counter-habitus, 'middling' is a process of amelioration between the neoliberal expectations of the school and the values in the home and community. In Phoenix's (2004) work on neoliberalism and masculinity, she found boys pursuing a 'middle position for themselves in which they could manage what they saw as the demands of masculinities, while still getting some schoolwork done' (p. 234). The desire to be perceived as ordinary also contributes to a lack of investment, for the boys often expressed they would 'make do' with whatever GCSE results they obtained. The 'make do' or 'wait and see' attitude is often a source of disadvantage for young people, as it results in them missing out on crucial information for their enhancing their best possible futures (Archer *et al.*,

2010: 96). The boys' egalitarianism, founded on the principle of 'not want-ing to be seen as better than others', shapes their learner identity and aspiration, where constructing subjectivities around average and ordinary allows for them to maintain a sense of value (Stahl, 2014a, 2014b).

Egalitarianism constitutes a working-class subjectivity of 'loyalty to self'

Throughout the research, it was clear the boys upheld a conception of 'loyalty to self', which was integral to their working-class subjectivity (Stahl, 2014b). Throughout this study there were consistent references to the participants' discomfort in acting like something they were not (Stahl, 2014a). 'Loyalty to self', which was deeply engrained in the egalitarian habi-tus, was how the boys constructed a working-class subjectivity beholden to a traditional working-class masculine culture of anti-pretentious humour, dignity, honour, loyalty and caring, pride and commitment to employment was represented (cf. Winlow, 2001; Skeggs, 2005). These values are well-documented aspects of working-class communities, especially with youth cultures in the face of deindustrialisation (Brann-Barrett, 2011). The impor-tance of these qualities, fostered through emotionally nurturing relationships, gains tremendous salience against the neoliberal prerogatives of the schooling where such relationships work to reaffirm the co-construc-tion and embodiment of egalitarianism.[1]

While the middle-class self may be able to operationalise capitals within fields and navigate different discourse communities, the working-class egali-tarian habitus resists this fluidity and the adoption of identities they perceive as 'fake'. For the boys, 'being yourself' was consistently valued, and to perform an identity that they perceived to be inauthentic became discon-certing, as it would have required an engagement with a habitus clivé and dexterous navigation between multiple fields and multiple subjectivities (Stahl, 2014b). The difficulties that arise in operating at the boundary of different fields suggest that, in order to be successful, my participants must continue to reduce their affiliation to a working-class identity and accept the aspiration rhetoric of the institutional habitus (Reay, 1998a). The dialectic between the institutional habitus of the school and the boys' counter-habitus is crucial to understanding how egalitarianism is formed and the degree of dexterity working-class students are able to deploy.

Egalitarianism resists a middle-class subjectivity of adaptability

In their research on undergraduate student experience, Bathmaker *et al.* (2013) illustrate how middle-class students are encouraged to enhance their employability and marketability through 'working on the self' in order to 'play the game', which often entails 'increasingly overt and conscious strategizing' to accrue capital in order to gain advantage in both education and the labour markets (pp. 725–726). Within modern prevailing discourses of individualisation and competition, middle-class students are often represented as motivated by the satisfaction of their own interests and sense of entitlement. Contending with high-status forms of employment that hold in esteem the ability to 'construct and market a new version of an individualised and reflexive identity', the boys contend with narratives of power and value (McDowell, 2012: 577). For working-class and non-traditional students, who do not necessarily consider higher education a natural step toward adulthood, successful attainment and progression into university involves a constant fashioning and refashioning of the self in order to 'fit in' or 'stand out' (Reay, Crozier, and Clayton, 2009) in a complex interworking of 'finding' and 'losing' oneself (Reay, 2001). While academic success is dependent on a close alignment to the embedded practices, values and norms of the educational system, it is also about the 'erasure' of 'working classness' (Reay, 2001: 334).

In his analysis of the durability of capital among the petite bourgeoisie, Bourdieu claims the possessors of durable educational capital and strong cultural capital 'enjoy a dual title of cultural nobility, the self-assurance of legitimate membership, and the ease given by familiarity' (Bourdieu, 1984: 74). Within this familiarity, or 'feel for the game', a middle-class habitus is bolstered by a portfolio of economic, cultural and symbolic capital that allows for a certain level of comfort when activating capital to their advantage. The middle class know this 'game' and play their cards accordingly; they are adept at skillfully activating different forms of capital dependent on the field (Hart, 2013: 55). The middle-class self is primarily upwardly mobile, fluid within many fields, economically comfortable, able to navigate different discourse communities through adopting new selves and understand what counts within certain fields, and, consequently, able to marshal resources accordingly (Lawler, 1999). Drawing upon the narrative of 'loyalty to self', the boys egalitarian habitus constitutes their working-class subjectivities as valuable, and through this reaffirmation they resist the neoliberal 'four Cs – change, choice, chances, and competition' (Phoenix, 2004: 229), which demand fluidity and adaptation. In establishing what they perceive as their authentic self, they distance themselves from a middle-class subjectivity.

Egalitarianism becomes a reflexive process

While reflexivity is a contentious area in sociology (cf. Farrugia, 2013), Bourdieu's (Bourdieu and Wacquant, 1992: 130) articulation reflexivity occurs when there is a lack of 'fit' between the habitus and the structuring conditions of the field. In these moments of disjuncture, the habitus is no longer able to easily produce meaningful or reasonable practices, creating the conditions for reflexivity where agents 'often have difficulty in holding together the dispositions associated with the different stages of the given field, and in adjusting to the newly established order' (Yang, 2013: 9). When the self becomes a 'reflexive project' (Giddens, 1991: 32), the middle-classes are able to form a profitable dialectical relationship with their fields, while their working-class counterparts are not as proficient, as reflexivity cannot be exercised in the same way for all individuals and is deeply structured by class experience.

Sweetman (2003) and Adams (2006) have recently attempted to develop a 'reflexive habitus', arguing that being reflexive has already become part of the habitus for those who live in the era of modernity. This work has been furthered by Threadgold and Nilan (2009), who contend the 'new' reflexivity constitutes an element of cultural capital for contemporary youth experiencing 'risk' where they show how the capacity for reflexive negotiation of future risks, both real and perceived, has become another form of what Bourdieu calls embodied cultural capital and is constituted differently for different class backgrounds.[2] The work on 'new' reflexivity and 'reflexive habitus' assumes that modernity impacts all individuals in the same way when its influence is fragmented, and, therefore, reflexivity is experienced to different degrees. Not all young people have the resources required to gain access to meaningful opportunities in work or education, so while they are required 'to be self-managers[,] their reflexivity is heavily circumscribed by immediate material disadvantage' (Farrugia, 2012: 689). While working-class experiences with education have historically been shaped by such disjunctures and reflexive processes, it is important to acknowledge how the habitus has the capacity to construct narratives to ameliorate against the 'injuries of class' (Bottero, 2009). An egalitarian habitus serves as a way of calibrating the self during reflexive processes that require a fashioning and refashioning of the self.

Egalitarianism provides a route to reaffirm normative boundaries and establish authenticity

In postmodern work on youth it has been argued that, in direct contrast to the class-based youth cultures of Birmingham's Centre for Contemporary Cultural Studies, youth identities are more 'fleeting, transitional and organized around individual lifestyle and consumption choices' (Shildrick, 2006: 63). If individualisation is understood to be a process of undoing traditional ways of life where both networks and boundaries of class (Beck, 1992) and gender identities are being reimagined (Adkins, 1999: 122), egalitarianism is where normative boundaries, as sites of negotiated tensions, are reaffirmed. Skeggs (2002: 2) argues respectability is one of the most 'ubiquitous signifiers of class', where it is a key mechanism by which subjects are pathologised, informing 'how we know who we are (or are not)', and what is valued and devalued. In contrast to fluid/adaptable identity constructions that privilege a middle-class self, an egalitarian habitus shows how the boys reaffirm traditional gender boundaries influenced by masculine identities, respectability, place and space as they construct an image of a 'Boremund Boy' in South London.

Through gendered, class and ethnic constructs regarding authenticity, some boys become 'locked' into a 'groove' of certain identities (Sewell, 1997: 4); the process of becoming fixed is sometimes beyond their control as they draw upon various context-specific capitals in order to establish their public identity (Reichert *et al.*, 2006). Individuals also draw on certain strategies, such as the practice of 'othering', a shallow form of displacement whereby identities are reaffirmed at the expense of the Other. As identity is increasingly 'hybridized', 'multiracialized' and 'entangled' (Archer and Yamashita, 2003), othering becomes a process of identity work undertaken to reconstitute and re-traditionalise certain modes of masculinity and masculine identity through policing acceptable boundaries and, thus, strives to construct a 'fixed' or consistent masculine identity. Othering is a strategy deployed through interactions with the field, to uphold an egalitarian habitus.

Egalitarianism disassociates from hegemonic masculinity

In gender theory, it has been argued that the 'presence of a competitive performance-oriented culture generates anxiety, especially among boys whose gender identity needs to be based on achieving power, status, and superiority' (Arnot, 2004: 35). Within work on boys in schooling, the hegemonic practices that constitute masculinity have been widely used in education studies to explore masculinities in classroom life (Connell, 2005: 832–833). Hegemony always refers to a 'historical situation, a set of circumstances in which power is won and held' and, in order to understand the demands and constraints associated with masculinity, researchers examine 'practices in which hegemony is constituted and contested' (Carrigan *et al.*, 1985: 594). Deeply contextual, the hegemonic is rendered through actions, behaviours and discourses, and remains a prominent force within identity construction as boys use the various strategies to preserve hegemonic masculinity and secure status (Connell and Messerschmidt, 2005; Howson, 2014). In considering the theoretical construct of hegemonic masculinity, the boys do not orient themselves toward gaining status and superiority, or admit to it, as to do so would conflict with their egalitarian habitus. An egalitarian habitus is not about accruing power over others; it instead upholds the inverse of such a practice. The hegemonic masculine identity in this case study is one infused with traditional working-class values of non-dominance; therefore, for my participants, the hegemonic is a resistance to the very concept of a hegemonic.

Throughout the research with the boys, I observed many daily practices commonly associated with hegemonic masculinity. However, despite being asked in multiple ways and through many different methods, none of the boys identified with an image of the hyper-masculine hegemonic that has been documented on other gender work. Analysing hegemonic masculinity from a psychological perspective, Wetherall and Edley's (1999) research with Open University students of diverse backgrounds found significant problems with the conceptual tool. They found men very rarely associated with a masculine imaginary position and argued it was not the principle method by which men constructed themselves as masculine. Instead, their participants sought to identify with the ordinary, or Mr Average, and resisted the ultra-masculine risk-infused stereotypes (Wetherall and Edley, 1999: 350). Arguably, the rejection of the hyper-masculine hegemonic (or a hegemonic in general) could be construed as a sanction for new social practices or a process of justifying autonomy from social conventions. The identification with Mr Average could also represent a shift in the hegemonic to a less masculine form of hegemonic masculinity. The denial of a hegemonic, and the disposition toward average-ness, was a process in which egalitarianism, as part of a counter-habitus, was reaffirmed.

Egalitarianism functions on a variety of levels. It becomes a process of reconciling aspirations with current social and economic inequalities, serving as both a central narrative and process of amelioration between the expectations of the school and communal and familial values. The boys acquire their egalitarian habitus through a socialisation process that reflects central structural elements such as solidarity, kinship rules and masculine virtues, which leads them to enact dispositions that resist embracing alternative lifestyles and where instead they draw on narratives of 'ordinariness' to reaffirm or re-fix cultural practices. Responsive to both their marginalisation and the logic of neoliberal ideology, egalitarianism is a pervasive element within the habitus that shapes the formation of the habitus and also its interactions within the educational field. The current dominant neoliberal discourse, which prioritises a view of aspirations that is competitive, economic and status-based, shapes the subjectivities of these young males. Field/habitus is a case of push and pull where the struggle stems from the habitus reconstituting itself in fields of contestation, though this only occurs in fields where the habitus has the capital to compete.

Functioning between positions and practices, habitus enables the social world to be read and understood. As a counter-habitus, there are echoes in egalitarianism of the relationship between emotional work, aspiration and communal values as well as guarding against the guilt associated with moving beyond one's place (Reay, 2003, 2009). Also, as with other studies that analyse counter-habituses, they can become durable across social fields and can counteract negative schooling experiences (Holt *et al.*, 2013). The words of the boys are infused with persistent tensions along the axis of presenting an 'authentic self' that values autonomy alongside deep belonging/connections. These working-class boys are clearly caught up in contemporary processes of individualisation and self-motivation, however, 'such processes are both ameliorated and framed by an overreaching sense of, and commitment to, collectivity and "the common good"' (Reay, 2003: 305).

The study

As my research questions focused on interactions, perceptions, attitudes and the construction of identity, my school-based qualitative approach was an attempt to comprehend the relationship between the boys' identity production and its relationship to the schooling process. I conducted the study with 23 boys, aged 14–16 years, who were preparing for GCSEs, which complete their last two years of compulsory schooling in the UK. I selected the boys using a variety of criteria, such as placement in certain academic or vocational sets, income (Appendix B) and level of parental qualifications (Appendix C). Except for two participants who were from a White Eastern European background, all of the participants identified as native White British. Seven stages of the research process were conducted over nine months in south London using a variety of visual, auditory and kinaesthetic methodologies (Appendix A).

Semi-structured interviews, focus groups and visual methods were used to ensure the same questions were covered with each student while maintaining flexibility and the opportunity for further probing. Due to a variety of factors (non-attendance, exclusions), not every participant completed all seven stages. Through the primary methodology of semi-structured interviews, I was able to explore vague or inadequate responses to certain questions. Identities and subjectivities do not simply reveal themselves in interviews; they need to be developed reflexively, and interviewers need to consider their positioning carefully in the interview process. As a researcher, my goal was not only to be open and non-judgemental within the social situation, but also cautious and respectful, and my longitudinal research design enabled for relationships to develop.

Three South London school sites were used: 1) a pupil referral unit (PRU); 2) a school where white working-class boys were a minority in a male-heavy cohort (World School); and 3) a school where white working-class were the majority with a more equal gender balance (London Academy). Each field contained many site-specific variables: subject choice, different expectations of participants, teacher quality and levels of individual expressions. Each institution had its own habitus, a set of dispositions, though within 'the same school institutional habituses are mobilized differentially for different pupils" (Reay, 1998a: 524). In order to provide a snapshot of each educational setting, I addressed the main features Delamont (1983) uses in the text *Interaction in the Classroom*: physical setting (spatial relationships, layout, décor); institutional setting (whole school ethos, organisation, procedures, assessments, dress, attendance); and institutional control (rules, policies concerning pupil conduct).

School site A: Pupil Referral Unit (PRU)

The PRU was an educational site that faced many daily challenges. Students, of which there was a small cohort in Year 11 of approximately 15 students, only attended the unit three days a week to complete work for their GCSEs, and the remaining two days a week they attended vocational placement training, which the majority of them appeared to enjoy. The teachers were faced with the task of teaching entire GCSE courses within the confines of three days a week and were further burdened by non-attendance. The GCSE is not designed to be taught in this way, and the chances of gaining qualifications were, therefore, systemically rendered as minimal. Despite colourful layout and engaging décor, the physical setting was extremely claustrophobic, which made it challenging to concentrate and difficult to handle high-level behaviour problems when they occurred. Pupil conduct was often problematic and when one student 'kicked off', it would spread quickly among the other students until some were excluded. The institution had a good organisational structure, but the transitory nature of the students made adopting a good ethos difficult to maintain. Students were not required to wear uniforms and lunch was provided to all students.

School site B: World School

World School was an educational site in the process of an entire school turnaround. The site I visited in May and June 2010 was completely obliterated and new buildings and facilities were created over the six-week summer holidays. While I was conducting the research, the school was coming to terms with a completely new school environment using the Gates model of small school structures, so, therefore, I only interacted with the small school of Years 10 and 11. The student intake was predominantly Afro-Caribbean with only a handful of white working-class boys per year group. The approximately 200 students in this small school were subjected to high levels of behaviour monitoring and authoritative discipline. Both staff and students were experiencing tremendous pressure centring on exam scores, and the achievement ideology permeated the educational space constantly. The environment was very restrictive and the strict methods of discipline were having an effect, as classroom behaviour improved substantially from September to April.

School site C: London Academy

London Academy is also a relatively new educational site, built in the late 1990s. The institution is a comprehensive school with a sixth form and above-average facilities. The open-plan layout made it conducive to fostering a sense of community and the majority of the teaching staff was female, young and energetic. The whole school ethos was focused on pupils attaining qualifications and the school timetable was about to be restructured so a higher percentage could take vocational Business and Technical Education Council (BTEC) qualifications, to increase the pass rate and enhance the reputation of the school. Though the quality of teaching was uneven, during the observation stage, I was witness to some exceptionally high calibre educators, even in the lower ability sets. What was most problematic about the school environment, and which made both staff and students anxious, was a white working-class girl 'gang culture'. A specific group of girls, mainly in Years 10 and 11, were testing the institutional control, contributing to high-level disruptive behaviour in lessons and they were, as a result, over-represented in the on-site referral unit.

Summary

My interest in the nexus of social and learner identities speaks to Bourdieu's aim of theorising human action as a dialectical relationship between objective structures and subjective agency. The research presented intends to use a blend of different qualitative approaches to 'work at and across the interface between social and learner identities in schools, to explore the relationships between the two' in order to 'recognize not only the regular convergences but also significant divergences' (Reay, 2010: 281). My study works selectively with Bourdieu's concepts of habitus, field and capital to explore how white working-class boys engage with education and how classed, gendered and ethnic meanings are constructed.

While the boys' accounts are a partial construction rather than a reflection of their true experiences, in Part II the data show how social structures shape agents' subjectivities and how the habitus of individuals 'resist and succumb to inertial pressure of structural forces' (McLeod, 2009: 139).

Notes

1   It should be noted that the investment in the peer group works against social mobility, as the social capital fostered has limitations in terms of conversion to other forms of capital.

2   In her critique of a reflexive habitus, Yang (2013: 13) notes 'reflexivity works against habitus; habitus has the tendency to perpetuate the social structure from which it is produced and it is below the level of consciousness, while the purpose of reflexivity is to raise the consciousness, trying to understand the complexity of the practice'.

References

Abrahams, J. and Ingram, N. (2013) The chameleon habitus: Exploring local students' negotiations of multiple fields. *Sociological Research Online*, 18(4). Online at: www.socresonline.org.uk/18/4/21.html

Adams, M. (2006) Hybridizing habitus and reflexivity: Towards an understanding of contemporary identity. *Sociology*, 40(3), 511–528.

Adkins, L. (1999) Community and economy: A retraditionalization of gender?. *Theory Culture Society*, 16(1), 119–139.

Archer, L. and Francis, B. (2005) Negotiating the dichotomy of boffin and triad: British-Chinese pupils' constructions of 'laddism'. *The Sociological Review*, 495–521.

Archer, L. and Francis, B. (2006) Challenging classes? Exploring the role of social class within the identities and achievement of British-Chinese pupils. *Sociology*, 40(1), 29–49.

Archer, L. and Leathwood, C. (2003) New times–old inequalities: Diverse working-class femininities in education. *Gender and Education*, 15(3), 227–235.

Archer, L. and Yamashita, H. (2003) Theorising inner-city masculinities: 'Race', class, gender, and education. *Gender and Education*, 15(2), 115–132.

Archer, L., Halsall, A. and Hollingworth, S. (2007a) Class, gender, (hetero) sexuality and schooling: Paradoxes within working-class girls' engagement with education and post-16 aspirations. *British Journal of Sociology of Education*, 28(2), 165–180.

Archer, L., Halsall, A. and Hollingworth, S. (2007b) 'University's not for me – I'm a Nike person': Urban, working-class young people's negotiations of 'style', identity, and educational engagement. *Sociology*, 41(2), 219–237.

Archer, L., Hollingworth, S. and Mendick, H. (2010) *Urban youth and schooling: The experiences and identities of educationally 'at risk' young people*. Berkshire: Open University Press.

Arnot, M. (2004) Male working-class identities and social justice: A reconsideration of Paul Willis's *Learning to Labor* in light of contemporary research. In N. Dolby, G. Dimitriadis and P. Willis (eds), *Learning to Labor in new times* (p. 231). New York: Routledge.

Ball, S. J., Maguire, M. and Macrae, S. (2000) *Choice, pathways, and transitions post-16: New youth, new economies in the global city*. London: RoutledgeFalmer.

Bathmaker, A. M., Ingram, N. and Waller, R. (2013) Higher education, social class, and the mobilisation of capitals: Recognising and playing the game. *British Journal of Sociology of Education*, 34(5–6), 723–743.

Beck, U. (1992) *Risk society: Towards a new modernity*. London: Sage Publications.

Bottero, W. (2009) Class in the 21st Century. In K. P. Sveinsson (ed.), *Who cares about the white working class?* (pp. 7–15). London: Runnymede Perspectives.

Bourdieu, P. (1984) *Distinction: A social critique of the judgement of taste*. Oxon: Routledge.

Bourdieu, P. (1999) The contradictions of inheritance. In P. Bourdieu (ed.), *Weight of the world: Social suffering in contemporary society* (pp. 517–551). Cambridge: Polity Press.

Bourdieu, P. and Accadro, A. (1993) *The weight of the world: Social suffering in contemporary society*. Stanford: Stanford University Press.

Bourdieu, P. and Wacquant, L. (1992) *An invitation to reflexive sociology*. Cambridge: Polity Press.

Brann-Barrett, M. T. (2011) Same landscape, different lens: Variations in young people's socio-economic experiences and perceptions in their disadvantaged working-class community. *Journal of Youth Studies*, 14(3), 261–278.

Butler, J. (1999) Performativity's social magic. In R. Shusterman (ed.), *Bourdieu: A critical reader* (pp. 113–128). Oxford: Blackwell.

Byrom, T. and Lightfoot, N. (2013) Interrupted trajectories: The impact of academic failure on the social mobility of working-class students. *British Journal of Sociology of Education*, 34(5–6), 812–828.

Carrigan, T., Connell, B. and Lee, J. (1985) Toward a new sociology of masculinity. *Theory and Society*, 14(5), 551–604.

Connell, R. W. (2005) *Masculinities*. Cambridge: Polity.

Connell, R. W. and Messerschmidt, J. W. (2005) Hegemonic masculinity: Rethinking the concept. *Gender and Society*, 19(6), 829–859.

Delamont, S. (1983) *Interaction in the Classroom*. London: Methuen.

Evans, G. (2006) *Educational failure and working class white children in Britain*. Palgrave: Macmillan.

Farrugia, D. (2012) Young people and structural inequality: Beyond the middle ground. *Journal of Youth Studies*, 16(5), 679–693.

Farrugia, D. (2013) The reflexive subject: Towards a theory of reflexivity as practical intelligibility. *Current Sociology*, 61(3), 283–300.

Giddens, A. (1991) *Modernity and self identity*. Cambridge: Polity.

Gillies, V. (2005) Raising the 'meritocracy': Parenting and the individualization of social class. *Sociology*, 39(5), 835–853.

Hart, C. S. (2013) *Aspirations, education and social justice: Applying Sen and Bourdieu*. London: Bloomsbury.

Hartas, D. (2010) Families' social backgrounds matter: Socio-economic factors, home learning and young children's language, literacy and social outcomes. *British Educational Research Journal*, 37(6), 893–914.

Holt, L., Bowlby, S. and Lea, J. (2013) Emotions and the habitus: Young people with socio-emotional differences (re)producing social, emotional, and cultural capital in family and leisure space-times. *Emotion, Space and Society*, 9, 33–41.

Howson, R. (2014) Re-thinking aspiration and hegemonic masculinity in transnational context. *Masculinities and Social Change*, 3(1), 18–25.

Jackson, B. and Marsden, D. (1966) *Education and the working class*. London: Penguin Books.

Lareau, A. (1987) Social class differences in family-school relationships: The importance of cultural capital. *Sociology of Education*, 60(2), 73–85.

Lareau, A. (2003) *Unequal childhoods*. Berkeley: University of California Press.

Lareau, A. and Horvat, E. M. (1999) Moments of social inclusion and exclusion: Race, class, and cultural capital in family-school relationships. *Sociology of Education*, 72(1), 37–53.

Lawler, S. (1999) 'Getting out and getting away': Women's narratives of class mobility. *Feminist Review*, 63(3), 3–24.

MacDonald, R., Shildrick, T. and Furlong, A. (2013) In search of intergenerational cultures of worklessness: Hunting the yeti and shooting zombies. *Critical Social Policy*, 34(2), 199–219.

McDowell, L. (2012) Post-crisis, post-Ford and post-gender? Youth identities in an era of austerity. *Journal of Youth Studies*, 15(5), 573–590.

McLeod, J. (2009) Youth studies, comparative inquiry, and the local/global problematic. *Review of Education, Pedagogy, and Cultural Studies*, 31(4), 270–292.

Phoenix, A. (2004) Neoliberalism and masculinity: Racialization and the contradictions of schooling for 11-to-14-year-olds. *Youth Society*, 36(2), 227–246.

Reay, D. (1998a) 'Always knowing' and 'never being sure': Familial and institutional habituses and higher education choice. *Journal of Education Policy*, 13(4), 519–529.

Reay, D. (1998b) Cultural reproduction: Mothers' involvement in their children's primary schooling. In M. Grenfell and D. James (eds), (pp. 55–74) *Bourdieu and education: Acts of practical theory*. Abingdon: RoutledgeFalmer.

Reay, D. (1999) 'Class acts': Educational involvement and psycho-sociological class processes. *Feminism and Psychology*, 9(1), 89–106.

Reay, D. (2001) Finding or losing yourself? Working-class relationships to education. *Journal of Education Policy*, 16(4), 333–346.

Reay, D. (2003) A risky business? Mature working-class women students and access to higher education. *Gender and Education*, 15(3): 301–317.

Reay, D. (2004) Rethinking social class: Qualitative perspectives on class and gender. In S. Hesse-Biber and M. C. Yaiser (eds), (pp. 140–155) *Feminist perspectives on social research*. Oxford: Oxford University Press.

Reay, D. (2009) *Making Sense of White Working Class Educational Underachievement*. London: Runnymead Trust.

Reay, D. (2010) Identity-making in schools and classrooms. In M. Wetherall and C. Talpade Mohanty (eds), *The Sage handbook of identities* (pp. 277–294). Los Angeles: Sage Publications.

Reay, D., David, M. E. and Ball, S. (2005) *Degrees of choice: Social class, race and gender in higher education*. London: Institute of Education.

Reay, D., Beedell, P., Crozier, G., James, D., Jamieson, F., Hollingworth, S. and Williams, K. (2007a) White middle classes and urban education. Conference paper for White Middle Classes and Urban Education, Metropolitan University.

Reay, D., Hollingworth, S., Williams, K., Crozier, G., Jamieson, F., James, D. and Beedell, P. (2007b) 'A darker shade of pale?' Whiteness, the middle classes and multi-ethnic inner city schooling. *Sociology*, 41(6), 1041–1060.

Reay, D., Crozier, G. and Clayton, J. (2009) 'Strangers in paradise'? Working-class students in elite universities. *Sociology*, 43(6), 1103–1121.

Reichert, M., Stoudt, B. and Kuriloff, P. (2006) Don't love no fight: Healing and identity among urban youth. *Urban Review*, 38(3), 187–209.

Savage, M. (2000) *Class analysis and social transformation*. Buckingham: Open University Press.

Savage, M. (2005) Working-class identities in the 1960s: Revisiting the affluent worker study. *Sociology*, 39(5), 929–946.

Savage, M., Bangall, G. and Longhurst, B. (2001) Ordinary, ambivalent, and defensive: Class identities in the northwest of England. *Sociology*, 35(4), 875–895.

Sewell, T. (1997) *Black masculinities and schooling: How black boys survive modern schooling*. Staffordshire: Trentham Books.

Shildrick, T. (2006) Youth culture, subculture, and the importance of neighbourhood. *Young: Nordic Journal of Youth Research*, 14(1), 67–74.

Skeggs, B. (2002) *Formations of class and gender*. Nottingham: Sage Publications.

Skeggs, B. (2004) *Class, self, culture*. London: Routledge.

Skeggs, B. (2005) The making of class and gender through visualizing moral subject formation. *Sociology*, 39(5), 965–982.

Stahl, G. (2014a) White working-class male narratives of 'loyalty to self' in discourses of aspiration. *British Journal of Sociology of Education*, forthcoming.

Stahl, G. (2014b) The affront of the aspiration agenda: White working-class male narratives of 'ordinariness' in neoliberal times. *Masculinities and Social Change*, 3(2), 88–118.

Sweetman, P. (2003) Twenty-first century dis-ease? Habitual reflexivity or the reflexive habitus. *The Sociological Review*, 51(4), 528–549.

Threadgold, S. and Nilan, P. (2009) Reflexivity of contemporary youth, risk and cultural capital. *Current Sociology*, 57(1), 47–68.

Vincent, C., Ball, S., Rollock, N. and Gillborn, D. (2013) Three generations of racism: Black middle-class children and schooling. *British Journal of Sociology of Education*, 34(5–6), 929–946.

Weis, L. and Cipollone, K. (2013) 'Class work': Producing privilege and social mobility in elite US secondary schools. *British Journal of Sociology of Education*, 34(5–6), 701–722.

Wetherall, M. and Edley, N. (1999) Negotiating hegemonic masculinity: Imaginary positions and psycho-discursive practices. *Feminism and Psychology*, 9(3), 335–356.

Winlow, S. (2001) *Badfellas: Crime, tradition and new masculinities*. Oxford: Berg.

Yang, Y. (2013) Bourdieu, practice and change: Beyond the criticism of determinism. *Educational Philosophy and Theory*, 45, 1–19.

Zipin, L., Sellar, S. and Hattam, R. (2012) Countering and exceeding 'capital': A 'funds of knowledge' approach to re-imagining community. *Discourse: Studies In The Cultural Politics of Education*, 33(2), 179–192.

Zipin, L., Sellar, S., Brennan, M. and Gale, T. (2013) Educating for futures in marginalized regions: A sociological framework for rethinking and researching aspirations. *Educational Philosophy and Theory*, 45, 1–20.

Part II

Chapter 4

Defining class and social class identification

It means the money you get is that you earned. If you do a hard day's work of building like a brick wall ... like something like manual labour or that ... you get paid. You get paid so much for it and you've actually earned it. You've actually stood and done your best, you've earned that money. And I reckon that's the difference between middle class and working class.

(Dan, Year 11, PRU)

Learner identities are regulated through many overlapping and competing fields that lend considerable weight to the intertwined relationship between social class, aspiration and neoliberalism. How these young men perceive the structures of social inequality remains an important access point for understanding why they engage or disengage with their education. However, class and class identity, particularly with young people, can be a challenging area to research as youth biographies are often 'structured in ways which do not map neatly onto traditionally understood class divisions, but are nevertheless implicated in the production of deeply entrenched structural inequalities' (Farrugia, 2012: 686). Today, expressions of class cultures 'are much more marked by reflexive attitudes – rueful, ironic, envious, reflectively proud – than was the case in the picture painted by Bourdieu in 1979' (Boyne, 2002: 119). Willis (2004: 185) writes, 'Most young working-class people in the United Kingdom would not thank you now for describing them as working-class'. As class identities involve highly emotive connotations and negative descriptors, the egalitarian habitus works to ameliorate such feelings. Asking the boys to consider social class required sensitivity as an interviewer as social class distinctions may give rise to emotions of 'shame and the fear of shame' (Reay, 2005: 923).

The relevance of class

When interviewing participants regarding their 'class antennae' (Sayer, 2005: 15) and social class identification, discussions were shaped not only by misrecognition and ignorance but also acute awareness. My participants had conflicted and conflicting views concerning social class, and discussions around class identity 'often provoked puzzlement and confusion' (Savage, 2005: 936). While the boys were hesitant about identifying themselves by their social background (Appendix B, C), I carefully tried not to impose common labels such as 'working class' and 'middle class'. As a researcher, being of a different nationality placed me in a unique position as my participants did not necessarily view me as being part of the British class system. While discussions concerning social class bring about feelings of self-worth, as well as 'injustice and moral evaluation' (Sayer, 2002, para. 1.4), we see how, by drawing upon an egalitarian habitus, the boys are able to dodge labels, judgements and distinctions in order to 'save face'. It has been well documented that individuals often articulate a belief that class does not touch them personally (Savage, 2000, 2010), where there exists a 'staunch denial of class thinking and feeling, especially one's own' (Reay, 2005: 923). Skeggs (2002) argues that unwillingness or reluctance to talk in class terms may not necessarily mean that people do not recognise the significance of class or their own class position. For Skeggs, the white working-class women in her study approached class reflexively and pursued strategies for 'improvement' in order to 'pass' for middle class, while always remaining insecure and never being certain that they had succeeded.

As part of the process of symbolic violence, the distancing from class as an effort to see society as open and equal, as opposed to shaped by disparate inequalities, has been addressed in other ethnographic work with working-class males (Weis, 1990; MacLeod, 2009). In her study of men in widening participation, Burke (2009: 90) found many do not openly identify with class, with some refusing to name a specific class position. A significant number of my participants felt class existed but was unimportant. The egalitarianism habitus, as a counter-habitus, explains some of the boys' unwillingness to articulate a belief in class, their resistance to accepting social inequality, and their own positionality within hierarchies:

> I think [people] make a big deal about nothing. I think there's nothing like that in our school. Well, obviously there are people that go to private schools and obviously they're the higher class. But that's about it.
>
> (Thomas, Year 11, London Academy)

> Well, it does exist because there's more rich people who do things, and do what's in their favour. But not so much I think. It is there but not too much.
>
> (Phillip, Year 11, London Academy)

> Calum: You mean like posh kids? Well, not in this school.
> Garth: So do you think social class is important?

Calum: No, absolutely not. Ain't important. There's either the rich, the middle or the poor. And we're pretty much the poor. We are the poor.

Garth: Ok, so when you say you don't mean its important – what do you mean by that?

Calum: Ain't important. Why do you want to boast about what social class you're in? There's no point in having it.

(Calum, Year 10, World School)

Calum's response is particularly striking in that he knows his position in the hierarchy, yet there is resistance in accepting the power of class to shape opportunities and life chances. Calum is resentful of class, claiming it 'ain't important' and 'there's no point in having it' becomes a mediation on class in relevance to his current circumstances. Sayer (2002) reminds us that people's resentment in regards to social inequality, or symbolic notions of class stigmatisation, is often more pronounced than their resentment over their lack of material wealth. Calum accepts class exists, 'we are the poor', and therefore accepts what Bottero (2009) calls 'class injuries', but then his habitus enacts strategies to make its significance negligible and reify his own self-worth. Calum's response raises wider questions regarding the significance of a so-called 'reflexive habitus' in an era of high modernity (Sweetman, 2003; Adams, 2006). Individuals are:

> evaluative beings, continually monitoring and assessing our behaviour and that of others, needing their approval and respect, but in contemporary society this takes place in the context of inequalities such as those of class, gender, and 'race' which affect both what we are able to do and how we are judged.
>
> (Sayer, 2005: 1)

While reflexivity may arguably constitute a new form of cultural capital (Threadgold and Nilan, 2009), reflexivity regarding inequality does not necessarily lead to agency. In subsequent interviews, Calum's reflexive work around class did not foster increased engagement with his education. While Calum is critical and aware, his evaluations and consequent dispositions are tempered by certain limitations as the egalitarian habitus seeks to accrue value within constraints.

For the boys to verbalise the existence of class and class inequality brushes against a habitus clivé where a destablised habitus may enable students to accept doxic discourses regarding education and upward mobility, while simultaneously maintaining their key dispositions in their habitus of origin. Within this tension, accepting social class is often about accepting a lack of opportunity and restriction; it is also accepting that judgement is placed upon the individual and that the individual, in turn, judges others. In preserving a sense of authentic self, it is often advantageous to ignore or reject wider repertoires of classed, gendered and ethnic hierarchies (cf. Whitman, 2013: 60–61). Toward the end of the data collection (Appendix A) the boys became more forthcoming in expressing their feelings regarding social class:

Garth: So do you think social class is something that really exists or maybe not so much?

Terry: It does because obviously there's people who do better jobs than other people. But it don't really effect – well, it does. It means that you like for instance might have more money but it don't really effect you really.

(Terry, Year 11, London Academy)

Keith: No, I don't think that there's different … like certain classes and that. So basically you get on with and like mix with everyone. And there's no like stereotypes involved with different classes.

Garth: Ok, in the wider world do you think there's social class?

Keith: Um – yeah, I think there is really. I ain't a racist or anything, yeah. But you get a group of white kids and you get a group of black kids, sometimes you … Like I have friends in both but if you go to Pluckham and there's loads of black kids, and then you stay in Boremund where there is loads of white kids … so where I hang about it's mixed.

(Keith, Year 10, London Academy)

Viewing social class only in terms of economic capital was quite common, with only Keith articulating a conception of social class along racialised boundaries. Whiteness is a category that is 'contested, determined and re-classified over time as part of an ongoing process of white racialisation' (Preston, 2009: 5). The boys consider gangs as a racialised performance; black males are in gangs, whereas white males are not. Regardless of their own experiences with gangs, not belonging to a gang becomes a part of the discourse of constituting themselves as authentic white working-class males. Within the wider data set there were references to gangs, but none of the boys admitted to being part of gang activity or witness to gang activity. Many expressed a disgust and fear of gangs that, they articulated, were prevalent in their community. In his response, Keith also closely aligns class, identity and place. For many working-class children, 'locality, identity and educational success are all powerfully connected' and stepping outside their local geographical context becomes a difficult negotiation (Ingram, 2009: 422). The social capital developed within their community offered many benefits:

Nowadays it really is the people you know. Like if you know all the people robbing, shooting, hurting people. If you know them and people recognise you with them ... then that's one of the main reasons ...If you're associated with them people, not really depending on your size... you could be small and all that... if you're associated with them then people will leave you alone because no one wants trouble with them.

(Dan, Year 11, PRU)

The prevalence of violence and reputation in this account show how the social space is characterised as complex and risk-intensive, which, arguably, impels Dan to reorient himself toward an egalitarian habitus that projects a simplified, non-hierarchical, idealistic view of the world. While Keith identified how social groupings were porous, the attention to social mix was not shared by all participants:

I'm not really sure. I don't know. Obviously like the lower-class are unemployed, they have a lot more problems than the upper class. But the upper class they're like in one group and the lower class are in one group, but you don't see them mix very often.

(George, London Academy)

Umm, I think [social class] exists. Like I've just said there's like a wide range of people. Like loads of people – there must be different ranges of poor people and really rich people. So yeah, it does it exist.

(Harry, Year 10, London Academy)

Ben: Depends on what kind of job they have. If they're doing a higher class [job] then they think they're higher than other people, but then in the middle class you think they are earning money but not earning enough as the other people ... then you got the poor people who got a job but don't earn enough.

Garth: You touched on money a couple of different times; do you think it's more about money than anything else?

Ben: I think so.

(Ben, Year 10, World School)

Habitus always implies a 'sense of one's place' but also a 'sense of the place of others,' and therefore, 'nothing classifies somebody more than the way he or she classifies' (Bourdieu, 1989: 19–20). Ben, as well as other participants, primarily defined social class in terms of economic capital, which is easily measured and easily understood, whereas there are difficulties associated with verbalising all the other subtleties associated with class. Ben's account also shows how certain forms of employment, in his view, could impact on how people perceive themselves and others.

Identifying through social class

Through an orientation toward an egalitarian habitus, the boys read the world around them and develop a set of strategies that allows them to feel value and a sense of belonging in society and determine what is, and is not, 'for the likes of us'. Over the course of the interviews and focus groups (Appendix A), there were moments of confusion where the boys contradicted themselves, arguably trying to uphold an egalitarian habitus that conflicted with their social and educational spaces. When I asked the boys to self-identify their own class status they ran into dilemmas:

Ben: Working class.
Garth: Why?
Ben: 'Cause I'm hard working and when I want to do something I do it.
Garth: What does the term 'working class' mean to you?
Ben: Like obviously it means like you get lower class people – like y'know people like that are on the streets and don't do nothing with their lives. It just like … it's just groups of individuals, people think of them.
Garth: So in terms of working class, what does that mean?
Ben: Like disadvantaged. That's what it means.
Garth: What does the term 'middle class' mean to you?
Ben: Normal.
Garth: So you said you would think of yourself as working class but … do you ever want to be middle class?
Ben: No, no.

(Ben, Year 11, London Academy)

In late modernity, young people are often theorised as engaging in forms of individualisation where 'fluidity and transgressive forms of identification' often exist alongside a 'dis-identification from class (or even a denial of class) as a potentially grounding principle in shaping youth subcultural activity' (Dillabough and Kennelly, 2010: 36). Threadgold and Nilan (2009), extending the work of Beck (1992), argue the relationship between individualisation and self-reflexive biographies require ongoing self-production where reflexivity becomes a capital. Arguments concerning individualisation emphasise a middle-class self that is more adaptable, fluid within many fields and able to marshal resources strategically. For members of the working class to successfully inhabit a neoliberal middle-class subjectivity, which requires embracing certain 'ways of being', they must confront class and their own positionality (Bourdieu, 1984). Class, with all its ambiguity, remains salient in identity construction:

Phillip: I guess I'd say working class.
Garth: Why do you say that?
Phillip: 'Cause we're not low-class sort of thing. Not celebrities or nothing.
Garth: What does the term 'working class' mean to you?
Phillip: Work. Bring home money. Have a decent house, a car.
Garth: What does the term 'middle class' mean to you?
Phillip: Like you have a little bit better job, like a higher job sort of thing. Like working-class work at Tescos, then they'd be the manager of Tescos.

(Phillip, Year 11, London Academy)

Mitchell defines class in terms of profession and lifestyle:

Garth: Given the categories of 'working class', 'middle class', and 'upper class' what social class would you consider yourself?
Mitchell: Working.
Garth: Why?
Mitchell: 'Cause my whole family works – like manual jobs like plumbing. My dad used to drive lorries, things like that, manual work.
Garth: What does the term 'working class' mean to you?
Mitchell: Manual, like manual labour. Plumbing, electrician. Things like that.
Garth: What does the term 'middle class' mean to you?
Mitchell: Uh – like. Like wannabe posh people. Like they made something of themselves, they forget like who they really are. They just become posh. Like people with banking jobs and all that.

(Mitchell, Year 11, London Academy)

The working classes are consistently constructed as having a hard life because they engage in physical labour, while the middle classes are perceived to have a life of ease due to having easier jobs and working less. Mitchell's reasoning behind his social class identification links back to 'loyalty to self' (Stahl, 2014). For Mitchell, to be 'disloyal to self' is to embrace fluidity and embody an identity that he sees as inauthentic, a performance (Archer and Leathwood, 2003: 233). According to Mitchell, the middle class are 'wannabes' and he objects to a middle-class subjectivity, which he sees as fake. Through becoming middle class and making 'something of themselves', they would have to change and 'forget who they really are'. Fluidity research shows how agents may or may not shift positions, adopting different identities depending on the field (Carter, 2005; Horvat and Lewis, 2010; Wilkins, 2011). Reay *et al.* (2009: 1105) assert that the high-achieving working-class students at an elite university, 'displayed the ability to successfully move across two very different fields with what are seen to be classically middle-class academic dispositions, a versatility that most had begun to develop in early schooling'.

However, while an ability may be present, it does not necessarily mean such movement is comfortable. Working-class boys have not found it easy to 'slip seamlessly in and out of different social fields' or negotiate different and often paradoxical fields (Ingram, 2011: 301). While some working-class students have the capacity for versatility, adopting different identities in different contexts, these identity shifts can have quite serious psychic and reparative costs (Reay, 2002; Reay *et al.*, 2007; Youdell, 2010). This fixity influences how working-class boys perceive their social worlds and how they construct aspiration. According to Ingram (2011), the ability to be versatile does not always enable reflexivity, for if reflexivity can become a capital, whether it can be operationalised or not is dependent on the field and habitus. Alen's response reveals many different layers to his understanding of class:

> Alen: Lower-class because my dad's disabled and can't work and my mum – I don't know why she don't want to work. But I ain't poor or anything, we got everything sorted out.
>
> I don't think I'm like lower-class only 'cause my dad don't work. I would put myself in the middle class because everyone says my house is nice and clean. When I go to other people's houses, their mum and dad's parents do work they still haven't finished decorating and stuff like that and I'm thinking my house is better than theirs.
>
> (Alen, Year 11, London Academy)

In terms of social class identification, reflexive deliberations are framed within ubiquitous discourses of negative representations of the working-class throughout the UK (Skeggs, 2004). Alen recognises that employment is essential to class, but, most importantly, his response to his class identification is highly defensive. While someone may categorise him as lower class according to certain criteria, he considers himself middle class, 'nice and clean'.

Keith, who is positioned in a top set and is widely considered by teachers and his parents to have the capability and motivation to pursue A-levels and university, articulates a specific aspiration:

> Keith: Lower. Lower. I don't want to be a doctor or a teacher or anything like that. I want to be an electrician or a career in the armed forces – that's obviously long hours and low pay.
> Garth: What does the term 'working class' mean to you?
> Keith: People that work hard for not a lot of money.

Garth: What does the term 'middle class' mean to you?
Keith: People that control everyone and tell everyone what to do and they get the credit for it.

(Keith, Year 10, London Academy)

However, Keith's reflexive knowledge of class does not necessarily impact on buying into the achievement ideology embodied in the institutional habitus where gaining qualifications is the only path to social mobility. In subsequent interviews, it was clear that Keith's knowledge of class disadvantage was also well informed as he is aware that the cost of university would be a struggle. Keith was also one of the few boys who was able to cite the nuances of class: 'Personality, looks, background and family – the way you speak probably. Like around here Cockney'. While his habitus aligned with the habitus of the institution in nearly every way (academic success, good behaviour), Keith's egalitarian habitus constrained his aspirations. Habitus is where perceptions and conceptions are conditioned by the structures of the environment in which they are engendered (cf. Allen and Hollingworth, 2013). In their classic work, Jackson and Marsden (1966) document the difficult identity negotiations facing working-class grammar-school boys, where educational achievement often resulted in painful separation from one's cultural origins. In the case of Keith, he excludes himself from what he is already excluded from. It can be argued Keith does not 'feel' the impact of social class because he has accepted their current circumstances through an egalitarian habitus that legitimises 'what will be, will be'.

Dan's articulation illustrates a sophisticated knowledge of class and elements of class hatred:

Dan: I say working class. Because I've asked my mum and dad what all that was … that middle class and that … and they said working class and they are. You look at upper-class [people] and that's obviously with those lords and all that, like Prince William and you look at middle-class which is like …
Garth: Teachers, lawyers…
Dan: Yeah, you see all them people are well off with their jobs and then you have like normal working-class and … they do alright but the jobs they do, the money they earn is alright …
Garth: Do you consider working class to be a bit more 'normal' because you used the word normal?
Dan: Yeah, because if you look at sort of middle-class people, their attitudes and that … they're on their own planet and they're so far up their own arse.
Garth: What does the term 'working class' mean to you?
Dan: It means the money you get is that you earned. If you do a hard day's work of building like a brick wall … like something

like manual labour or that ... you get paid. You get paid so much for it and you've actually earned it. You've actually stood and done your best, you've earned that money. And I reckon that's the difference between middle class and working class. 'Middle class' means above average. They've got sort of office jobs and all that ... it probably is hard work in some degree. For what they do they earn more than the average.

(Dan, Year 11, PRU)

Habitus can be used to understand 'the ways in which the socially advantaged and disadvantaged play out the attitudes of cultural superiority and inferiority ingrained in their habitus', and established through daily interactions (Reay, 1998: 33). In despising middle-class attitudes and snobbishness, claiming they are 'so far up their own arse', Dan's habitus celebrates a working-class identity that 'earns' money through manual labour and through 'doing their best'. Dan constitutes a working-class subjectivity that has been noted in other research on white working-class males, 'a muscular Puritan work ethic (honesty, loyalty, self-sufficiency, "a fair day's work for a fair day's pay")' (Nayak, 2003: 309).

The participants' conceptualisation of middle-class people influences their aspirations; it became part of a rationale in which they dis-identified from a lifestyle that was largely beyond their reach. Reflexivity is central to understanding the way that the boys compose identities in relation to structural inequalities. However, such reflexive processes are not straightforward as young people are also 'not homogeneously reflexive, and those who are reflexive do not necessarily gain much advantage from this in their work or educational lives' as reflexivity is dependent on structural conditions (Farrugia, 2012: 686). Dan's words reveal how he sees social class identification and employment as inseparable. His response shows how reflexive youth subjectivities are formed and shaped by inequality, but this is very much a negotiation within the egalitarian habitus that seeks to constitute itself as valuable, 'You've actually stood and done your best'.

The importance of place

The research was conducted in a time of moral panics concerning gangs, anti-social behaviour and young working-class males who exist in urban spaces that are continually pathologised as 'unfit' and 'undesirable' (Archer et al., 2010), where they are constructed as 'rubbish' and 'shit' (Lucey and Reay, 2002). The interconnectedness of locality, or territory, social class identity and working-class masculinity is significant (Willis, 1977; McDowell, 2003; Deuchar and Holligan, 2010). An attachment to locality was also framed by long-standing history, as the majority of the boys in the study had parents and grandparents who grew up in the area. Like other studies focused on the identity work of working-class youth (Lucey and Reay, 2000a; Evans, 2006), it was quite clear from the data that the white working-class boys balanced a tension between detesting their local area and taking pride in it, and their conception was tied to how they negotiated social class, crime and risk:

Garth: How would you describe the area?
Mitchell: What, seriously?
Garth: Yeah.
Mitchell: A shithole.
Garth: Why?
Mitchell: Boremund is a shithole.
Garth: What makes it a shithole?
Mitchell: The people that live here like. People who can't go out and get jobs and just sit around and like basically drink all day. Just losers.

(Mitchell, Year 11, London Academy)

Garth: How would you describe the area?
Thomas: It's alright but there's, like, too many crimes going on, like, people ... there's always stuff, like someone getting robbed or some shops always getting broke into, something like that.

(Thomas, Year 11, London Academy)

Garth: How would you describe the area?
Ryan: A tough place to be – grow up.
Garth: Why? What makes it tough?
Ryan: The gangs and the violence and drugs and stuff like that.

(Ryan, Year 10, London Academy)

Loic Waquant (1996: 238–239) reminds us in his study of low income, socially-excluded urban areas in Paris and Chicago, 'To dwell in a ... low-income estate means to be confined to a branded space, to [dwell in] a blemished setting experience[d] as a trap', which he terms as 'territorial stigmatization' where pejorative labels stick because those who are located within these communities have little power to reject them. The data indicate that the boys engage in a psychic negotiations (Reay, 2005) to reconcile pride/disgust, trap/freedom, belonging/mobility. The Boremund community was a place of contradiction in their minds. South-east London was not a good place, but their part of it, their house, their street, their section, was the 'nice', 'peaceful' part. The ambivalent view that their locality was 'good enough' has been argued as a form of working-class resilience (Lucey and Reay, 2000a); a view some of the boys echoed:

Garth: How would you describe the area?
Billy: I like it. My opinion of it is that it's basically a family – that's
           what I think of the area. Because everyone's behind each
           other, telling each other what to do … so yeah.

                                        (Billy, Year 11, London Academy)

Charlesworth (2000: 21) writes that the phenomena around working-class
place-based experience is 'exemplified in the constant remarking, by working
people, of the social decline' where his participants often 'speak of feeling
"dragged down" and invaded by what is around them'. It is important to
note the boys, regardless of their description of their locale, feel a strong
sense of belonging with very few desiring to leave the area if viable opportunities were made available, which Pugsley (1998) notes is common in
working-class culture. The working-class preference toward locality, referred
to as 'territory' by McDowell (2003) and 'placism' by Evans (2006), and
their reluctance to associate with middle-class people (Skeggs, 2002), and
conversely the middle-class reluctance to associate with them (Reay *et al.*,
2007), is problematic when one considers that social capital is produced
through relationships, connections and group membership. Working-class
young people in London, especially young working-class men, move
through incredibly small parts of the city (Gidley, 2007). More specifically,
such movement is largely restricted by class identity and a sense of belonging
(Evans, 2006). Lucey and Reay (2000b), for example, found white middle-
class boys from Camden who were adept at London mass transport travelling
vast distances across the city, while their white working-class counterparts
rarely travelled off their estates. Whereas the London middle classes, in
possession of economic or cultural capitals, are able to transcend their urban
spaces, the working class are often relegated to pathologised spaces such as
council estates (socialised housing) and 'sink' inner-city comprehensive
schools (Archer *et al.*, 2010: 32). The working class lack the power to associate with whomever they choose, combined with the middle-class practices
of exclusion, ensure they are 'put in their place'. Locality, place, fixity and
displacement form an essential foundation influencing how young people
structure their lives and aspirations. In bearing the weight of their worlds, the
egalitarian habitus allows these young men to engage in the dual process of
refusal and reclassification as a coping mechanism.

Summary

Through the words of the participants, it is clear that articulations around
class are steeped in conceptions of shame around poverty, self-doubt and lack
(Stahl, 2013). Pejorative depictions of the working class have resulted in an
erosion of working-class pride where it can no longer be used as a positive
source of identity (Skeggs, 2004). Prior to conducting this research, I

expected, given the vibrant history of the docklands in South London, a degree of class honour; however, at no point did working-class pride explicitly play a role in the discussions with participants in this research. While the lack of the articulation does not necessarily mean working-class pride was not present, it does indicate that social positioning and traditional working-class employment are perhaps no longer areas for valorisation and/or validation. In constituting the dispositions that form their egalitarian habitus, the boys attach certain attributes to each social class. The boys describe the working classes as hard-working, decent and ordinary people, while the middle classes are depicted as people with well-paid jobs who earn more for doing less. While we must remain sceptical of the level of experience the boys had with different social classes, these characterisations have the potential of lowering these boys' aspiration into such professions. The boys who dis-identified with the potential impact of class drew upon certain strategies in order to maintain value in light of exclusionary processes and opportunity denials (Abrahams and Ingram, 2013).

References

Abrahams, J. and Ingram, N. (2013) The chameleon habitus: Exploring local students' negotiations of multiple fields. *Sociological Research Online*, 18(4). Online at: www.socresonline.org.uk/18/4/21.html

Adams, M. (2006) Hybridizing habitus and reflexivity: Towards an understanding of contemporary identity. *Sociology*, 40(3), 511–528.

Allen, K. and Hollingworth, S. (2013) 'Sticky Subjects' or 'Cosmopolitan Creatives'? Social class, place, and urban young people's aspirations for work in the knowledge economy. *Urban Studies*, 50(3), 499–517.

Archer, L. and Leathwood, C. (2003) New times – old inequalities: Diverse working-class femininities in education. *Gender and Education*, 15(3), 227–235.

Archer, L., Hollingworth, S. and Mendick, H. (2010) *Urban youth and schooling: The experiences and identities of educationally 'at risk' young people*. Berkshire: Open University Press.

Beck, U. (1992) *Risk society: Towards a new modernity*. London: Sage Publications.

Bottero, W. (2009) Class in the 21st Century. In K. P. Sveinsson (ed.), *Who cares about the white working class?* (pp. 7–15). London: Runnymede Perspectives.

Bourdieu, P. (1984) *Distinction: A Social critique of the judgement of taste*. Oxon: Routledge.

Bourdieu, P. (1989) Social space and symbolic power. *Sociological Theory*, 7(1), 14–25.

Boyne, R. (2002) Bourdieu: From class to culture: In memorium Pierre Bourdieu 1930–2002. *Theory Culture Society*, 19(3), 117–128.

Burke, P. J. (2009) Men accessing high education: Theorizing continuity and change in relation to masculine subjectivities. *Higher Education Policy*, 22, 81–100.

Carter, P. (2005) *Keepin' it real: School success beyond Black and White*. New York: Oxford University Press.

Charlesworth, S. J. (2000) *The phenomenology of working class experience*. Cambridge: University Press.

Deuchar, R. and Holligan, C. (2010) Gangs, sectarianism and social capital: A qualitative study of young people in Scotland. *Sociology*, 44(1), 13–30.

Dillabough, J. A. and Kennelly, J. (2010) *Lost youth in a global city: Class, culture and the urban imaginary*. New York: Routledge.

Evans, G. (2006) *Educational failure and working class white children in Britain*. Palgrave: Macmillan.

Farrugia, D. (2012) Young people and structural inequality: Beyond the middle ground. *Journal of Youth Studies*, 16(5), 679–693.

Gidley, B. (2007) Youth culture and ethnicity: Emerging youth interculture in South London. In P. Hodkinson and W. Deicke (eds), *Youth cultures: Scenes, subcultures, and tribes* (pp. 145–159). New York: Routledge.

Horvat, E. M. and Lewis, K. S. (2010) Reassessing the burden of 'acting white': The importance of peer groups in managing academic success. *Sociology of Education*, 76(4), 265–280.

Ingram, N. (2009) Working-class boys, educational success, and the misrecognition of working-class culture. *British Journal of Sociology of Education*, 30(4), 421–434.

Ingram, N. (2011) Within school and beyond the gate: The complexities of being educationally successful and working class. *Sociology*, 45(2), 287–302.

Jackson, B. and Marsden, D. (1966) *Education and the working class*. London: Penguin Books.

Lucey, H. and Reay, D. (2000a) 'I don't really like it here but I don't want to be anywhere else': Children and inner-city council estates. *Antipode*, 34(4), 410–425.

Lucey, H. and Reay, D. (2000b) Identities in transition: Anxiety and excitement in the move to secondary school. *Oxford Review of Education*, 26(2), 191–205.

Lucey, H. and Reay, D. (2002) Carrying the beacon of excellence: Social class differentiation and anxiety at a time of transition. *Journal of Education Policy*, 17(3), 321–336.

McDowell, L. (2003) *Redundant masculinities?: Employment change and white working class youth*. Malden, MA: Blackwell Pub.

MacLeod, J. (2009) *Ain't no makin' it*. Boulder, CO: Westview Press.

Nayak, A. (2003) 'Ivory lives': Economic restructuring and the making of whiteness in a post-industrial youth community. *European Journal of Cultural Studies*, 6(3), 305–325.

Preston, J. (2009) *Whiteness and class in education*. Dordrecht: Springer.

Pugsley, L. (1998) 'Throwing your brains at it.' Higher education markets and choice. *International Studies in Sociology of Education*, 8(1), 71–90.

Reay, D. (1998) *Class work: Mothers' involvement in their children's primary schooling*. London: UCL Press, Taylor and Francis Group.

Reay, D. (2002) Shaun's story: Troubling discourses on white working-class masculinities. *Gender and Education*, 14(3), 221–234.

Reay, D. (2005) Beyond consciousness?: The psychic landscape of social class. *Sociology*, 39(5), 911–928.

Reay, D., Hollingworth, S., Williams, K., Crozier, G., Jamieson, F., James, D. and Beedell, P. (2007) 'A darker shade of pale?' Whiteness, the middle classes and multi-ethnic inner city schooling. *Sociology*, 41(6), 1041–1060.

Reay, D., Crozier, G. and Clayton, J. (2009) 'Strangers in paradise'? Working-class students in elite universities. *Sociology*, 43(6), 1103–1121.

Savage, M. (2000) *Class analysis and social transformation*. Buckingham: Open University Press.

Savage, M. (2010) The politics of elective belonging. *Housing, Theory and Society*, 27(2), 115–161.

Sayer, A. (2002) What are you worth?: Why class is an embarrassing subject. *Sociological Research Online*, 7(3). Online at: www.socresonline.org.uk/7/3/sayer.html

Sayer, A. (2005) *The moral significance of class*. Cambridge: Cambridge University Press.

Skeggs, B. (2002) *Formations of class and gender*. Nottingham: Sage Publications.

Skeggs, B. (2004) *Class, self, culture*. London: Routledge.

Stahl, G. (2013) Habitus disjunctures, reflexivity, and white working-class boys' conceptions of status in learner and social identities. *Sociological Research Online*, 18(3). Online at: www.socresonline.org.uk/18/3/2.html

Stahl, G. (2014) The affront of the aspiration agenda, white working-class male narratives of 'ordinariness' in neoliberal times. *Masculinities and Social Change*, 3(2), 88–118.

Sweetman, P. (2003) Twenty-first century dis-ease? Habitual reflexivity or the reflexive habitus. *The Sociological Review*, 51(4), 528–549.

Threadgold, S. and Nilan, P. (2009) Reflexivity of contemporary youth, risk and cultural capital. *Current Sociology*, 57(1), 47–68.

Wacquant, L. (1996) Red belt, black belt: Racial division, class inequality, and the state of the French urban periphery and the American ghetto. In E. Minione (ed.) *Urban poverty and the underclass* (pp. 234–274). Oxford: Blackwell.

Weis, L. (1990) *Working class without work*. New York: Routledge.

Whitman, K. (2013) The 'Aussie battler' and the hegemony of centralising working-class masculinity in Australia. *Australian Feminist Studies*, 28(75), 50–64.

Wilkins, A. (2011) Push and pull in the classroom: Competition, gender, and the neoliberal subject. *Gender and Education*, 24(7), 1–17.

Willis, P. (1977) *Learning to labour: How working class kids get working class jobs*. New York: Columbia University Press.

Willis, P. (2004) Twenty-five years on: Old book, new times. In N. Dolby, G. Dimitriadis and P. Willis (eds), *Learning to Labor in new times* (p. 231). New York: RoutledgeFalmer.

Youdell, D. (2010) Identity traps or how black students fail: The interactions between biographical, sub-cultural, and learner identities. *British Journal of Sociology of Education*, 24(1), 3–20.

Chapter 5

Social class influence and educational engagement

I mean – I don't know anything about the middle and working class, but posh people they're usually all stuck-up. And like only care about themselves and that … Where working-class and maybe some middle-class would think about others, like, and all that.

(Thomas, Year 11, London Academy)

In this chapter I analyse how the boys apply their conceptualisations of social class to education. There is a complex relationship between how the boys come to understand social class and their engagement with their formal schooling. Both societal discourses and urban schooling practices, grounded heavily in social class, foster pupils' conceptualisations of themselves as learners and their education-based aspirations. Learning and engagement with one's education is not simply a cognitive process, but is socially, culturally and emotionally produced through interaction and 'intimately bound up with self-hood' (Hollingworth and Archer, 2010: 591). In constituting themselves as learners, the participants confront neoliberal discourses of social mobility that require them to juggle multiple subjectivities. As a result of this delicate balancing act, there are convergences and overlaps between social class and learner identities as 'pupils construct themselves and are constructed by others as particular types of learners in relation to both other pupils and their teachers' (Reay, 2010: 279).

Social class, education and influence

According to Bottero (2009: 10), '"Class" is always about invidious comparison, and when people talk about "class" their accounts often shift easily from social description, to social evaluation, to social abuse'. There exists a fine line between belonging to the legitimised working class and the poverty underclass (Lawler, 2004; Reay, 2005). While working-class experiences with education have historically been shaped by the 'injuries of class' (Bottero, 2004), the habitus has the capacity to both acknowledge social inequalities and construct narratives to ameliorate against such injuries. As learners, the reflexivity of working-class boys, which stems from disjunctures between the field of origin and subsequent fields, is experienced to different degrees as it is 'heavily circumscribed by material disadvantage' (Farrugia, 2012: 689). An egalitarian habitus serves as a way of calibrating the self during reflexive processes; however, it is a fragmented process as dispositions struggle for dominance. While the boys' accounts are a partial construction of their reflexive experiences, the data show how social structures shape and reshape agents' subjectivities and how the habitus of individuals 'resist and succumb to inertial pressure of structural forces' (McLeod, 2009: 139). When responding to questions regarding how social class may or may not have the capacity to influence how well individuals do in school, the boys show a significant degree of reflexivity:

> Yeah. Because obviously people in upper class they wouldn't want their children going to a lower-class school. So the upper class obviously going to do well, but the lower class have less chance of doing well.
>
> (George, Year 10, London Academy)

> Kind of. Like if you ain't got no money then you can't pay for equipment but if you have the money you can pay for extra learning, extra ... if you have money then you have more of an opportunity than the people that ain't.
>
> (Keith, Year 10, London Academy)

While the influence of class was an uncomfortable area to research, given the often bleak backgrounds the boys came from, my outsider status may have enabled the boys to be more open with me and articulate things they would not have necessarily admitted to a white, middle-class male with a British accent. When asked if social class impacted on an individual's feeling about themselves, the boys' words contain elements of evaluation, preserving authenticity and resistance:

> Umm – sort of, I reckon. Because they think differently about themselves and it's not always about what money they got or nothing. They could be happy with what they've got and it doesn't matter, but ... some people might think they need more, or want more and they might not be happy.
>
> (Phillip, Year 11, London Academy)

> Terry: They might think to themselves, like, I more need to be up ... more likely to be middle class – get a better job.
> Garth: Do you agree with that?
> Terry: No. 'Cause either way you are earning money.
>
> (Terry, Year 11, London Academy)

It's more; it's what they think of themselves. Like middle-class people think of themselves as 'Yeah, I got a good job and I got some money' and they like to brag about it. But working-class people just think of themselves as average people.

(Harry, Year 10, London Academy)

If they're middle class then they may think they're better than working class.

(Frankie, Year 11, London Academy)

If they let it ... Yeah ... it depends on the person themself. If it doesn't really affect the way you are than no. Because if people know who you are, how you are and where you are then ... no it doesn't. If you don't rub it in their face then no they don't. They see you as a normal person.

(Dan, Year 11, PRU)

Dan draws attention to an authentic self that can resist the constraints of social class and where such a self is bolstered against class judgements. Through Dan's words we see an attention to establishing a subjectivity of 'normal' where class matters only if and when it becomes a problem. Dan's 'loyalty to self' contains inflections of dignity and of not losing oneself; to fully embrace social mobility would require the boys to concede dispositions of their working-class identity embodied in the egalitarian habitus (Reay, 2009). As power relationships become internalised in the habitus as categories of perceptions, these processes of categorising become essential to how the boys' constitute themselves as 'average' and ordinary (Stahl, 2013). Through ascribing to such subjectivities, the boys are able to resist the potency of class hierarchies. Social class often concerns accepting that judgement is placed upon the individual and that the individual, in turn, judges others. Embracing a middle-class lifestyle would require the boys to change what they are (Reay, 2001); they would become judgemental and think themselves 'better than working-class', according to Frankie. Embracing a middle-class lifestyle requires challenging identity negotiations and re-appropriations, which for many working class boys means the losses would be greater than the gains (Reay, 2002).

As a counter-habitus, egalitarianism is how the boys come to understand the cards they have been dealt. The habitus incorporates the immanent structures of the neoliberal field and is established in relation to dominant or privileged cultures. As neoliberal subjects, the middle classes are dealt better cards in the high-stakes game and are able to compete through economic and cultural advantages; they know how best to play their hands in order to secure an advantageous position. Mitchell acknowledges how the game works:

'Cause like the middle class – their parents pay for them to go to a private school or a grammar school and they just get some of the best education in the country. And they're probably going to pass and get really high grades, go on. Like a working-class person they care more about what, like, people think and what they look like than grades they get more. That's what I think.

(Mitchell, Year 11, London Academy)

The habitus is where class is internalised and individual aspiration is mediated alongside collective history. In acknowledging the complexities regarding social class, Alen and Calum show how certain doxic discourses exist that work to actively structure their subjectivities. In regards to queries regarding if social class had the capacity to influence how individuals felt about themselves, the two boys remarked:

Alen: Yeah. Definitely because you ... want ... to feel like ... dunno ... obviously you don't want to be, like, doing bad in life and like being lower class. Obviously you want to be up there.
Garth: Do you think that is true of everyone, though? Don't you think some people are quite content where they are?
Alen: Yeah, there are some people but money don't always make you happy. Money can't buy you everything. Love, happiness.

(Alen, Year 11, London Academy)

Yeah, definitely. If you're ... if you're born from poverty you're going to have to ... I wouldn't say you're definitely going to come up with knife crime and that, but it's definitely going to be a big part in your life. If you come up with all that surroundings. But if someone came from ... I dunno ... again, 'The Waltons' then you know ...

(Calum, Year 10, World School)

Throughout the dialogues with participants there was reflexivity in regards to how class influenced self-worth, aspiration and barriers. These accounts show how egalitarianism, a counter-habitus against feeling of inferiority and shame, has the capacity to become a process of mitigation, of reconciling aspirations with current social positioning. In terms of understanding class, the boys arguably have the beginnings of a 'reflexive habitus' (Sweetman, 2003; Adams, 2006). At times, the boys may lack ways of articulating the nuances of class, but that does not mean that the participants are unreflexive nor does possessing reflexivity necessarily lead to agentic responses. In fact, two students, Luke and Mitchell, who had taken GCSE sociology and who, therefore, had increased academic knowledge of social class, had already taken steps to ensure they would remain in the same social class by opting not to attend a local private/faith school for fear of not fitting in, and enrolling in a post-16 trade programmes. When considering how the social status of an individual influences their feelings about themselves, Keith said:

> Kind of because if someone says to you, 'oh you're lower class' then I'm going to think I'm poor. Basically … and if someone says you're upper class, you're rich and that. Basically, middle class I'd probably think … you'd think high of yourself.
>
> (Keith, Year 10, London Academy)

The egalitarian habitus represents both the 'mental structures through which they apprehend the social world and simultaneously a product of that world' (Bourdieu, 1989: 18), but this is a social world that is constantly changing and where the traditional codes that define social class, as well as gender norms, are influenced by globalisation and modernity. Our current generation of white working-class boys face an uncertain future where the historic infrastructures of respectable employment, which have been the traditional bases of white male power, 'have eroded rapidly' (Weis, 1990: 6). Young men, particularly those from lower and working-class backgrounds, have to negotiate their identity work around rapidly changing discourses of aspiration and power where they become 'reflexive subjects trying to fill the void left by the demise of traditional codes and early-modern ideologies' (Mouzelis, 2007).

Social class and learner identities

Learning is a process of orientation to a particular identity that is socially validated and socially constituted, and there exist many overlaps and conflations between learner identities with social identities (Reay, 2010: 279). In their study of vocational courses in a British further education (FE) college, Colley et al. (2007: 488) set forth an argument for a 'vocational habitus' where:

> [the] learner aspires to a certain combination of dispositions demanded by the vocational culture. It operates in disciplinary ways to dictate how one should properly feel, look and act, as well as the values, attitudes and beliefs that one should espouse. As such, it is affective and embodied, and calls upon the innermost aspects of learners' own habitus.

How these boys look and act and the attitudes they espouse in their schooling is established through learning cultures that are comprised of sets of common practices and certain discourses (James et al., 2007). Identities are shaped in a system where these young men are forced to play for high stakes in a 'finely calibrated hierarchy of credentialised achievement [which] has been flattened into winners and losers' (Brown, 2013: 685). The egalitarian habitus is always co-constructed with field(s) not only where structure and agency combine to render the process of acculturation but also where the habitus does not passively absorb, as dispositions adopt, subvert and adapt the prerogatives of different discourses. As they make sense of their positioning, the boys make connections between social and learner identities where the boys consistently see social class as part of the learner identity and vice versa:

Harry: I think [other students] are lower class because they don't keep on track and stuff and they mess around in class and stuff.

Garth: You are in the habit of going over each other's houses and stuff, so would you say they live in or their families live in similar ... similar to your parents or different?

Harry: Yeah. I think they're like ... I've only been to a couple of my friends' houses but I think they're working class as well. Because their mums have good jobs and they don't have a lot of children and they don't just live on benefits and stuff like that.

(Harry, Year 10, London Academy)

Garth: What social class do you think your friends are?

Ryan: Well, some of 'em are at the bottom. Some in my maths class are at the middle; especially in science they're middle. They think 'I'm better than you at this', 'I'm better than you at that'. Too big headed and some of my mates are just working.

Garth: Is it important for you to have friends of different social classes?

Ryan: Want them to have same background as myself.

(Ryan, Year 10, London Academy)

Through Ryan's interview we see a convergence of social and learner identities where he expresses disapproval of those he sees as performing an identity that is 'disloyal' to his disposition, oriented toward ordinariness or averageness with 'big headed' and 'better than you'. The majority of the participants saw their learner identities and aspiration as adequately fulfilled by a drive towards 'middling', and through this process they reaffirm their own place in both the social and neoliberal hierarchies (cf. Stahl, 2014a, 2014b). When I queried Ryan further about his aspirations to become a professional football player, he drew upon his egalitarian habitus to ameliorate feelings around class injuries:

Garth: You said you don't like posh people because they are 'up there' and 'full of themselves' but if you were to become a professional footballer, would you be one of those posh people or not?

Ryan: No. If I had a lot of money I would be giving charity a lot of money. Getting nice clothes, trainers – just look after my family and that … ain't going to be …
Garth: So you'd give it back in some way.
Ryan: I would go on, I wouldn't go to people 'do you want me to buy you a pair of trainers?' and that … I'd just be normal and that. Just myself. Just keep the money close to me.

(Ryan, Year 10, London Academy)

Ryan aspires to reap the financial rewards associated with being a football celebrity, but he is careful to articulate that he would not change and that he would always give back to his family and be 'normal'. While people are equipped with different capitals that are advantageous depending on the field, the boys in this study mentioned numerous times that thinking one is better than someone else, or putting on a show, was an affront to how they think boys like them should behave. The difficulties that arise in operating at the boundary of different fields suggest that, in order to be successful, individuals must often reduce their affiliation to their working-class identity. Yet, an egalitarian habitus allows Ryan to balance multiple conceptions of success where he can have wealth but also have a 'loyalty to self' unchanged by the opportunities that would be afforded to him. Ryan wants to embody what Carter (2006) calls a cultural straddler: someone who is strategically able to dexterously navigate the cultural codes of multiple fields and multiple subjectivities; however, this requires an ongoing reflexive engagement with habitus clivé.

Interest in middle-class and upper-class lifestyles

In McDowell's (2000) research on white working-class boys, she notes, 'Many of them were not verbally adept, perhaps unused to exploring their views and feelings with a stranger' (p. 209). In planning the research, I considered that many of my participants would respond 'more easily to visual, rather than lexical prompts' (Prosser and Schwartz, 1998: 123). The research utilised visuals, music, film and kinaesthetics to elicit richer responses from the boys (Appendix A) and break down power imbalances to forge 'deeper ties with participants' (Eglinton, 2013: 256). As an ethnographer who lived and worked in the area for five years, I felt I had a solid knowledge of the visual repertoires the boys experienced, a 'sense of the visual and technological cultures' (Pink, 2007: 45) of my participants in this South London locale. Many of the pictures that were chosen were taken from Facebook, internet sites, or from magazines. I recognise that in choosing the photographs, I imposed certain visual representations upon the participants, thus structuring the discussion. A variety of rationales were employed in the selection of the images; however, the chief rationale was that they should introduce participants to a large amount of information and encouraged them to scrutinise the photographs (Johnson, 2008: 83). The majority of the boys were fascinated by middle-class and upper-class boys, but equally unsettled by the foreignness of their dramatically different lifestyles. When provided with pictures of middle-class and upper-class masculinities, my participants often selected the picture of Etonians (Picture 5.1):

> The ones that appeal to me [Figure 5.1]. 'Cause I'm not really familiar with that sort of ... I mean obviously I know that's a school. I am not familiar with that uniform. There is still the premises itself; if I was in that situation it would be completely new to me.
>
> (Dan, Year 11, PRU)

Keith: Because [Figure 5.1] shows you posh boys coming out of a college or something like that dressed really smartly. And it shows you like their family is upper class.

Garth: Ok, why does that appeal to you or does that appeal to you?

Keith: Because it shows that. I don't know about it. It just shows you what people are like and how family money effects people's education.

(Keith, Year 10, London Academy)

Figure 5.1 Etonians
Source: Christopher Furlong/Getty Images

Discussions with Figure 5.1 consistently resulted in the boys describing them as 'unfamiliar', which has implications for the boys' willingness to mix socially if the opportunity was to present itself (Hollingworth and Williams, 2009). The social, cultural and economic capitals influence young people's positioning as they move through spaces acquiring different kinds and forms of capital and resources; therefore, '[i]dentifications develop not through consciousness, but through distinctions from others' (Tolonen, 2013: 58). Leitch (2008: 38) writes that through the use of visual images participants 'have the opportunity to narrate for themselves and be their own audience, children have occasion to articulate perceptions, emotions, and viewpoints which are latent or less conscious as and when they emerge'. In contrast to Bathmaker *et al.* (2013), there were no examples, in the data set, of frustration in regard to the advantages of their more privileged counterparts, as the egalitarian habitus, as part of a process of symbolic violence, ameliorated such feelings. Yet there were feelings of negativity and anxiety:

Garth: Why [Figure 5.1]?
Mitchell: Middle class, upper class. Yeah, that's what it looks like.
Garth: Ok, and why do you find that unappealing?
Mitchell: 'Cause I don't relate to it.
                              (Mitchell, Year 11, London Academy)

'Cause it looks like – they look like posh kids all coming out of university of a boarding school or something like that. I like normal schooling and that. Normal school, being where all my mates are.
                              (Phillip, Year 11, London Academy)

Dan: I'd say [Figure 5.1] doesn't appeal to me. That looks sort of middle-class sort of schooling. I wouldn't feel comfortable there. Even though the education is probably better than what you'd get in average, I wouldn't like it. That sort of just knowing …
Garth: You feel outsiderish?
Dan: Yeah.
Garth: Different?
Dan: Yeah, like spoilt in the way. I wouldn't like that feeling.
                              (Dan, Year 11, PRU)

Mitchell feels not 'able to relate to it', while Phillip references a desire for 'normal' schooling where his 'mates are', revealing how the boys see this middle- and upper-class lifestyle as a place that could bring about feelings of inferiority. We glimpse what Bourdieu (1999) refers to as the most unexpected of all the potential conflicts that emanate from upward mobility: 'the feeling of being torn that come from experiencing success as failure, or, better still, as transgression' (p. 510). Dan recognises the education would be better, but that ultimately he would feel 'spoilt'. Through making sense of their own positionality, the boys also stereotyped working-class, middle-class and upper-class people:

> I mean – I don't know anything about the middle and working class, but posh people they're usually all stuck-up. And like only care about themselves and that ... Where working-class and maybe some middle-class would think about others, like, and all that.
>
> (Thomas, Year 11, London Academy)

Most sociological research tends to focus on the pathologisation of the working classes by middle classes; however, the boys' reflexive response indicates they have the capacity to pathologise the 'snob' middle classes who they characterise as self-centred and uncaring. In wider discourses, certain elements of working-class culture have been socially constructed as inferior such as 'the creative hedonism; the anti-pretentious humour, the dignity, the high ethical standards of honour, loyalty, and caring' (Skeggs, 2004: 88). A significant aspect of egalitarianism is the caring for others, a commitment to collective well-being. These standards have been well-documented as aspects of working-class communities, especially with youth cultures in the face of de-industrialisation (Brann-Barrett, 2011). Within neoliberal educational discourses, the commitment is toward the individual who is valued solely through the acquisition of credentials. An ethos of caring and support was not a part of the school environment in this study. I can draw on very few examples from my field notes where boys were asked to work cooperatively, to teach and support one another, or to engage in community service. Whilst this does not necessarily illustrate how the school fails to recognise working-class communal values, it is worth considering this as evidence of a certain prerogative within the education system, which contributes to the construction of identity.

Attaching certain behaviours to perceptions of social class is a very different process compared to simply defining social class through income and material possessions. Where early on in the research process the boys discussed class in economic terms, as time went by, and we became more familiar, the boys verbalised the behavioural connotations attached to social class status. The use of visual images opened up a space for more nuanced dialogues regarding how social class was constructed for the boys:

> Yeah, posh kids and middle-class kids are excellent behaved and the working-class kids ain't.
>
> (Mitchell, Year 11, London Academy)

> Yeah, 'cause if you have a bunch of lower-class or working-class people in the room ... then obviously they are going go to mess about but if

you have a higher-class then they're going to sit there and pay attention.

(Keith, Year 10, London Academy)

Luke: Probably the middle-class [people] are more stuck up.
Garth: Where working-class people are not?
Luke: They want to express themselves, they don't care what people
         think of them.

(Luke, Year 11, London Academy)

The conception of the working classes as valuing self-expression free from social constraints has a long history, and through this expression working-class boys often become labelled as 'disrespectful' (Willis, 1977; Humphries, 1981; McDowell, 2007). Respectability is one of the most 'ubiquitous signifiers of class', where it is a key mechanism by which subjects are 'othered' and pathologised, informing 'how we know who we are (or are not)', what is valued and what is devalued (Skeggs, 2002: 1). As Sayer (2002: 415) suggests, the working classes are caught in a bind that produces 'acute inner turmoil as a result of the opposing pulls of both wanting to refuse the perceived external judgements and their criteria and wanting to measure up to them – both to reject respectability and to be respectable'. Winlow (2001) documents how, in pre-neoliberal times of economic stability, there existed a 'shop floor masculinity' comprised of physical strength, a lack of respect towards authority, having a 'laff' and the desire to be released from the bonds of responsibility (p. 38). In an era of high modernity, where media and consumerist culture is far more robust, what constitutes respectable working-class masculinity and positionality is no longer straightforward (Allen and Mendick, 2012).

While there exists many complexities surrounding class, it is clear from the data that the boys are reflexive and aware of class, though not always necessarily aware of their own positionality, their limited opportunities, or the processes which work to fix them in place:

Garth: What makes a working-class person and what makes a middle-
         class person?
Dan: Middle class is sort of … I dunno if middle class is sort of born
         into it or … 'cause you get the sort of odd working-class
         person whose gone into middle class – like they're well off and
         all that. That they've earned it and all – and you can tell
         they've come from working class because it's all new to them
         and they're happy that they're there. They're excited that
         they've got all this sort of thing. You can tell that even in their
         speech, they talk like every sort of working-class person … in
         their speech and all that and the things that they do, the enjoy-
         ment they get out of it basically. The pleasures of it. You can

tell but middle class are sort of born into it so it's normal for
them – they wouldn't get excited of getting up into the house
and in their garden and all that stuff. They wouldn't necessarily get excited about getting up in that sort of flat and looking
out into a sort of car park. Sort of things like that. That's sort
of the same. It's normal for them.

Garth: It's all relative to their situation. Do certain social classes have
certain behaviours you associate with them? Or do you think
people behave the same?

Dan: I reckon people behave the same but you get more sort of
working class people – its normal for them to not follow rules
and things like that. It's normal, it's what they grew up with.
They haven't really had the structure or parents to tell them
this and that. Yet some people who have come from middle-
class backgrounds, they've had a structure – they start sort of
misbehaving for the thrill of it, of not doing things and behaving in a certain way because they like it.

Garth: Yeah, they act out for different reasons …

Dan: Yeah. They can control what they do. They know it's wrong,
but they still do it 'cause they've never done it, never experienced it before. Then you have the working-class kid who
doesn't know another way. He doesn't know to control it or
to do that because no one's told him.

(Dan, Year 11, PRU)

Dan's perception of what constitutes a working-class person and a middle-
class person touches on parental influence, marginalisation and doxic
representations of aspiration among other factors. The narrative indicates
that class can be emulated but cannot be acquired by money alone. Dan is
aware of social mobility where working-class people can make the transition
to a middle-class lifestyle because 'they've earned it', 'they're happy that they
are there', and 'they're excited that they've got all this sort of thing'. While
some working classes may have a similar volume of economic capital as their
middle-class counterparts, they will always be at best, the pretentious inauthentic Other where 'their speech', for example, gives them away. Such a
transition to the middle class does not necessarily change the working-class
individual as they are still working class in 'everything that they do', placing
'enjoyment' and 'pleasure' as a high priority. Class is also portrayed here as a
pre-given reality where people are 'born into it', where class difference is
normalised and naturalised.

Dan perceives a middle-class person as one with an easy life, a person born
into privilege but who does not know or appreciates it. Middle-class children
are perceived as the ones with all of the choices, all of the good opportunities
and a solid foundation that allows them to succeed in education: 'they've had

a structure'; therefore, they can 'control what they can do' in education. While the working-class children are doomed to fail, for the middle-class children, educational success is theirs to lose ... for 'not doing [the right] things' and/or 'behaving in certain way because they like it'. One can also infer from Dan's comment, 'then you have the working class kid who doesn't know another way. He doesn't know to control it', that he perceives his current circumstance as class-related. In this sense, Dan is reflective of his current situation. Dan sees his social origin as not only influencing his world-view: 'working class people, it's normal for them not to follow rules and things like that, it's what they grow up with', but also as determining his present circumstances. During this interview, which was conducted in a pupil referral unit, Dan was very reflective in regards to class, but his egalitarian habitus, which privileges an equal opportunity structures, allowed him to be positive in what was a severely restricted education. Despite his awareness of social class and his own positionality, Dan's learner identity remained positive:

> ... if I get a good education I'm going to get good jobs and that. I reckon that if there was a group of important things then [education] would be one of the top three or something. 'Cause we spend ten years on learning alone so that must have some importance. Ten years of it ... I want to try to get an apprenticeship for construction and sort of learn on the job. Like normal apprenticeships really – like not full-time, like I'm working and learning as well. And they're paying me as well. So I want to do that and then after a few years ... once I understand, once I sort of know the ins and outs of the industry then I'll start looking into more detail into more jobs that I want to do, I can do and all that.
>
> (Dan, Year 11, PRU)

Despite having a fragmented educational biography, Dan values his education and sees it as part of successfully achieving his goals with very little risk of educational failure. Students, according to Byrom and Lightfoot (2013: 818), 'get caught up in discourses that present education as an equal playing field where decisions, choices and outcomes are influenced by the individual' where the impact of educational failure becomes challenging to reconcile with their career aspirations. As his habitus is permeable to neoliberalism, Dan recognises there is a sense of achievement; however, his egalitarian habitus questions how such achievement may ring false depending on the person. There are echoes here of what Archer *et al.* (2010: 96) call 'a strategy of defer-ment' where he has intent but also a level of flexible hope which enables him to 'minimise the identity costs (such as, disappointment and shame) posed by the risk of failure'. While Dan's plan to pursue trade work may be possible, when he encounters barriers to his goals, a strategy of deferment may allow him to not blame himself for his lack of attainment, as noted in other research on working-class male aspirations (MacLeod, 2009; Reichart *et al.*, 2006).

Summary

The tension between an egalitarian habitus and neoliberal middle class 'success' has contributed to the boys' fractured relationship with social class and achievement. Through the boys' conceptions of class we show how the habitus, as a way people see the world, becomes embedded and where the arbitrariness of power relations becomes naturalised (Grenfell, 2008: 96). Furthermore, the interaction between habitus and field strengthens symbolic violence and people's perceptions that things are as they are because of the natural order, rather than through the influence of a culturally determined principle. The habitus is agentic, and the boys seek to constitute themselves as having value. The general perception among the boys is not only are they aware of social class but also of its potential to influence educational success. Educational attainment is closely linked to their understanding of social class and interlinked with their negative perception of the middle classes. Overall, the boys seem to accept and believe that to become middle class, which is an integral part of the neoliberal rhetoric, one needs not only the necessary qualifications but also the changing of dispositions in order to adopt certain behaviours.

References

Adams, M. (2006) Hybridizing habitus and reflexivity: Towards an understanding of contemporary identity. *Sociology*, 40(3), 511–528.

Allen, K. and Mendick, H. (2012) Keeping it real? Social class, young people, and 'authenticity' in reality TV. *Sociology*, 47(3), 460–476.

Archer, L., Hollingworth, S. and Mendick, H. (2010) *Urban youth and schooling: The experiences and identities of educationally 'at risk' young people*. Berkshire: Open University Press.

Bathmaker, A. M., Ingram, N. and Waller, R. (2013) Higher education, social class, and the mobilisation of capitals: Recognising and playing the game. *British Journal of Sociology of Education*, 34(5-6), 723–743.

Bottero, W. (2004) Class identities and the identity of class. *Sociology*, 38(5), 985–1003.

Bottero, W. (2009) Class in the 21st Century. In K. P. Sveinsson (ed.), *Who cares about the white working class?* (pp. 7–15). London: Runnymede Perspectives.

Bourdieu, P. (1989) Social space and symbolic power. *Sociological Theory*, 7(1), 14–25.

Bourdieu, P. (1999) The contradictions of inheritance. In P. Bourdieu (ed.), *Weight of the world: Social suffering in contemporary society* (pp. 517–551). Cambridge: Polity Press.

Brann-Barrett, M. T. (2011) Same landscape, different lens: Variations in young people's socio-economic experiences and perceptions in their disadvantaged working-class community. *Journal of Youth Studies*, 14(3), 261–278.

Brown, P. (2013) Education, opportunity, and the prospects for social mobility. *British Journal of Sociology of Education*, 34(5–6), 678–700.

Byrom, T. and Lightfoot, N. (2013) Interrupted trajectories: The impact of academic failure on the social mobility of working-class students. *British Journal of Sociology of Education*, 34(5–6), 812–828.

Carter, P. (2006) Straddling boundaries: Identity, culture, and school. *Sociology of Education*, 78(3), 304–328.

Colley, H., James, D., Diment, K. and Tedder, M. (2007) Learning as becoming in vocational education and training: Class, gender, and the role of vocational habitus. *Journal of Vocational Education and Training*, 55(4), 471–498.

Eglinton, K. A. (2013) Between the personal and the professional: Ethical challenges when using visual ethnography to understand young people's use of popular visual material culture. *Young*, 21(3), 253–271.

Farrugia, D. (2012) Young people and structural inequality: Beyond the middle ground. *Journal of Youth Studies*, 16(5), 679–693.

Grenfell, M. (2008) *Pierre Bourdieu: Key concepts.* Durham: Acumen.

Hollingworth, S. and Archer, L. (2010) Urban schools as urban places: School reputation, children's identities and engagement with education in London. *Urban Studies*, 47(3), 584–603.

Hollingworth, S. and Williams, K. (2009) Constructions of the working-class 'other' among urban, white, middle-class youth: 'Chavs', subculture, and the valuing of education. *Journal of Youth Studies*, 12(5), 467–482.

Humphries, S. (1981) *Hooligans or rebels? An oral history of working-class childhood and youth 1889-1939.* Oxford: Basil Blackwell Publisher Limited.

James, D., Biesta, G., Colley, H., Davies, J., Gleeson, D., Hodkinson, P., Maull, W., Postlethwaite, K. and Wahlberg, M. (2007) *Improving learning cultures in further education.* London: Routledge.

Johnson, K. (2008) Teaching children to use visual research methods. In P. Thomson (ed.), *Doing visual research with children and young people* (pp. 77–95). Oxon: Routledge.

Lawler, S. (2004) Rules of engagement: Habitus, power and resistance. *Theory Culture Society*, 20(6), 110–128.

Leitch, R. (2008) Creatively researching children's narratives through images and drawing. In P. Thomson (ed.), *Doing visual research with children and young people* (pp. 37–58). Oxon: Routledge.

McDowell, L. (2000) The trouble with men? Young people, gender transformations and the crisis of masculinity. *International Journal of Urban and Regional Research*, 24(1), 201–209.

McDowell, L. (2007) Respect, respectability, deference and place: What is the problem with/for working class boys? *Geoforum*, 38(2), 276–286.

MacLeod, J. (2009) *Ain't no makin' it.* Boulder, CO: Westview Press.

McLeod, J. (2009) Youth studies, comparative inquiry, and the local/global problematic. *Review of Education, Pedagogy, and Cultural Studies*, 31(4), 270–292.

Mouzelis, N. (2007) Habitus and reflexivity: Restructuring Bourdieu's theory of practice. *Sociological Research Online*, 12(6). Online at: www.socresonline.org.uk/12/6/9.html

Pink, S. (2007) *Doing visual ethnography: Images, media, and representation in research.* London: Sage.

Prosser, J. and Schwartz, D. (1998) Photographs within the sociological research process. In J. Prosser (ed.), *Image-based research* (pp. 115–130). London: Falmer Press.

Reay, D. (2001) Finding or losing yourself? Working-class relationships to education. *Journal of Education Policy*, 16(4), 333–346.

Reay, D. (2002) Shaun's story: Troubling discourses on white working-class masculinities. *Gender and Education*, 14(3), 221–234.

Reay, D. (2005) Beyond consciousness?: The psychic landscape of social class. *Sociology*, 39(5), 911–928.

Reay, D. (2009) Making sense of white working class educational underachievement. In K. P. Sveinsson (ed.), *Who cares about the white working class?* (pp. 22–28). London: Runnymede Perspectives.

Reay, D. (2010) Identity-making in schools and classrooms. In M. Wetherall and C. Talpade Mohanty (eds), *The Sage Handbook of Identities* (pp. 277–294). Los Angeles: Sage Publications.

Reichert, M., Stoudt, B. and Kuriloff, P. (2006) Don't love no fight: Healing and identity among urban youth. *Urban Review*, 38(3), 187–209.

Sayer, A. (2002) What are you worth?: Why class is an embarrassing subject. *Sociological Research Online*, 7(3). Online at: www.socresonline.org.uk/7/3/sayer.html

Skeggs, B. (2002) *Formations of class and gender*. Nottingham: Sage Publications.

Skeggs, B. (2004) *Class, self, culture*. London: Routledge.

Stahl, G. (2013) Habitus disjunctures, reflexivity, and white working-class boys' conceptions of status in learner and social identities. *Sociological Research Online*, 18(3). Online at: www.socresonline.org.uk/18/3/2.html

Stahl, G. (2014a) The affront of the aspiration agenda: White working-class male narratives of 'ordinariness' in neoliberal times. *Masculinities and Social Change*, 3(2), 88–118.

Stahl, G. (2014b) White working-class male narratives of 'loyalty to self' in discourses of aspiration. *British Journal of Sociology of Education* (forthcoming).

Sweetman, P. (2003) Twenty-first century dis-ease? Habitual reflexivity or the reflexive habitus. *The Sociological Review*, 51(4), 528–549.

Tolonen, T. (2013) Youth cultures, lifestyles and social class in Finnish contexts. *Young*, 21(1), 55–75.

Weis, L. (1990) *Working class without work*. New York: Routledge.

Willis, P. (1977) *Learning to labour: How working class kids get working class jobs*. New York: Columbia University Press.

Winlow, S. (2001) *Badfellas: Crime, tradition and new masculinities*. Oxford: Berg.

Chapter 6

Narratives in reconstituting, reaffirming and the self

'Othering' the non-normative

They're trying to do something that isn't working.

(Luke, Year 11, London Academy)

We have seen the role an egalitarian habitus plays in how the boys decipher and code their social worlds, and this chapter will extend this analysis to considering the practice of 'othering' as a strategy to police normative identity boundaries. White working-class boys acquire their habitus through a socialisation process that reflects central structural elements (kinship rules, masculine virtues, etc.), and, therefore, they engage in behaviours that serve to reproduce these structural elements. Through the use of visual methods, the data illustrate the 'ways of doing' white masculinity in Boremund, which are centred upon the dispositions of 'fitting in' and 'ordinariness' – both grounded in the collective 'we' that values solidarity and anti-performativity. In educational settings, the boys' social class identity comes to the forefront where they ascribe to the disposition of 'no one is better than anyone else' in order to constitute themselves as valuable. However, an egalitarian habitus operates in a very different way outside the classroom where gender identity, specifically heteronomativity, comes to the forefront and where they subjugate forms of non-normative masculinity. Using Bourdieu's tools alongside the conceptual lens of heteronormativity, I explore how, when traditional working-class masculine values are inverted, othering becomes a structuring practice where my participants engage with 'intra-habitus tensions' or 'general incongruences between dispositions', and are thus pushed to reflexively secure their own sense of identity (Mouzelis, 2007). Contemporary youth cultures have been argued to be 'fleeting, transitional, and organized around individual lifestyle and consumption choices' (Shildrick, 2006: 63) and no longer underpinned by the conventions of gender and class (Deutsch and Eleni, 2009). While some youth may operate as cultural omnivores (Peterson, 1992) and embrace alternative identity expressions in a time of high modernity, this chapter explores the boys' reflexivity regarding masculinity practices combined with an egalitarian habitus which reorients white working-class boys' masculinity in a process of identity stabilisation.

Othering as a practice of reaffirming

Othering as a practice of identity formation has been documented in the fields of class-based research (Bourdieu, 1989; Lareau, 2003; Sayer, 2005; Bottrell, 2007) and theoretical work on gender (Mills and Lingard, 1997; Archer and Francis, 2005; Francis, 2006). The practice of othering is also apparent in youth culture literature concerning friendship groups (McCulloch *et al.*, 2006; Hollingworth and Williams, 2009), peer networks (Byrom and Lightfoot, 2013; Papapolydorou, 2013), ethnicity/race (Preston, 2010), place (Dillabough and Kennelly, 2010) and sexuality (Brewis and Gavin, 2010). Othering is often enacted through hyper-masculinity, which enhances heterosexual reputation, surveillance, distancing from the feminine and increased capacity to subjugate the Other (Papapolydorou, 2013). However, this is just one possible way in which the strategy of othering manifests. In her analysis of othering, 'doing other' and 'being other' Renold (2004: 249) writes:

> Alternative masculinities are imbued with power relations, and boys who stray or contest the hegemonic ideal (which is contextually and culturally contingent and thus can vary between schools and communities) can incur high social and emotional costs and be subjected to a number of Othering practices in which their deviation from hegemonic norms are subordinated and pathologized.

This chapter examines how working-class hegemonic masculinity is structured through attempts to pathologise others, in order to reaffirm boundaries of authenticity. Othering is always contextual and arguably more salient within neoliberal contexts where identities are bounded by multiple and shifting logics of capital. In the decade between *Working Class Without Work* (1990) and *Class Reunion* (2004), Lois Weis (2008) argues neoliberal ideology introduced a more agentic and autonomous self, inciting the white males in her study to engage in othering, which she argues is an effort toward 'fixing' identities in place in order to 'stabilize' one's own identity (pp. 296–297). Othering, therefore, has the capacity to reconstitute traditional identities that have become fragmented through uncertain transitions into adulthood in deindustrialised places.

Constituting a heteronormative through othering

Gender, as a social practice (ie. performance, 'process' or project) toward understanding one's identity, occurs in relation to other identities (Renold, 2004: 253). Within symbolic or discursive structures, gender is always a 'lived social relation' (McNay, 2004). According to her three-fold model of masculine identity, consisting of power (e.g. subordination of women), production (e.g. division of labour) and cathexis (e.g. emotional attachments), Connell (2005) shows how gender intersects with race and class where white masculinities are constructed in relation to all Others, whether it be white women, black men, Asian women, etc. Connell and Messerschmidt (2005: 4–5) assert that it is 'the Other, the relation to what it is not, to precisely what it lacks', which becomes an essential ingredient to how identity is constructed. Masculinities, as discursively constructed and positioned, are constantly reworked and always in the process of 'becoming'. In an effort to understand the relationships between different masculine identities, Martino (1999) utilises Foucault's polymorphous techniques of power to examine adolescent masculinities and how subjects constitute themselves; specifically, he shows how modalities of power are channelled, through normalising regimes of practice, to permeate individual modes of behaviour. Martino introduces the concept of the heteronormative, where there exists a particular form of masculinity marked out and consistently policed, including boys who model it and excluding boys who do not. There exist many theoretical overlaps between hegemonic masculinity, heteronormativity and othering.

In the analysis of the gendered identity construction of these young men, I want to draw attention to how masculinity is constituted within the habitus, which carries 'the traces of the lines of division and distinction along which the social is organized' where 'class, race, gender, sexuality and so on, are all marked' (Lawler, 2004: 112). Coles (2009: 36) argues masculinity, as a Bourdieusian field, represents:

> sites of domination and subordination, orthodoxy (maintaining the status quo) and heterodoxy (seeking change), submission and usurpation. Individuals, groups, and organizations struggle to lay claim to the legitimacy of specific capital within the field of masculinity. Those in dominant positions strive to conserve the status quo by monopolizing definitions of masculinity and the value and distribution of capital, while subordinate challengers look to subversive strategies, thus generating flux and mechanisms for change.

Within value-laden domains (fields) where there is often constant change, the boys engage in othering to maintain dominant positions 'monopolising' a specific form of authentic masculinity. Adkins (2004: 6), citing Moi, argues that while class has the capacity to structure social fields, so does gender where gender is not an autonomous system but influencing every other category it comes in contact with. While there may be elements of domination and subordination in the field according to Coles (2009), the habitus wants to accrue value and, therefore, processes surrounding gender identity can be conceived as the maintenance of symbolic capital (Skeggs, 2002, 2004). An egalitarian habitus is how the boys create a sense of value and how they gain a sense of where to invest their energies, as egalitarianism ultimately orients their sense of 'normality' within their social space (cf. Winlow, 2001; MacLeod, 2009). In McNay's (1999) work on how gender identity functions within the habitus, she remains critical of the overemphasis on the alignment that the habitus establishes between 'subjective dispositions and the objective structure of the field with regard to gender identity' (p. 107) in favour of an approach that includes attention to a greater instability in gender norms in an era of high modernity. In contrast to Coles, for McNay (2004) gender is not a field at all but a form of symbolic violence in the cultural field where masculinities/femininities are not bounded entities but ambiguous, contradictory and unstable. McNay's argument is particularly relevant when considering how the egalitarian habitus reorients white working-class boys in an ongoing process of identity stabilisation. The rest of this chapter considers gender identity and habitus reaffirmations as I explore how these young men distinguish non-normative behaviour.

Othering Emos

As a gender-based practice of subjugation, my participants othered the subculture of the Emos (who were of the same locale, gender, ethnicity and socio-economic status); through this process they enacted a strategy to reaffirm a heteronormative masculinity within their habitus. McCormack and Anderson (2010) argue that in modern times we are witnessing a dramatic shift in gender relations where there exists persistent change that leads to contemporary masculinity becoming somewhat 'softened'. While pluralities of masculinity may exist in times of persistent change (cf. Roberts, 2012), these masculinities exist alongside the policing of normative boundaries. During the course of the research, the strong dislike my participants had for the Emos occurred unexpectedly through discussions of the picture of a boy dressed in an Emo style. From my time in the area I knew Emos were a noticeable part of the South London locale, but I knew less about how the process of othering worked between social groups in this particular field; the majority of my participants perceived the Emos to be artificial, inferior and inauthentic.

Emos, through their fluid, alternative style, embrace an alternative masculinity that deviates from normative white masculinity construction. Emos typically wear black clothing and have black hair with 'sweeping, dramatic bangs [and] heavy eyeliner' (Peters, 2010: 129) as well as other styling, such as 'tight or over-sized jeans, t-shirts with slogans or band logos on them, canvas or chunky trainers, heavy boots' (Ward, 2013: 8). Emos, as 'hyperstylized almost-punkers', often portray an apathetic and unemotive image (Peters, 2010: 129). In gender terms, male androgyny within the Emo scene is an ideal that is highly valued (Brill, 2007: 115). Within the social space of South London, partaking in an Emo style is about actively creating difference as opposed to creating 'sameness', which the Boremund Boys hold in high regard. As the Emos disassociate themselves from the typical Boremund white working-class style of track pants, Drummond jacket, grey hoodie and Ralph Lauren sneakers for a 'trans-global form of youth culture known as the "alternative scene"' (Ward, 2013: 2), my participants see this self-selection, the 'alternative' expression of identity, as an affront to their masculinity.

Thornton's (1995: 163) work on contemporary dance culture suggests within subcultures – where 'microstructures of power' operate – there are always elements of acceptance and resistance. Extending Bourdieu's concepts of cultural capital and distinction, Thornton introduces a compelling argument for 'subcultural capital', a mark of distinction which can be objectified (e.g., jewellery, hair, make-up, music tastes, clothing, etc) or embodied (e.g., 'cool' demeanour) and through which concepts of status and power are conferred as a process of maintaining respectability. Within the subculture, Thornton maintains there are powerful patterns of inclusion and exclusion at play as the subculture renders itself distinctive. The othering of the Emos by my participants allows for consideration of how masculine domination works as a form of symbolic violence, where male power is constituted through everyday symbolic processes that structure the habitus. In Atencio et al.'s (2009) work on exclusivity within all-male skateboarding cultures, they use Bourdieu's conceptual tools to 'shed light on how embodied masculinities and femininities became interpolated in normative and hierarchical ways within this field' (p. 6), where agents enact various strategies that constitute their subjectivities and where thought processes occur within the constraints of the social fields. Othering is a strategic process employed selectively depending on the social context, where it is both embodied and an act, not only signifying an outsider, but simultaneously defining the self (Lawrence, 2013).

Through a reflexive process, my participants draw upon egalitarianism, which serves as a foundation for exclusionary practices where Emos are discursively constructed as being different from the ideals of dominant (Anglo) white masculinities within the Boremund community. The social space, for the boys, functions as symbolic space. 'Knowing the game', or knowing the social world, enables these boys not only to 'negotiate and manipulate the positional challenges they experience daily' (MacLeod, 2009: 139) but also to define the boundaries of that social world, resisting an alternative style. Habitus operates in relation to the field, but habitus also arguably 'ensures that removal from the field – or entry into a new game – will generate a different set of responses dependent upon one's "feel" for the game with which one is now confronted' (Sweetman, 2003: 534). Self-reflexivity does not offer the uncoupling of agency from structure; rather, 'self-reflexivity itself depends upon access to resources and concomitant forms of capital' (Skeggs, 2004: 60). Through their style, the Emos blur gender norms, inverting a 'Boremund Boy' heteronormative. While gender may be characterised by reflexivity, this reflexivity is not a freedom from gender norms; it is rather a reworking of gender categories (Adkins, 2004: 9). The Emos are fluid in their identity shifts, whereas my participants hold close to what they perceive as an authentic self. The egalitarian habitus contests and resists fluidity and the adoption of identities perceived as 'fake'.

In terms of Martino's concept of the heteronormative, my participants do see the Emos as embodying a specific model of masculinity; therefore, their othering is primarily focused on their individualised performativity and self-exclusion. In his analysis of a masculine habitus as distributed cognition, Connolly (2006: 144) argues habitus:

> helps us move away from the idea that a boy's masculine identity is static and fixed; that it is something simply acquired and then located in their head and that it remains the same and unchanged regardless of the differing contexts he will move between.

There exist many forms of masculinity, but the pluralism of masculinities, represented in this case by the picture of the Emos, pushes the participants to reaffirm a specific form of heternormative masculinity. While white Boremund boys have brushed against different masculinities, some of which are more individualised and fluid, such exposure has only served to adhere my participants to a set, fixed image, usually grounded in strong sense of place (McCulloch et al., 2006).

While there may be 'no core masculine identity that an individual boy (or group of boys) has and which they then take with them and express across a range of contexts and situations' (Connolly, 2006: 150), I would argue that the agent's ability to dexterously draw on different masculinities at different times is advantageous and has been documented to have a significant impact on learner identities (Archer and Yamashita, 2003; Youdell, 2010; Stahl and Dale, 2013). Gilbert and Gilbert (1998) cite the tremendous anxiety many adolescent boys experience within the school environment and how this pushes them to 'folly' by fixating on one form of masculinity, a 'form of masculinity which is narrow, rigid and inflexible, and whose integrity and viability depends on its opposition to femininity and more diverse concepts of masculinity' (p. 222). Prudence Carter's (2006) work with African-American and Latino youth in New York supports fluidity as capital with learner identities, as she documents how some working-class students could temporally embrace middle-class fluidity, moving back and forth among different fields, turning 'cultural codes on and off' and reflexively identifying 'with their multiple social identities simultaneously operating in a variety of cultural spheres' (p. 322).

To view habitus as overtly unconscious and pre-reflexive underestimates the actors' rationality and reflexivity (Sayer, 2005). When habitus confronts a field that challenges it, in this case the subculture of the Emo, reflexivity is incited through the disjuncture. Through this encounter of habitus and field, the (unconscious) habitus is destabilised, and it is where identity transformation is both vacillating between a desire to change and a desire to maintain. Therefore, while Bourdieu's conception of reflexivity is where 'the individual will renounce his or her doxic attitude toward the world, or better, toward specific elements or dimensions of the social order' (Krais, 2006: 130), reflexivity is also a practice where certain doxic attitudes, in this case heteronormativity, are reaffirmed. Within the fixed and fluid dichotomy, reflexivity plays a significant role, but it is not straightforward. For example, Lahire (2011) emphasises that a modern reflexivity is not inconsistent with Bourdieu's emphasis on social practice, but that thinking about habitus as unified is reductive. As Farrugia (2013: 11) explains:

> Lahire argues that it is impossible for modern subjects to operate according to a single set of assumptions about the social world which are somehow transposable across different social contexts. Rather, Lahire argues that, in order to understand modern social practice it is necessary to recognise the contemporary need to deal with multiple structural logics.

As youth deal with a multiplicity of structural logics, Threadgold and Nilan (2009) claim the reflexive, individual negotiation of risk is where reflexivity 'embodied the idea of self-referring, even sense-constitutive in a continuous and ongoing way – a kind of feedback loop of information and reinvention' (p. 510). In previous chapters we have seen a high level of sophistication where the boys have exhibited reflexivity in regard to class. Modernity requires them to negotiate a variety of structural logics, and, through this negotiation, my participants reconstitute their egalitarian habitus in a continual way, perpetually marking off boundaries and creating a sense of value.

Othering the non-normative

We have seen an egalitarian habitus foster exclusionary practices that discursively construct the ideals of dominant (Anglo) white, heteronormative masculinities within the Boremund community. Typically, othering has been documented as intertwined with racism, sexism, homophobia and hypermasculinity, which become powerful forms of legitimate capital for white working-class men who, in a post-industrial landscape of bleak unemployment and fragmented rites of passage, 'displace their rage toward historically and locally available groups' (Weis, 1990: 66). I would argue we must consider how 'othering' practices can also work for boys to distance themselves from identities and behaviours they see as excessive. My participants object to hypermasculinity, or more specifically, the overt 'laddish' and 'bad boy' performativity. The boys pathologise hypermasculine performances, especially if such performances are seen as inauthentic and thus unacceptable, in order to construct boundaries around a Boremund Boy identity. The egalitarian habitus resists fluidity and the adoption of gendered identities they perceive as 'fake'. For the boys, 'being yourself' was consistently valued, and to perform an identity that they perceived to be inauthentic became disconcerting, as it would have required an engagement with a habitus clivé and dexterous navigation between multiple fields and multiple subjectivities (Stahl, 2014).

Whilst there is no set methodology for the use of photo elicitation in the social sciences, Cappello's (2005) approach was used, in which my participants were asked to separate out certain images that caught their attention and explain why they believed them to be more interesting. The use of photographs gave 'research participants a means to reflect on aspects of their lives that they may usually give little thought to' (Rose, 2007: 238). Extending our understanding of egalitarianism and how the boys are highly influenced by what they see as a 'disloyalty to self', the picture below irritated and alarmed many of the participants because the boys, in their eyes, performed a behaviour that they viewed as counter-ethnic, counter-hegemonic and counter-normative.

Luke, for example, objects to the behaviour demonstrated by the boys in Figure 6.1, and, in terms of authenticity, the act the boys are engaged in just 'isn't working':

> Garth: Why [Figure 6.1]?
> Luke: Um – I don't think they know what they're doing.
> Garth: What's your reading about what's happening in the picture?
> Luke: They're trying to do something that isn't working.
> Garth: You noticed the Ps they're making.
> Luke: Yeah, gang sign. They're mocking it, trying to do it.
>
> (Luke, Year 11, London Academy)

The P-sign hand gesture, or what will be referred to as the PK sign, is associated with Afro-Caribbean gang culture in Pluckham, a predominantly Afro-Caribbean area that borders Boremund. Recently there has been a re-emergence of the importance that place and class play in the shaping of identities of young people (Nayak, 2003b; Dillabough and Kennelly, 2010). Othering is interwoven with both a sense of place and masculine identity formation (cf. Renold, 2004; Archer and Francis, 2005; Dalley-Trim, 2007), and this is especially salient in areas where heavy industry has declined and traditional hegemonic masculine identities have been challenged and occasionally subverted (Nayak, 2003a). Youth identities are continually being played out through gender and racial boundaries that interlink with a community's specific industrial, social, cultural and political history.

Figure 6.1 Two 'middle-class' boys posing

Source: Facebook, with permission from photo subjects

Boremund has been shaped by 'white flight' to the outer parts of London and surrounding counties and the result is what Gulson (2006) calls 'crisis populations', where there are longstanding tensions between the white population, who 'have not got out', and the recent non-white migrant influxes. The influence of mobility contributes to how the normative, as an identity boundary, becomes highly ethnicised and place-based.

The use of the Figure 6.1 illustrates how authenticity is constituted; the boys in Figure 6.1 could never be part of an Afro-Caribbean Pluckham gang, and their actions are therefore, in the mind of these white working-class boys, disloyal to oneself (cf. Stahl, 2014). In discussions of gangs, the boys in my study often articulated how gangs were a non-white phenomenon. In Figure 6.1, the white boys are 'mocking' this racialised symbolic gesture. My participants reject the excessive performative nature, and they do not see the humour of parodying a white identity when they are striving to establish the boundaries of authenticity. An egalitarian habitus is not simply shaped by the field but rather the tension and contestation between the field and the habitus. However, the habitus, as generative, is also shaped through a process of 'othering'. The habitus is both a system of schemes of production of practices and a system of perception and appreciation of practices (Bourdieu, 1989). Therefore, through the process of 'othering' images they viewed as transgressive, my participants engage in a continuous process of reaffirming their habitus. In regards to Figure 6.1:

Terry: That looks like they're doing something. They're having fun. They're just standing there with their little fingers up thinking they look good.
Garth: Thinking they look cool?
Terry: When they don't.

(Terry, Year 11, London Academy)

Calum: That's actually really weird because they're both ... they look like proper idiots. He's doing that which is the Pluckham sign ... ya ...
Garth: And clearly ...
Calum: He doesn't look like he should be in Pluckham.

(Calum, Year 11, World School)

In his study of white identity in Essex schools, Preston (2009) captures what occurs when the dominant social constructions of whiteness influence behaviour, where whiteness became enacted and students took pleasure in language, humour, play and what the male students referred to as 'larging it', and where the white 'Essex-ness' was jested with and parodied (p. 55). Clearly the boys in Figure 6.1, who came from a more middle-class background and felt comfortable playing with their whiteness, dexterously navigate between multiple fields and multiple subjectivities (one even placed the image as his Facebook profile picture), yet my white working-class participants find such performativity quite disconcerting. As Liam says:

Stupid thing to do, isn't it?

(Liam, Year 10, London Academy)

There exist tremendous overlaps between ethnic, class and gender identity, where the boys territorialise boundaries they see as highly important to their identity construction while looking for ways to reconstitute themselves as authentically 'white'. The performativity element in the photographs inverts 'sameness' and 'ordinariness' and therefore conflicts with an egalitarian habitus. Furthermore, it is clear whiteness enables the 'interpretation of bodies in a particular place, and their association with cultural forms that are deemed "not like ours"' (Garner, 2012: 451). Alfie, like Liam, views Figure 6.1 as very serious and a high-risk behaviour:

> Alfie: Because the way they're acting, one day they're going to end up getting hurt because that guy's got the PK sign. And this guy. If they were walking around the street there they would probably end up getting stabbed.
> Garth: Do you think they're putting on a bit of a show?
> Alfie: Yeah. Because he's making a 'P' with his hands and he should-n't be doing that because he could be killed for that.
> Garth: He's making a what with his hands?
> Alfie: A 'P'. Like that? You can be killed for that. If you do it in the wrong place. If you do it in Pluckham, basically you'll end up getting stabbed.
> Garth: Is it like a gang thing?
> Alfie: Yeah, it's like a gang thing. So you don't want to be doing it in [Pluckham].
>
> (Alfie, Year 11, PRU)

My participants did not emulate 'hard' black masculinities and they did not 'act black' like Nayak's 'B-Boyz' (2003a) or become 'white wannabes' (Sewell, 1997), although such pretence does sometimes occur in parts of South London. Preston (2010: 335) reminds us that, 'Rather than being "born white", whiteness has to be made' and remade; it is enacted and performed where ultimately 'overcoming and simultaneous re-inscribing of whiteness requires whiteness to be written against the "other"'. While the boys in the image are mocking an 'other', they are also creating an 'other' of inauthentic hypermasculinity infused with stereotypes of black gang culture. My participants object to non-normative white masculine behaviours because it inverts the normalisation of their whiteness and Figure 6.1 'deterritorialises' boundaries they see as highly important to their identity construction. In rejecting the picture, the boys reaffirm a 'loyalty to self', which they see as being transgressed.

Summary

How Boremund boys reflexively define limits and create identity markers involves a process of meaning-making where they establish and police boundaries. The othering of heteronormativity is grounded in a process of representation and recognition, where the economy of symbolic goods is a field of power relations, where agents struggle to increase their symbolic capital, and where power is exercised over those perceived as either less or inauthentic. In understanding how young people engage in an 'active negotiation of their cultural worlds' (Allen and Mendick, 2012: 3), the habitus 'shapes what is perceived ab/normal, un/desirable and im/possible' (Archer *et al.*, 2007: 220). Constantly moulded by social, cultural and economic capital, the white working-class collective habitus draws upon conventional cultural signifiers in order to form their own sense of respectability. The use of photo elicitation allowed me to explore the reflexive processes around normative masculinity, where the pictures allowed the boys to make sense of 'intra-habitus conflicts' (Mouzelis, 2007). The inception of critical reflexivity lies in the mismatches between habitus and field where there is dissonance and, ultimately, where identity-making is fostered (Mouzelis, 2007). The data illustrate the identity work involved with the 'stabilising' and 'fixing' processes with gender subjectivities. The tension within the field of masculinity shows how the participants' habitus, through a process of reorientation, reconciles competing and contrasting conceptions of what it is to be an authentic white, working-class male in South London.

References

Adkins, L. (2004) Introduction: Feminism, Bourdieu and after. *Theory Culture Society*, 20(6), 3–18.

Allen, K. and Mendick, H. (2012) Young people's uses of celebrity: Class, gender, and 'improper' celebrity. *Discourse: Studies in the Cultural Politics of Education*, 34(1), 1–17.

Archer, L. and Francis, B. (2005) Negotiating the dichotomy of Boffin and Triad: British-Chinese pupils' constructions of 'laddism'. *The Sociological Review*, 495–521.

Archer, L. and Yamashita, H. (2003) Theorising inner-city masculinities: 'Race', class, gender, and education. *Gender and Education*, 15(2), 115–132.

Archer, L., Halsall, A. and Hollingworth, S. (2007) 'University's not for me – I'm a Nike person': Urban, working-class young people's negotiations of 'style', identity, and educational engagement. *Sociology*, 41(2), 219–237.

Atencio, M., Beal, B. and Wilson, C. (2009) The distinction of risk: Urban skateboarding, street habitus, and the construction of hierarchical gender relations. *Qualitative Research in Sport and Exercise*, 1(1), 3–20.

Bottrell, D. (2007) Resistance, resilience, and social identities: Reframing 'problem youth' and the problem of schooling. *Journal of Youth Studies*, 10(5), 597–616.

Bourdieu, P. (1989) Social space and symbolic power. *Sociological Theory*, 7(1), 14–25.

Brewis, J. and Gavin, J. (2010) Consuming chavs: The ambiguous politics of gay chavinism. *Sociology*, 44(2), 251–268.

Brill, D. (2007) Gender, status and subcultural capital in the goth scene. In P.

Hodkinson and W. Deicke (eds), *Youth cultures: Scenes, subcultures, and tribes* (p. 280). New York: Routledge.

Byrom, T. and Lightfoot, N. (2013) Interrupted trajectories: The impact of academic failure on the social mobility of working-class students. *British Journal of Sociology of Education*, 34(5–6), 812–828.

Cappello, M. (2005) Photo interviews: Eliciting data through conversations with children. *Field Methods*, 17(2), 170–182.

Carter, P. (2006) Straddling boundaries: Identity, culture, and school. *Sociology of Education*, 78(3), 304–328.

Coles, T. (2009) Negotiating the field of masculinity: The production and reproduction of multiple dominant masculinities. *Men and Masculinities*, 12(1), 30–44.

Connell, R. W. (2005) *Masculinities*. Cambridge: Polity.

Connell, R. W. and Messerschmidt, J. W. (2005) Hegemonic masculinity: Rethinking the concept. *Gender and Society*, 19(6), 829–859.

Connolly, P. (2006) The effects of social class and ethnicity on gender differences in GCSE attainment: A secondary analysis of the youth cohort study of England and Wales 1997–2001. *British Educational Research Journal*, 32(1), 3–21.

Dalley-Trim, L. (2007) 'The boys' present ... Hegemonic masculinity: A performance of multiple acts. *Gender and Education*, 19(2), 199–217.

Deutsch, N. L. and Eleni, T. (2009) Aspiring, consuming, becoming: Youth identity in a culture of consumption. *Youth and Society*, 1–26.

Dillabough, J. A. and Kennelly, J. (2010) *Lost youth in a global city: Class, culture and the urban imaginary*. New York: Routledge.

Farrugia, D. (2013) Addressing the problem of reflexivity in theories of reflexive modernisation: Subjectivity and structural complexity. *Journal of Sociology*, 49(5), 1–15.

Francis, B. (2006) Heroes or zeroes? The discursive positioning of 'underachieving boys' in English neo-liberal education policy. *Journal of Education Policy*, 21(2), 187–200.

Garner, S. (2012) A moral economy of whiteness: Behaviours, belonging and Britishness. *Ethnicities*, 12(4), 445–464.

Gilbert, R. and Gilbert, P. (1998) *Masculinity goes to school*. London: Routledge.

Gulson, K. (2006) The white veneer: Education policy, space and 'race' in the innter city. *Discourse: Studies in the Cultural Politics of Education*, 27(3), 259–274.

Hollingworth, S. and Williams, K. (2009) Constructions of the working-class 'other' among urban, white, middle-class youth: 'Chavs', subculture, and the valuing of education. *Journal of Youth Studies*, 12(5), 467–482.

Krais, B. (2006) Gender, sociological theory and Bourdieu's sociology of practice. *Theory Culture Society*, 23(6), 119–134.

Lahire, B. (2011) *The plural actor*. Cambridge: Polity.

Lareau, A. (2003) *Unequal childhoods*. Berkeley: University of California Press.

Lawler, S. (2004) Rules of engagement: Habitus, power and resistance. *Theory Culture Society*, 20(6), 110–128.

Lawrence, S. (2013) *On white men's representations of 'race', whiteness, masculinities. and 'otherness': A critical race study of men's magazines, racialisation and athletic bodies*. (Unpublished Doctoral Dissertation). Leeds Metropolitan University, Leeds, UK.

McCormack, M. and Anderson, E. (2010) 'It's just not acceptable any more': The erosion of homophobia and the softening of masculinity in an English state school. *Sociology*, 44(5), 843–859.

McCulloch, K., Stewart, A. and Lovegreen, N. (2006) 'We just hang out together': Youth cultures and social class. *Journal of Youth Studies*, 9(5), 539–556.

MacLeod, J. (2009) *Ain't no makin' it*. Boulder, CO: Westview Press.

McNay, L. (2004) Agency and experience: Gender as a lived relation. *Theory Culture Society*, 20(6), 175–190.

McNay, L. (2000) *Gender and agency: Reconfiguring the subject in feminist and social theory*. Cambridge: Polity Press.

McNay, L. (1999) Gender, habitus and the field: Pierre Bourdieu and the limits of reflexivity. *Theory, Culture, Society*, 16(1), 95–117.

Martino, W. (1999) 'Cool boys', 'party animals', 'squids', and 'poofters': Interrogating the dynamics and politics of adolescent masculinities in school. *British Journal of Sociology of Education*, 20(2), 239–263.

Mills, M. and Lingard, B. (1997) Masculinity politics, myths and boys' schooling: A review essay. *British Journal of Educational Studies*, 45(3), 276–292.

Mouzelis, N. (2007) Habitus and reflexivity: Restructuring Bourdieu's theory of practice. *Sociological Research Online*, 12(6). Online at: www.socresonline.org.uk/12/6/9.html

Nayak, A. (2003a) 'Boyz to Men': Masculinities, schooling and labour transitions in de-industrial times. *Educational Review*, 55(2), 147–159.

Nayak, A. (2003b) *Race, place and globalization: Youth cultures in a changing world*. Oxford: Berg.

Papapolydorou, M. (2013) 'When you see a normal person ...': social class and friendship networks among teenage students. *British Journal of Sociology of Education*, 1–19.

Peters, B. M. (2010) Emo gay boys, and subculture: Postpunk queer youth and (re)thinking images of masculinity. *Journal of LGBT Youth*, 7(2), 129–146.

Peterson, P. E. (1992) The urban underclass and the poverty paradox. *Political Science Quarterly*, 106(4), 617–637.

Preston, J. (2009) *Whiteness and class in education*. Dordrecht: Springer.

Preston, J. (2010) Prosthetic white hyper-masculinities and 'disaster education'. *Ethnicities*, 10(3), 331–343.

Renold, E. (2004) 'Other' boys: Negotiating non-hegemonic masculinities in the primary school. *Gender and Education*, 16(2), 247–265.

Roberts, S. (2012) Boys will be boys ... won't they? Change and continuities in contemporary young working-class masculinities. *Sociology*, 47(4), 671–686.

Rose, G. (2007) Making photographs as part of a research project: Photo-elicitation, photo-documentation and other uses of photos. In Rose, G., *Visual methodologies: an introduction to the interpretation of visual materials* (pp. 237–257). Los Angeles: Sage.

Sayer, A. (2005) *The moral significance of class*. Cambridge: Cambridge University Press.

Sewell, T. (1997) *Black masculinities and schooling: How black boys survive modern schooling*. Staffordshire: Trentham Books.

Shildrick, T. (2006) Youth culture, subculture, and the importance of neighbour-hood. *Young: Nordic Journal of Youth Research*, 14(1), 67–74.

Skeggs, B. (2002) *Formations of class and gender*. Nottingham: Sage Publications.

Skeggs, B. (2004) *Class, self, culture*. London: Routledge.

Stahl, G. (2014) White working-class male narratives of 'loyalty to self' in discourses of aspiration. *British Journal of Sociology of Education* (forthcoming).

Stahl, G. and Dale, P. (2012) Creating positive spaces of learning: DJers and MCers identity work with new literacies. *The Educational Forum*, 76(4), 510–523.

Sweetman, P. (2003) Twenty-first century dis-ease? Habitual reflexivity or the reflexive habitus. *The Sociological Review*, 51(4), 528–549.

Thornton, S. (1995) *Club cultures: Music, media and subcultural capital.* Cambridge: Polity Press.

Threadgold, S. and Nilan, P. (2009) Reflexivity of contemporary youth, risk and cultural capital. *Current Sociology*, 57(1), 47–68.

Ward, M. R. M. (2013) Working paper 150: The emos: The re-traditionalisation of white, working-class masculinities through the 'alternative scene'. *Cardiff School of Social Sciences Working Paper Series.* University of Cardiff: University of Cardiff.

Weis, L. (1990) *Working class without work*. New York: Routledge.

Weis, L. (2004) Revisiting a 1980s 'moment of critique': Class, gender, and the new economy. In N. Dolby, G. Dimitriadis and P. Willis (eds), *Learning to Labor in new times* (p. 231). New York: RoutledgeFalmer.

Weis, L. (2008) Toward a re-thinking of class as nested in race and gender. In L. Weis (ed.), *The way class works: Readings on school, family and the economic* (pp. 291–304). New York: Routledge.

Winlow, S. (2001) *Badfellas: Crime, tradition and new masculinities.* Oxford: Berg.

Youdell, D. (2010) Identity traps or how black students fail: The interactions between biographical, sub-cultural, and learner identities. *British Journal of Sociology of Education*, 24(1), 3–20.

Chapter 7

Aspirations

Myths, reality and ambivalence

> I dunno. I'm just going to see what qualifications I get and what I could get with them. If I get high then I have a lot to choose from.
>
> (Dan, Year 11, PRU)

Aspirations are social processes, and youth today draw 'not just on dominant policy and populist ideologies but on multiple social–cultural resources' (Zipin *et al.*, 2013: 4). Aspirations are constituted within a societal shift toward an 'ideology of performocracy' where performativity is grounded in a market ideology 'where it is a winning performance that counts' and where the daily goal is to '"achieve" a competitive advantage, whether for individuals in the competition for credentials, jobs, or income' (Brown, 2013: 687). Youth construct aspirations within fragmented rites of passages and contradictory social contexts, which results in complex identity work in order to constitute themselves as subjects of value. As neoliberal subjects, youth are enmeshed in processes of individualisation and individualised failure, yet, through drawing upon an egalitarian habitus, the boys attempt to constitute themselves as valuable individuals where egalitarianism becomes a process of amelioration, contestation or resistance. As a result of the tension between what the boys witnessed in their own reality and the neoliberal ethos of the school, the data set contains certain interwoven paradoxes. In the study of aspiration and life trajectories, Bourdieu and Wacquant (1992: 130) remind us that:

> People are not fools; they are much less bizarre or deluded than we would spontaneously believe precisely because they have internalized, through a protracted and multisided process of conditioning, the objective chances they face. They know how to 'read' the future that fits them, which is made for them and for which they are made (by opposition to everything that the expression 'this is not for the likes of us' designates).

The boys in this study experienced an ongoing reflexive process of internalisation of possibilities, shaped by the conditions of both material poverty and a poverty of opportunity. Their limited means, juxtaposed against a rhetoric of aspirations that were competitive, economic and status-based, created a dynamic that directly influenced how their gendered, classed and ethnic masculinities came into being.

Innate to the study of aspiration, mobility and engagement are the concepts of risk, cost and benefit (Archer and Yamashita, 2003). In the research, risk and uncertainty were constructed through a multiplicity of discourses, the most central being the high levels of unemployment in the community (especially among men) and the school-based discourses regarding preserving one's 'worth' through accruing qualifications. Similar to recent research, my participants' aspirations were diverse and still in a process of formation, where multiple aspirations were embraced simultaneously (cf. Archer et al., 2010; Hart, 2013). The contradictory, fluid and dynamic nature of aspirations 'can be read as a pragmatic strategy adopted by those who are exposed to high levels of risk and uncertainty in their lives' (Archer et al., 2010: 80). The multiple aspirations the respondents held could be understood as an active management of risk against current circumstances, both simultaneously influenced by a historically problematic relationship between the working class and an education shaped by 'relatively low levels of the kind of material, cultural, and psychological resources that aide educational success' (Reay, 2009: 24). As a result of these constraints, boys engage in behaviour in which they acquire semi-permanent labels within their educational institutions. Within the neoliberal agenda, which emphasises human capitalisation and entrepreneurship, these young men are often 'constructed as "failed citizens" who do not "add value"' (Zipin et al., 2012: 185). Sitting in the staff room, I observed conversations among the teachers peppered with derogatory and pejorative labels such as 'silent non-worker', 'lazy', 'pathologically immature' and 'thick', 'toe-rag', 'jack-of-the-lads' and 'bastard'. These labels fix certain dispositions and attributes in the mind of teachers, and, obviously, fix certain reductive identities for the boys.

The study of aspirations is in no way straightforward, as it is a complex intermeshing of agency/investment, hegemonic discourses, available opportunities, generational history, current economic climate, adaptability/trade-offs, resistance, labels/categorisation, awareness/ignorance and mentoring/guidance. As Hattam and Smyth (2003: 383) argue, 'It is not possible to understand the complex processes of youth identity formation without understanding the interplay between young people's desire for economic independence and their struggles to establish, confirm and in many cases endure, a sociocultural identity'. When considering student aspirations, I draw attention to how aspiration has been theoretically represented as a negotiated and complex process. Drawing both on the theoretical tools of Bourdieu and Sen in her study of aspiration and agency, Hart (2013) documents the correlations between the level of agency and identified aspirations. For example, if aspirations were identified by her participants in terms of low individual agency, it was because the individual did not agree with the aspirations others had of them; conversely, if the participants had a high level of individual agency, the aspirations were more self-selected (p. 85). Hart (2013) employs a typology of aspirations using terms like 'revealed, concealed, adapted' and 'apparent', which illustrates how in various stages of development certain aspirations come to the forefront, moving, as she describes, 'from latent (not yet formed) aspirations to true (actual) aspirations' (p. 86).

In an analysis of learner identities, Mac an Ghaill's *Young, Gifted, and Black* (1988) shows how schools embed inequalities through the valuing of particular forms of knowledge and culture. Mac an Ghaill uses two typologies: the Warriors, who exhibit resistance through non-compliance and deviance, and the Black Sisters, who resist through adopted strategies. The Black Sisters' strategy involved a seemingly positive attitude towards schooling but was explicitly described by the girls as a political strategy designed to gain social mobility. They were simply playing by the rules to get ahead, rules that they viewed as unfair. Mac an Ghaill's study shows not only how schools and certain teachers privilege certain capitals and marginalise others, but also how learners are responsive to the culture of the school. In relation to the white middle-class ethos of the school, other racial, ethnic and class values that simply do not fit with the ideal clientele are denounced (Youdell, 2004). School-constituting practices and their dialectical relationship to student agency are also apparent in other works focused upon learning subjectivities, pedagogy and engagement (cf. Wexler, 1992; Youdell, 2004; Hattam and Prosser, 2008).

Valuing earning, trade work and ambivalence

The boys in my study exhibit a wide range of ambitions, some very realistic and some very unrealistic (Stahl, 2012). Within the cohort, 18 out of 23 mentioned the importance of a job or career in terms of their future plans and what they wanted out of life. Such articulations were infused with many contradictions regarding financial return, social mobility, class inferiority and ambivalence. Largely they did not desire to achieve increased social status; most boys' occupational aspirations were based on an underlying desire to secure a steady income. Throughout the interviews and focus groups, 14 of the 23 boys referred to specific types of jobs when they described what they wanted in life: four of them aimed for jobs related to sports (football or boxing), four described skilled manual jobs, two discussed having their own business, one talked about working for the UK Border Agency, one said banking, one said cooking and one said being a musician, while some mentioned more than one job over the course of the data collection. As noted in other studies of student aspirations and social class identities (Bathmaker *et al.*, 2013), the majority of my participants were aware of the financial recession, austerity measures and the limited opportunities available in the employment market. As a researcher I was not only interested in what the boys wanted out of life, but also how they perceived success. When responding to the question, 'What do you think you want most in life?', the results suggest that earning money was of significant importance to the majority of the respondents where they showed an interest in 'quick money' and 'quick rise' professions:

> Money. A nice girlfriend. Big house. Footballer. That's it.
> (Ryan, Year 10, London Academy)

> To become a professional footballer.
> (Thomas, Year 11, London Academy)

> Phillip: To have a good job. Money. Nice house.
> Garth: So what would be a good job in your eyes?
> Phillip: Boxer. [laughter]
> (Phillip, Year 11, London Academy)

> Have a good life. Work. Have my own house and my own car. Good job.
> (Connor, Year 10, London Academy)

Within the neoliberal discourse, attaining wealth through some blend of meritocratic talent and hard work is often embodied in hegemonic discourses as a 'solution to poverty and its attendant effects' (Zipin *et al.*, 2012: 186). Equating 'success' with financial return, the data suggest that, to a certain extent, the boys accept the dominant neoliberal rhetoric transmitted through the structures and processes that surround them, and they are in a process of sense-making (Giroux, 2004). The use of sport to gain a celebrity lifestyle has been cited in research among young males (Swain, 2000; Skelton, 2010). Within the cohort, Thomas actually had a realistic chance of using sport as a route to financial success (and indeed he now plays professionally in London), whereas the other participants largely did not. As the subjectivities of the boys are influenced by the rhetoric, and entrenched in consumerism, the boys are open about their economic and lifestyle goals:

> I want to have a nice job … I want to have a nice job and that, getting paid a nice bit of money.
> (Terry, Year 11, London Academy)

> Garth: What do you think you want most in life?
> Frankie: To be successful.
> Garth: Like …
> Frankie: To have a lot of money.

Garth: That's how you determine success.
Frankie: Yeah.

                                    (Frankie, Year 11, London Academy)

Garth: What do you think you want most in life?
Keith: Money.
Garth: Money?
Keith: Yeah, it's got to be.
Garth: Why money?
Keith: 'Cause …
Garth: 'Cause you can afford to buy everything else.
Keith: Everything, everything is money like this school costs money,
            everything I'm wearing costs money.

                                    (Keith, Year 10, London Academy)

The attraction to money (and economic stability) also influenced the boys' desire for immediate trade work that was locally based and usually accessed through family connections. This opposition between 'learning and earning' has been noted in other studies as the reason why some working-class men opt out of post-compulsory education in pursuit of economic stability (Archer *et al.*, 2001; Burke, 2007). Similar to Willis' lads, the division between the practical and the academic was underscored by a gendered and classed association of working-class masculinity as 'active', set against the passivity of middle-class easy living. As Archer *et al.* (2010: 62) point out, boys construct a 'rigid classed and gendered dichotomy between "education/learning" and "work/earning" rendered post-compulsory education both unthinkable and undesirable in their eyes'.[1] Trade jobs, perceived by the boys as mature and responsible employment, were consistently viewed through an idealistic lens, where these forms of employment were devoid of risk and where the boys felt they would be most comfortable. Paid work can offer young people independence and it is where they gain social status and acceptability as an adult (Nayak, 2003). Trade work was associated with a lack of competition,[2] seeing a job done well and the physicality of the tasks. As Archer *et al.* (2010: 61) note, in working-class boys' desire to leave school and earn money, the 'anxiousness to leave was palpable'. Traditional trade work also represents a way of avoiding the dominant neoliberal prerogative that emphasises aspirant pathways valuing choice and flexibility.

It should be noted that, despite shifts in aspiration over time, the majority of participants drew on conventional conceptions of 'known' working-class male employment, as for the most part the boys' aspirations were highly classed, representing intelligible versions of working-class masculinity. As seen in the work of both MacDonald and Marsh (2005) and Nayak (2003), their participants' aspirations occur within strong, locally embedded, class-cultural frames of reference that continue to structure their expectations, even when the structural conditions for these expectations are either endangered or no longer exist. In terms of ambivalence, trade work for many of the boys served as a valid and respected alternative if they were 'unlucky' in their GCSE attainment:

Garth: What do you think you want most in life?
Billy: To be successful. Just successful.
Garth: But how do you define successful?
Billy: Hopefully, I want out of my life … say I want to have my own business when I'm older, a plumbing company.
                                    (Billy, Year 11, London Academy)

Garth: What do you think you want most in life?
Liam: A good education to be able to get a good job.
Garth: What's like a good job for you?
Liam: I'm not sure what I want to do yet. Hopefully I do get a good job.
                                    (Liam, Year 10, London Academy)

Garth: What's a 'good' job for you?
Mitchell: I like going into the cooking industry maybe. Like I was think-ing my stepdad's a plumber so if nothing works out. Say if I don't get sixth form because I'm applying to colleges as well … I could do a construction course so …
Garth: So construction or sixth form?
Mitchell: Basically, college to do construction or sixth form to carry on with my studies … whichever one accepts me.
                                    (Mitchell, Year 11, London Academy)

In this case, Mitchell's non-negotiable aspiration is occupational, but he is ambivalent about the route to it. His preference is to follow the educationally aspirational route of sixth form if possible, but this is not crucial to him because there is not just one route to his central goal of full-time employment. Like him, many of the boys tepidly value a 'Plan A' where they claim they would follow the academic trajectory favoured by the dominant neoliberal ideology if the grades come through, yet they also have a 'Plan B' guided by local and familial ties (social capital) that will lead them to traditional work-ing-class occupations. The boys present themselves as aspiring to be serious, hardworking and responsible by their decision to leave education and become a 'grafter' (Gunter and Watt, 2009). Research shows how, for many young working-class men, the role of male breadwinner 'held currency and was employed to defend their aspirations for leaving education' (Archer *et al.*, 2010: 63; Archer and Yamashita, 2003), as further education would have delayed access to steady employment and an authentic adult masculinity.

While trade work was consistently devalued by the school, it was paradoxically a part of the school:

Liam: I do a course, a construction course. That's at – It's part of the school. I go every Tuesday. And my other interests are like football and stuff like that.

Garth: So tell me about this construction course …

Liam: Basically, when you're in school and you're not achieving the highest levels you can – you go to this place and this place is like woodwork but you get two qualifications out of doing it.

Garth: Do you enjoy it?

Liam: Yeah, it's alright.

Garth: What do you like about it?

Liam: Instead of sitting down in the classroom and doing work, it's like practical …

(Liam, Year 10, London Academy)

According to Bourdieu and Wacquant (1992), the school inclines young people to generally reject manual labour and working-class conditions, which 'leads them to reject the only future accessible to them but without giving any guarantee for the future that it seems to promise' (p. 185). As an instrument of social reproduction, the education system plays a key role in shaping both the image people have of their destinies (e.g. their perceived choices) and the resources (capital) available to them to achieve their goals. Within this case study, the school sites were not necessarily about raising aspiration and instead remained heavily focused on the attainment of GCSEs, with trade work typically available to those who had reached certain levels of disengagement in the eyes of administrators. In theorising aspiration according to risk, cost and benefit, many of the boys were realistic and pragmatic in setting themselves on a vocational track:

Billy: I just applied for college doing a plumbing course. Which is like if you do Level 1, if you pass that you go onto Level 2, pass that – even if it's volunteer you got to get a job or an apprenticeship then you do Level 3. So you get three qualifications out of plumbing.

Garth: How long would that take?

Billy: Three years. To do Level 3. It's a one year course, each thing.

(Billy, Year 11, London Academy)

Dan: I don't really know what I want really. Go day by day really. Do what I can for the day – whatever happens happens. I don't really have …

Garth: And what's for you after GCSEs?

Dan: I dunno. I'm just going to see what qualifications I get and what I could get with them. If I get high then I have a lot to choose from. If I get low then there are certain things … they're going to hold me back from getting certain things. Yeah, it's fairly structured what I want to do.

(Dan, Year 11, PRU)

As a focus of research, discussion of aspirations provides a space to examine the 'interplays of identities and inequalities within young people's lives' (Archer *et al.*, 2013: 3). As we see in Dan's words, he not only recognises how a lack of qualifications will impact his future – 'hold me back from getting certain things' – but also conceptualises his future ambivalently – 'go day by day really' – where he will see what his qualifications may bring. In examining why white working-class boys have historically opted out of education, Marks (2003) argues how ambivalence has remained constant, but the reasons for its manifestation have altered alongside the rise of neoliberal ideology, economic restructuring and gender roles. According to Marks, in the 1950s and 1960s, the white working class rejected education in deference to the middle or upper class, where it was 'not for the likes of us'; in the 1970s and 1980s, education had little relevance to one's future and, instead, working-class boys 'had a laff' as they went straight from school to the labour market or vocational training (pp. 86–87). Due to deindustrialisation, Marks (2003) articulates that today, the concept of 'Learning to Labour' has shifted to a 'generation of 'lost boys' from the 'sink' estates' who, he argues, are 'Learning to Loaf' when they see that education cannot guarantee a career and thus question the point of it (p. 85). My research into occupational aspirations reaches less pessimistic conclusions than those of Marks, as all the participants valued employment.

Neoliberalism and the rhetoric of exclusion

In the investigation of how the habitus becomes a site of mediation, Byrom and Lightfoot (2013: 816) discuss a 'habitus in tension' where the trajectories of students differ substantially from that of their parents, where going back was not an option and where going forward was fraught with challenges. The dialectical confrontation between habitus and field (other than the field of origin) results in a degree of accommodation where the habitus accepts the legitimacy of the new field's structure and is, in turn, structured by it, thus enabling a modification in the habitus. Habitus is an internal matrix of dispositions where choices are bounded by the framework of opportunities and constraints the person finds him/herself in (Reay, 2004b). The process of social mobility and transformation results in an emerging secondary habitus, a 'cleft habitus' (Bourdieu, 1999) or habitus clivé, where a destabilised habitus enables students to accept the particular messages about education and upward mobility but simultaneously maintain their key dispositions in their habitus of origin. The aspiration of these young men is contingent on accepting their structural constraints, while the egalitarian habitus allows them to reaffirm traditional working-class family values in order to constitute a 'good life' (Stahl, 2012). Or, as Mitchell put it:

> I want a family. I want a nice wife. Kids. Good job. Nice house.
> (Mitchell, Year 10, London Academy)

Habitus does not operate alone; it interacts with capital (resources, which can be economic, cultural, social or symbolic). Individuals, who are not winners in the game of accumulating capital, experience different degrees of inferiority that potentially have longstanding emotional effects. Such experiences of abjection influence aspirations 'which are structurally constrained in subtle ways that present significant difficulties for the less advantaged' (Zipin et al., 2012: 187). A habitus divided against itself is in continual negotiation with itself and therefore, arguably, destined to a kind of duplication, to a double perception of the self, to enact multiple identities (Bourdieu, 1999: 511). There is a complex negotiation that exists in the habitus where working class students engage in an internalisation of possibilities that is simultaneously a process of resistance and acceptance, ever evolving. Egalitarianism represents the creative capacity of the habitus where the boys make an effort to contest/ignore/subvert inequalities in recognition and distribution, becoming a means of maximising their capacity to negotiate potential failure. The boys were, after all, aware they went to schools where the majority of students did not attain GCSEs and did not have high aspirations. As Harry demonstrates, the participants in this research hold to their conception of egalitarianism in contestation against a potential cleft habitus:

> I don't want people to think that I love money. I want them to think I give something back, that, like, it works both ways, that I'm not greedy.
> (Harry, Year 10, London Academy)

Skeggs (2004) argues that Bourdieu's theoretical framework fails to acknowledge values such as altruism, integrity, loyalty, and investment in others, which she characterises as 'non-accumulative, non-convertible values' (p. 30). Harry's investment in emotional capital will not likely accrue him other capitals, as emotional capital has limited exchange value (Reay, 2004a). Harry knows he does not possess the capital to successfully play at the game; therefore, his process of sense-making is a process of both amelioration and compromise, 'reworking older traditions of working class mutual aid and collective self-improvement' (Brown, 2013), as the habitus seeks to accrue value. In other research on working-class subjectivities, Reay (2003: 306) notes that the working class were not focused on the neoliberal project of the self in their educational advancement but instead ultimately wanted to give back to others, where altruism allowed her participants 'to reconcile difficult contradictions between wanting to escape from, whilst seeking to preserve, their working-class identities'. As Harry puts it:

Garth: What do you think you want most in life?

Harry: A good education, a good job and a good family. [I admire] My dad because he's got a good job and loves his children and his wife. And he like supplies. He brings home the bacon to my family basically.

(Harry, Year 10, London Academy)

Many working-class boys come to see academic success as a symbolically legitimated form of value that not only falls largely beyond their grasp but also beyond their desire. Of the 23 boys in the study, 18 did not see qualifications as empowering, and, in discussions, several called attention to celebrities without qualifications such as Richard Branson, Cristiano Ronaldo and David Haye who worked their way up with limited education. In considering aspiration from a Bourdieusian perspective, Lamont and Lareau (1988) define four types of exclusion. First, self-elimination refers to the process by which individuals adjust their aspirations to their perceived chances of success. They do this according to lack of ease in specific social settings and a lack of familiarity with their cultural norms. Second, over-selection refers to the obstacles faced in social settings by individuals with less valued cultural resources, when they are expected to outperform their cultural 'handicap'. Relegation, the third form, occurs when individuals receive less from their educational investment because they have landed in a less desirable position. The last form is direct exclusion. Operating within constraints, and as both collective and individual trajectories/histories, the habitus mediates what is possible from a limited range of possibilities. The end result is these working-class boys exclude themselves from what they are already excluded from (Bourdieu and Passeron, 1977), and they strategise in order to constitute subjectivities that are comfortable.

The act of aspiring

Currently, for a working-class young person to aspire to employment, rather than university study, is often evidence of a responsible and rational decision, given the risks of pursuing higher education. In the pursuit of further education, the risks are greater for working-class students in terms of their investment of time and money, their relationships with family and friends, and their sense of self (Archer and Yamashita, 2003). Reay *et al.* (2005) show how the potential benefits of higher education are fewer because working-class students, lacking in social capital, are more likely to attend lower status institutions and consequently attain lower-paid jobs afterwards. During the time of data collection, university fees were trebled and some of the boys were aware of this potential barrier. The boys were all aware that going to university would make them eligible for more lucrative employment, but that did not always translate into a desire to engage with the learning required for university qualifications.

While some white working-class boys may ascribe fully to the aspiration rhetoric and gain academic capital, such a tremendous commitment to over-coming significant barriers is often done at the cost of emotional well-being; more precisely, a relentless focus on academic achievement has the potential to depreciate 'emotional capital while simultaneously augmenting cultural capital' (Reay, 2004a: 69). Even if university was to be successfully navigated, McDowell (2012) notes many young working-class men are undesirable to employers in a service economy where 'their class, their accents, their perfor-mative masculinity are seen by employers as a challenge to the attributes required in a service economy' (p. 581).[3] Qualifications alone will not simply open doors to professional and managerial employment. If the boys, who have a high probability of lacking both social and educational capital, find themselves in higher-status jobs, it will be in low positions where they will 'often find it difficult to produce the required workplace performance, seeing deference and courtesy, bending to the will of both superiors and service sector customers, as a challenge to their sense of themselves as masculine' (McDowell, 2012: 581). Young males from lower socioeconomic status backgrounds often disengage from various life trajectories and powerful narratives that are largely inaccessible, often finding themselves in service-sector employment where they adopt strategies to ensure their masculine identity (Roberts, 2012) as they reconcile aspirations with everyday contexts. Yet, some do aspire to something beyond trade employment, though their articulations were tepid at best:

> I want to be a musician and I want to travel. I'll probably stay here to like study [but then] I'd like to move around.
>
> (George, Year 10, London Academy)

> To be a football coach. Yeah, I'm doing stuff on Wednesday with Victory – like this Sports thing – they need someone to help out and I do it. My PE teacher organised it for me.
>
> (Ben, Year 10, World School)

> I want a job in like a bank because I'm good at maths.
>
> (Lewis, Year 10, London Academy).

In Burke's (2007) study of working-class men in a foundation course lead-ing to higher education, she illustrates when men can construct their educational participation 'as a project of becoming a (better man)', the form of hegemonic (or respectable) masculinity they aspire to is 'university educated, engaged in intellectual rather than manual labour, comfortable (but not too wealthy) and financially able to support a family' (p. 422). Positioned across different and competing formations of identity, the men, according to Burke (2009), 'draw upon imagined hegemonic masculinities in their struggle towards success and respectability' (p. 91).

Drawing on neoliberal infused doxic aspirations that 'reiterate populist messages about dreams to which one might aspire' (Zipin *et al.*, 2013: 9), Alen and Luke view Figure 7.1 as representing a man they consider to be 'smart' and 'respectable', but, ultimately, their interviews and the use of visual methods reveal that they wavered in their desire for this lifestyle:

He's in a suit and looks respectable.

(Luke, Year 11, London Academy)

I reckon that if I met him he'd be a bit stuck-up 'cause like he looks like someone with money. He just thinks about money really. Yeah. But I

Figure 7.1 Businessman
Source: Getty Images

reckon that he's could have a kind and gentle personality but I reckon he's just stuck up – really.

(Keith, Year 10, London Academy)

Garth: What image appeals to you?
Alen: [selects number 1]
Garth: Why number 1?
Alen: Smart man.

(Alen, Year 11, London Academy)

As noted in previous chapters, being 'stuck-up' was detestable to the boys, and Keith highlights that the man in the picture would only 'think about money'. Figure 7.1 serves as a stimulus where the boys distance themselves from a lifestyle they already know is inaccessible and where they lack the necessary skills. Keith, who perhaps had the best chance of securing middle-class status through his education, was vocal about not wanting to be part of the middle class; instead he has a desire to be in the military, which he fully recognised as a form of employment that would pay him very little but where he would be comfortable.

Variations in aspiration

While this research focused on non-migrant white working-class boys, two white students of Eastern European heritage, Alen and Amin, provide an example of how aspiration is shaped by culture but also mediated by locale and quality of schooling. Similar to Platt's research (2007), there were differences in aspiration between these young men, who had been raised in London from an early age, and the indigenous white British in the study. In the UK, Anglo-whiteness, as an ethnic construct, remains largely an unmarked aspect of identity, 'invisible' yet dominant. In her analysis of white Eastern European migrants, Moore (2013) shows how whiteness becomes a performative act where whiteness is continually made and remade, and within 'shades of white' other points of distinction rise to the surface such as 'language, physical appearance, perceived "traits" or "qualities"' (p. 6), even aspiration. Both Alen and Amin self-identify as Boremund Boys, yet they attempt to constitute themselves as different in terms of aspiration:

My dad always said, 'Always want more in life' and that's what I'm going to keep doing. Pushing myself. Well, I'm thinking about coming back to this sixth form and carrying on with Business and ICT. And hopefully I'll go up to university and carry on with business – hopefully I'll just work for a company and once I get used to it and understand everything then I'll try and start my own business.

(Alen, Year 11, London Academy)

> Amin: I'm interested in art and making stuff. When I grow up I want
>   to be a graphic designer. My sister told me to go to Germany
>   and live with her for like two years – to learn the language.
>   Then go to school there, university there. Then give me a
>   Deutsche Bank – like an intern[ship], like something you go
>   to when you're a student …
> Garth: Like an internship?
> Amin: Yeah. 'Cause she works there. She's going to get me into that.
>   From then on I'm going to choose to go into financial busi-
>   ness or like the graphic design. I want to go to like college – I
>   think it's London College of Communication … Yeah, Yeah
>   … I want to go there 'til I'm like eighteen and then I'll move
>   to Germany.
>
>   (Amin, Year 10, World School)

Amin and Alen had more thoroughly developed educational aspirations,
which again were ultimately linked to occupational goals; both cited a higher
degree of parental pressure with the main source of this pressure coming
from their fathers. For the most part, Amin and Alen made explicit reference
to long-term career goals and university. While their aspirations were higher,
they also were potentially likely to experience shock at the lost viability of
pursuing intended futures, as their educational, social and economic capitals
were still limited. Both participants engaged in a process of making sense of
middle-class aspirations, which contrasted greatly with the aspirations of their
immediate, white, working-class peer group. When asked, 'How do you
want teachers to see you?' Alen responded:

> I want them to see that I will get somewhere in life and that I'm not just
> a joker. Stuff like that. Certain lessons, like the ones I want to do good
> in, that I want to carry on doing, that's the only ones I doing good and
> I care about. I know you need as much GCSEs as you can get but
> sometimes you don't even need GCSEs; it's who you know as well. Trust
> me.
>
>   (Alen, Year 11, London Academy)

Zipin *et al.* (2013) argue that habituated aspirations are often 'simplified
verbal expressions' which 'do not reveal the more complex strategic calculus
underlying them'; nonetheless, aspirations highlight the 'contradictions
between universalistic doxic aspirations on the one hand, and the felt sense
(within habitus) of situated possibility on the other', where both are often
present in the same interview (p. 9). In the extract above, Alen voices the
neoliberal ideology espoused in the school by buying into the mantra that
qualifications will gain him solid employment; yet his social identity diluted
the neoliberal rhetoric in which he claimed he could gain employment

without his qualifications. He contests the neoliberal project of 'entrepreneur of the self' and the pursuit of education to become 'what one is' (Beck, 1992), yet he simultaneously acknowledges he desires to not be seen as a 'joker'. Furthermore, Alen, who often vocalised university as a pathway to 'success', did not cite money or prestige as an ultimate goal:

> I want friends. Because without friends ... I dunno, I think friends are everything.
>
> (Alen, Year 11, London Academy)

Alen holds very tightly to his peers because friendship and loyalty for him are proxies of working-class success, and this disposition is essential to understanding why he may or may not pursue middle-class, academic, university-orientated success. I would argue that Alen's habitus is fragmented, and if he were to pursue a middle-class mobile trajectory, he would need to distance himself from the peer group. In following McLeod's (2002) work on the post-feminism 'transformation of intimacy' and gendered subjectivities, Alen values being with his mates, as linked to a wider spectrum of masculine activities that allow him to validate his gender identity. However, by putting his friends first, before his academic work, we glimpse a 'retraditionalised masculinity that is anchored not in paid work, but in relationships' (McLeod, 2002: 220). Alen represents not only the complex relationship between doxic aspirations and risk but also a desire for safety/security and reaffirmation.

Conceptions of failures

Within the neoliberal rhetoric, as Lucey and Reay (2002) observe, the notion of academic excellence and success cannot exist without reference to its other side: failure. When asked to select a photo that did not appeal to them, the boys were quickly able to articulate their concept of failure. The boys' responses to the visual task reveal how occupational aspirations are shaped, as they saw work in retail work and stacking shelves, depicted in the image of a Tesco worker, as extremely undesirable:

> I wouldn't want to like stack shelves.
>
> (Alen, Year 11, London Academy)

> That would never be a career of mine. It doesn't appeal to me.
>
> (Mitchell, Year 10, London Academy)

> Boring. Doing the same job everyday.
>
> (Luke, Year 11, London Academy)

Garth: Why is that unappealing to you?

Dan: Yeah, because if I was ever in his situation I would just feel like
          I underachieved. I don't belong there, I should be achieving
          better things than cashiering.

(Dan, Year 11, PRU)

Working service levels jobs is consistently constructed in the school context
as representing failure, as 'undesirable'. The contemporary post-Fordist
economy, underpinned by a neoliberal profit-driven prerogative toward
short-term contracts, presents working-class people with significant challenges where what can be realistically obtained is 'routine, subservient,
low-paid and often insecure' (Roberts, 2012: 647). The construct of the
individual who has few qualifications and, consequently, works a menial job
was referenced often in classrooms by teachers during my observations,
where it was generally a method of behaviour management and a way of
motivating students who were apathetic. For the boys, the reason that a retail
job was considered unappealing was not only because it was 'boring' involv-
ing 'doing the same job every day' but also because it represents an
employment route that the school is consistently negative about.

Throughout the entire study, failure and barriers to success were topics of
discussion. While their employment interests were varied, the pervasive aspiration rhetoric of self-made individuals, individual choice and entrepreneurial
selves significantly influenced how the boys conceptualised their futures
where 'success' and 'failure' were individualised. The boys appear to be of
the view that failure or success is entirely within the control of the individual; thus, their words often represent the neoliberal emphasis on individual
responsibility where if one works hard and chooses their friends carefully,
they could become successful. The broader implication here is that if the
boys see success and failure in this way, they will blame themselves when they
encounter barriers or fail, and, at this point, they may be more likely to
accept the social construction of the working classes' inferiority.

Wanting power and not wanting power

The final part of my argument, concerning how an egalitarian habitus structures the boys' aspirations, considers their conceptualisations of power over
other people, as well as power broadly. Sayer (2005) notes, in Bourdieusian
analyses of the social field, little attention is paid to the moral aspects of class,
instead privileging 'the habitual and instrumental character, as if a combina-
tion of habit and the pursuit of status and power animated everything' (p.
16). Perceptions of power can be difficult to access as power takes different
forms in each field, yet largely my participants produce subjectivities
grounded in a distancing from power. As a way of accessing their perception
of power, participants were provided with an activity that consisted of eleven

items to prioritize (Figure 7.2). Participants were then asked to rank in order the priorities from most important (1) to least important (11). In introducing the kinaesthetic activity, I was careful in my wording, wanting my participants to simply 'prioritise what is important to you today', and I purposely did not use language commonly associated with aspiration.

The prioritising activity served as a way of exploring what the boys considered to be important and, while each participant came up with a different list, there were clear commonalities. In researching youth and youth culture, visual and kinaesthetic methods (Appendix A) and subsequent discussions have an important role to play in accessing the contradictory and deeply contextual interpretations underlying symbolic images (Dillabough and Kennelly, 2010: 60). As a researcher I was surprised by how seriously the boys took the task, preferring not to rush through it and sometimes changing their lists several times, in order to ensure that it was a precise representation of their priority structure.

The activity was intended to serve as an exploratory stimulus that would provide an orientation to subsequent questions which intended to explore how dispositions were adjusted and where there were tensions within the habitus. Through the activity I consider how the boys engaged with a 'mode of subjectification', where individuals were invited/incited to recognise their moral obligations in balance with societal expectations as representative of certain priorities (Drummond, 2003). In creating their lists, the boys deliberated around priorities they consider important, but they also strategised presenting a certain self they considered to be ethical and valuable.

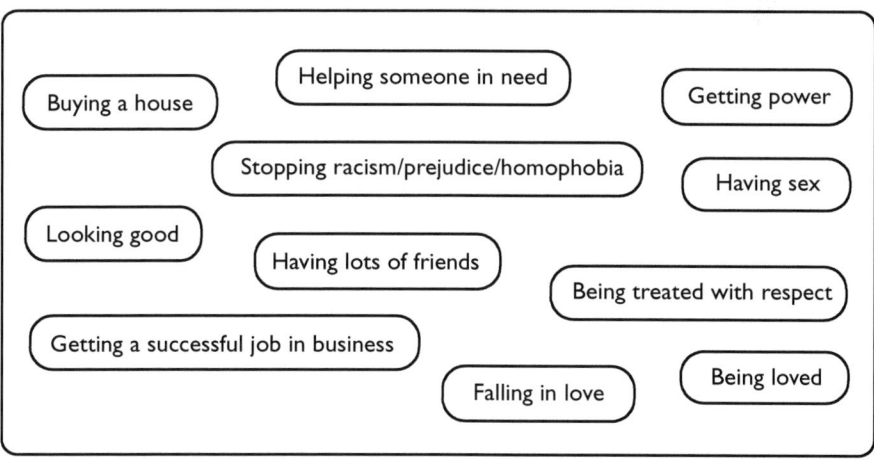

Figure 7.2 List of priorities

While each list was distinct to the individual, when the lists were averaged together certain themes became clear that were highly paradoxical. While my participants ranked 'getting a job in business' highly – over half of the boys listed it as the highest priority with an average rank of 3.1, they did not equate a job in business with gaining respect nor did they see qualifications as empowering. Ten of the students did not equate having qualifications with gaining power, six said qualifications 'sort of' led to power or was at least a starting point, while only three students felt that possessing qualifications (or a university degree) would increase their power. 'Being loved' (average rank of 4.7), 'having lots of friends' (5.2) and 'helping someone in need' (5.5) were all about in the middle. While high-status employment was ranked highly, 'getting power' was nearly universally placed as a low priority. By placing 'getting power' as a low priority, the activity suggests the boys' relationship to power is complex, a theme that was explored in subsequent questions. As will be apparent in the interviews, the activity also revealed the subjectivity of language surrounding terms like 'power' and 'respect', which can often be used interchangeably, but, for my participants, these words have fixed definitions. 'Being treated with respect' ranked high on their priority lists for the majority of participants, but, in follow-up dialogues, I learned respect came from family or peers, as opposed to an educational achievement or occupation. When reading over their individual lists, I questioned the rationale behind the conceptions of power:

Garth:	Why have you put having power there [pointing lower in the list]?
Terry:	'Cause you don't need to have a lot of power. Like obviously you need a bit of power or otherwise people just think you're nothing no matter what he thinks or whatever. You need power.
Garth:	When you say the words 'getting power', what immediately jumped to your mind?
Terry:	Having people that are respectful.

(Terry, Year 11, London Academy)

Garth:	So why have you put 'getting power' there?
Harry:	'Cause I don't care if I'm not powerful. I just want to be an everyday person. I don't want to be like upper class and stuff like that.
Garth:	Okay, is there a relationship between this one 'Getting power' and this one 'Being treated with respect'? Or is there not a relationship?
Harry:	A little bit. In order to get power you have to be treated with respect, so they link together like that.

(Harry, Year 10, London Academy)

I don't really care about having power over people. It's not the way I am.

(Luke, Year 11, London Academy)

As we can see from Harry's response, he draws upon an egalitarian habitus, desiring to be considered an 'everyday person'. As an important part of understanding power and attaining power, averageness and ordinariness are reflective of the disposition that draws on working-class values of 'fitting in' and where 'no one is better than anyone else'. As Bourdieu (1984: 11) argues:

> To strive for distinction is the opposite of distinction; firstly because it involves recognition of a lack and a disavowel of self-seeking aspiration, and secondly because, as can easily be seen ... consciousness and reflexivity are both cause and symptom of failure of immediate adaptation to the situation which defines the virtuoso.

The boys do not strive and are suspicious of power. Instead, they draw upon a strong identification with being an 'everyday person' grounded in having a 'loyalty to self', which, in turn, allows them to resist discourses that feel inauthentic (Stahl, 2014). In my interviews with Tom and Alen, an attempt was made to access the subjectivity around the words 'power' and 'respect':

Garth: 'Getting power' is at the end of your list. Why is it at the end?
Tom: Just no need. Dunno.
Garth: So would it be true to say that when you put 'getting power' beside 'gaining respect', getting respect is much more important?
Tom: Yeah, I'd say so.
Garth: So when you see 'getting power' what do you think I mean?
Tom: I'd say like people are scared of you or something like that.

(Tom, Year 11, London Academy)

Garth: 'Getting power' is your second one from the end of the list?
Alen: Because there's no power I want to get. I just want to be an average person who just works and makes enough money to pay the bills and stuff.
Garth: With 'getting power' – when you see those two words, what did you see in your mind?
Alen: Leader of some sort.

(Alen, Year 11, London Academy)

In these responses, the rejection of power can be interpreted as a component within the habitus, produced through social positioning and experience, resulting in dispositions that can contribute to, or reinforce, their perceptions of their social world. In their analysis of symbolic violence, Connolly and Healy (2004) state that the habitus gradually internalises the 'acceptance of those ideas and structures that tend to subordinate' as individuals progressively 'develop taken-for-granted ways of thinking and behaving that reflect this lived experience' (p. 16). When queried, Alen references a desire to 'be an average person', and by constituting his subjectivities in this way, a process of self-making becomes evident where he make sense of where to invest his energies as he adjusts 'virtualities, potentialities, eventualities' within his social space (Bourdieu and Wacquant, 1992: 135). Through how these young men understand concepts like 'power', 'respect' and 'priorities' we glimpse what occurs when habitus and field do not accord and there are disjunctures. Such disjunctures push the boys to reaffirm egalitarian working-class dispositions:

> Garth: Why is 'getting power' there [pointing low on the list]?
> George: Because getting power is not important in my life.
> Garth: So is it that 'respect' is more important than 'power'?
> George: Definitely.
>
> (George, Year 10, London Academy)

> Garth: 'Getting power' … it's come down low for you.
> Lewis: Everyone has their own power. You don't feel you have to get power because you have your own power. Like you don't really need others to see.
>
> (Lewis, Year 10, London Academy)

> Because everyone wants respect. No one wants to take you like a joke in life.
>
> (Alen, Year 11, London Academy)

When 'power' is seen as 'respect', my participants valued it quite highly; however, when the boys saw power as having power over other people or control, they universally dis-identified with the concept. Disassociating themselves from power remains a reoccurring theme in the data. Through their dialogues regarding power, the boys engage in processes of confrontation where they self-represent themselves through resisting modern subjectivities of neoliberalism. In their maintenance work around the neoliberal rhetoric of power and aspiration, the boys contend with feelings of 'pain, fear, estrangement, guilt, and desire that complicate attempted "escapes" from a disadvantaged class position' (Allen, 2013: 5). Resistance to gaining power could be seen as a rejection of neoliberal discourses of mobility and competitiveness as my participants look for stability and dependability in times of fragmented rites of passage and an infrastructure of dwindling respectable trade-based occupations that were previously the traditional bases of white, male, material power (Weis, 1990; Winlow, 2001). By not admitting to a desire for power and contesting competition, these working-class boys prepare for post-industrial employment or the 'McJob' (Bottero, 2009: 9), where there exists a high probability they will 'learn to serve' (McDowell, 2003). Some of the boys even highlighted how power is a force that had the potential to corrupt:

> Garth: When you see the words 'getting power' what do you think of?
> George: How – like usually when you have power people don't act the same around you. You know what I mean.
> Garth: Ok ... like they see you as ...
> George: Yeah, but they won't say anything to you because you're ...
> Garth: ... the one that has the power.
>
> (George, Year 10)

> Garth: When you see the words 'getting power' what do you think of?
> Calum: It kinda reminds me ... Reminds me of the dates between 1939 and 1945 ... reminds me a bit of Adolf. I don't think of it in a good way.
>
> (Calum, Year 10)

I concede there are significant conflicting elements at play, especially in the subjectivity of language, and this activity in no way represents a perfectly accurate reading of how the boys' aspirations were regulated and shaped. Through drawing upon the affective and emotional landscape within which class inequality is lived, embodied and shaped (Reay, 2005), I focus not on the activity itself but the process around the activity, addressing how the boys present a conflicted identity in how they conceptualise power. The habitus is permeable to the neoliberal field of the school and the boys elected to rank 'Getting a job in business' highly, as to position it as a low priority would admit certain deficits and constraints and a devaluing or their working-class dispositions. The activity became a value-laden process where the boys managed the 'petty mundane humiliations ... class recognitions, visceral aversions, and feelings of inferiority and superiority' in class-making (Reay, 2005: 917).

Summary

This research seeks to make a contribution to untangling the 'aspiration-engagement, aspiration-achievement, and aspiration-choice equations' (Archer *et al.*, 2010: 80). Originating from a nexus of learner and social identities, the boys' aspirations are heavily influenced by neoliberal educational practices while concurrently attempting to constitute a good life (Stahl,

2012). Bourdieu's tools allow for a nuanced analysis of contradictory demands and the complex interweaving of available categories, the emotional meaning participants attach to these categories, and the stories/narratives/myths through which they make sense of these discourses. The boys articulate a doxic logic drawing upon socio-historical conditions, where their funds of aspirations generally take place within two registers of meaning and action, internalising two career trajectories: an ideal option (football star, musician, graphic designer) and a realistic option (bricklayer, plumber, etc.).

There were few clear or discernable patterns in relation to achievement and aspiration. The boys who wanted to leave school immediately following their GCSEs did not have noticeably lower patterns of attainment. Building on the concept of habitus, Zipin *et al.* (2013) put forth a three-part conceptual framework for rethinking aspirations: (1) a 'doxic' logic for aspiring, founded 'upon populist–ideological mediations'; (2) a 'habituated' logic for aspiring that draws upon 'biographic–historical conditions and embodied as habitus among people in given social–structural positions'; and (3) 'emergent' senses of possible futures grounded in lived social-cultural resources they call 'funds of aspiration' (p. 5). In each approach, aspiration is constructed in relation to discourses, contributing to the formation subjectivities where the dispositional structures of the habitus come to embody 'possibilities-within-limits of given social–structural positions' and where the habitus becomes 'self-limiting possibility' in terms of probable futures (Zipin *et al.*, 2013: 9).

Notes

1   Archer *et al.* (2010) also provide some evidence that shows the black boys were more likely to envisage staying in post-compulsory education than leaving to find work. Aspiration as ethnicised is supported by other recent research (Gunter and Watt, 2009).

2   Ironically, with the recent influx of Eastern European migrants, trade work in South London has become increasingly competitive.

3   McDowell (2012: 582) writes, 'Employers read the surface signals of bodily demeanour, dress and language as indicators of the underlying qualities they are seeking, or more typically as characteristics they are careful to avoid. If these young men did find work, often their sexualised, aggressive embodied interactions, especially with women co-workers and superiors, disqualified them, as many of them found it hard to perform the deferential servility required in the service economy'.

References

Allen, K. (2013) 'Blair's children': Young women as 'aspirational subjects' in the psychic landscape of class. *Sociological Review*, 61(4), 1–20.

Archer, L. and Yamashita, H. (2003) 'Knowing their limits'? Identities, inequalities, and inner city school leavers' post-16 aspirations. *Journal of Educational Policy*, 18(1), 53–69.

Archer, L., Pratt, S. D. and Phillips, D. (2001) Working-class men's constructions of masculinity and negotiations of (non) participation in higher education. *Gender and Education*, 13(4), 431–449.

Archer, L., Hollingworth, S. and Mendick, H. (2010) *Urban youth and schooling: The experiences and identities of educationally 'at risk' young people*. Berkshire: Open University Press.

Archer, L., DeWitt, J. and Willis, B. (2013) Adolescent boys' science aspirations: Masculinity, capital, and power. *Journal of Research in Science Teaching*, 51(1), 1–30.

Bathmaker, A. M., Ingram, N. and Waller, R. (2013) Higher education, social class, and the mobilisation of capitals: Recognising and playing the game. *British Journal of Sociology of Education*, 34(5–6), 723–743.

Beck, U. (1992) *Risk society: Towards a new modernity*. London: Sage Publications.

Bottero, W. (2009) Class in the 21st Century. In K. P. Sveinsson (ed.), *Who cares about the white working class?* (pp. 7–15). London: Runnymede Perspectives.

Bourdieu, P. (1984) *Distinction: A social critique of the judgement of taste*. Oxon: Routledge.

Bourdieu, P. (1999) The contradictions of inheritance. In P. Bourdieu (ed.), *Weight of the world: Social suffering in contemporary society* (p. 517–551). Cambridge: Polity Press.

Bourdieu, P. and Passeron, J.C. (1977) *Reproduction in education, society, and culture*. London: Sage Publications.

Bourdieu, P. and Wacquant, L. (1992) *An invitation to reflexive sociology*. Cambridge: Polity Press.

Brown, P. (2013) Education, opportunity, and the prospects for social mobility. *British Journal of Sociology of Education*, 34(5–6), 678–700.

Burke, P. (2007) Men accessing education: Masculinities, identifications, and widening participation. *British Journal of Sociology of Education*, 28(4), 411–424.

Burke, P. J. (2009) Men accessing high education: Theorizing continuity and change in relation to masculine subjectivities. *Higher Education Policy*, 22, 81–100.

Byrom, T. and Lightfoot, N. (2013) Interrupted trajectories: The impact of academic failure on the social mobility of working-class students. *British Journal of Sociology of Education*, 34(5–6), 812–828.

Connolly, P. and Healy, J. (2004) Symbolic violence, locality and social class: The educational and career aspirations of 10–11-year-old boys in Belfast. *Pedagogy, Culture and Society*, 12(1), 15–33.

Dillabough, J. A. and Kennelly, J. (2010) *Lost youth in a global city: Class, culture and the urban imaginary*. New York: Routledge.

Drummond, J. (2003) Care of the self in a knowledge economy: Higher education, vocation and the ethics of Michel Foucault. *Educational Philosophy and Theory*, 35(1), 57–69.

Giroux, H. (2004) Public pedagogy and the politics of neo-liberalism: Making the political more pedagogical. *Policy Futures in Education*, 2(3 and 4), 494–505.

Gunter, A. and Watt, P. (2009) Grafting, going to college and working on road: Youth transitions and cultures in an East London neighbourhood. *Journal of Youth Studies*, 12(5), 515–529.

Hart, C. S. (2013) *Aspirations, education and social justice: Applying Sen and Bourdieu.* London: Bloomsbury.

Hattam, R. and Prosser, B. (2008) Unsettling deficit views of students and their communities. *The Australian Educational Researcher,* 35(2), 89–106.

Hattam, R. and Smyth, J. (2003) 'Not everyone has a perfect life': Becoming somebody without school. *Pedagogy, Culture and Society,* 11(3), 379–398.

Lamont, M. and Lareau, A. (1988) Cultural capital: Allusions, gaps and glissandos in recent theoretical developments. *Sociological Theory,* 6(2), 153–168.

Lucey, H. and Reay, D. (2002) Carrying the beacon of excellence: Social class differentiation and anxiety at a time of transition. *Journal of Education Policy,* 17(3), 321–336.

Mac an Ghaill, M. (1988) *Young, gifted, and black: Student-teacher relations in the schooling of black youth.* Milton Keynes: Open University Press.

MacDonald, R. and Marsh, J. (2005) *Disconnected youth? Growing up in Britain's poor neighbourhoods.* Basingstoke: Palgrave Macmillan.

McDowell, L. (2003) *Redundant masculinities?: Employment change and white working class youth.* Malden, MA: Blackwell Pub.

McDowell, L. (2012) Post-crisis, post-Ford and post-gender? Youth identities in an era of austerity. *Journal of Youth Studies,* 15(5), 573–590.

McLeod, J. (2002) Working out intimacy: Young people and friendship in an age of reflexivity. *Discourse: Studies in the Cultural Politics of Education,* 23(3), 211–226.

Marks, A. (2003) Welcome to the new ambivalence: Reflections on the historical and current cultural antagonism between the working-class male and higher education. *British Journal of Sociology of Education,* 24(1), 83–93.

Moore, H. (2013) Shades of whiteness? English villagers, Eastern European migrants, and the intersection of race and class in rural England. *Critical Race and Whiteness Studies,* 9(1), 1–19.

Nayak, A. (2003) 'Boyz to Men': Masculinities, schooling and labour transitions in de-industrial times. *Educational Review,* 55(2), 147–159.

Platt, L. (2007) Making education count: The effects of ethnicity and qualifications on intergenerational social class mobility. *The Sociological Review,* 55(3), 485–508.

Reay, D. (2003) A risky business? Mature working-class women students and access to higher education. *Gender and Education,* 15(3), 301–317.

Reay, D. (2004a) Gendering Bourdieu's concepts of capitals? Emotional capital, women and social class. *Theory Culture Society,* 20(6), 57–74.

Reay, D. (2004b) 'It's all becoming habitus': Beyond the habitual use of habitus in educational research. *British Journal of Sociology of Education,* 25(4), 431–444.

Reay, D. (2005) Beyond consciousness?: The psychic landscape of social class. *Sociology,* 39(5), 911–928.

Reay, D. (2009) Making sense of white working class educational underachievement. In K. P. Sveinsson (ed.), *Who cares about the white working class?* (pp. 22–28). London: Runnymede Perspectives.

Reay, D., David, M. E. and Ball, S. (2005) *Degrees of choice: Social class, race, and gender in higher education.* London: Institute of Education.

Roberts, S. (2012) Boys will be boys ... won't they? Change and continuities in contemporary young working-class masculinities. *Sociology,* 47(4), 671–686.

Sayer, A. (2005) *The moral significance of class.* Cambridge: Cambridge University Press.

Skeggs, B. (2004) Context and background: Pierre Bourdieu's analysis of class, gender and sexuality. *The Sociological Review*, 52(2), 19–33.

Skelton, C. (2010) 'A passion for football': Dominant masculinities and primary schooling. *Sport, Education and Society*, 5(1), 5–18.

Stahl, G. (2012) Aspiration and a good life among white working-class boys in London. *Journal of Qualitative and Ethnographic Research*, 7(8–9), 8–19.

Stahl, G. (2014) White working-class male narratives of 'loyalty to self' in discourses of aspiration. *British Journal of Sociology of Education* (forthcoming).

Swain, J. (2000) 'The money's good, the fame's good, the girls are good': The role of playground football in the construction of young boys' masculinity in a junior school. *British Journal of Sociology of Education*, 21(1), 95–109.

Weis, L. (1990) *Working class without work*. New York: Routledge.

Wexler, P. (1992) *Becoming somebody: Toward a social psychology of school*. London: The Falmer Press.

Winlow, S. (2001) *Badfellas: Crime, tradition and new masculinities*. Oxford: Berg.

Youdell, D. (2004) Engineering school markets, constituting schools, and subjectivating students: The bureaucratic, institutional, and classroom dimensions of educational triage. *Journal of Education Policy*, 19(4), 407–431.

Zipin, L., Sellar, S. and Hattam, R. (2012) Countering and exceeding 'capital': A 'funds of knowledge' approach to re-imagining community. *Discourse: Studies in the Cultural Politics of Education*, 33(2), 179–192.

Zipin, L., Sellar, S., Brennan, M. and Gale, T. (2013) Educating for futures in marginalized regions: A sociological framework for rethinking and researching aspirations. *Educational Philosophy and Theory*, 45, 1–20.

Chapter 8

Conclusions and recommendations

The research explored how working-class young men are conducting and managing their lives within schooling that is robustly shaped by a neoliberal agenda of 'continually changing the self, making informed choices, engaging in competition, and taking chances' (Phoenix, 2004: 229). Their conceptions of meritocracy and social class identity have a substantial influence on how the boys negotiate their learner identity, engage with education, and form their masculine identity. Through the data we are reminded that young people's engagement with their schooling 'depends in part on the sense they make of themselves, their community and their future, and in part on the adaptive strategies they use to accept, modify, or contest the institutional identities made available to them' (Hattam and Smyth, 2003: 387).

The habitus remains a site where these white working-class boys internalise new experiences and schemes of perception, which can lead to a newly reconfigured habitus made up of conflicting dispositions. An egalitarian habitus, where symbolic violence becomes a mediating force, is where the boys gradually internalise structures, mediated through their working-class communal values, thus reproducing their own subordination. Identities are not distinct from discourses but, instead, produced by and through them; my participants are neoliberal subjects despite efforts made to counteract such discourses and establish a self of value. Identity work involves daily strategising surrounding 'value' and insecurity/anxiety as they negotiate familiar/unfamiliar terrain; the boys may want to do well but, simultaneously, they do not want to do *too* well.

Undertaking research with young people, specifically young men, raises complex questions about access, reliability and power (McDowell, 2000). Participants are cautious in how they represent themselves as individuals and concerned with judgements of the dominant value system. Researchers thus need to be aware of this and to display a lack of attachment to hegemonic values and theories of 'self' (Skeggs, 2004b: 88). The research was focused on how individuals define and interpret situations, negotiate meanings and co-create social reality (Woods, 1986: 4–6). There are considerable dangers of reifying biographies and focusing too much attention on how young people's lives may/may not conform to the discourses of identity available to them (McLeod, 2002: 222). Throughout this work, an attempt has been made to keep the social context and individual biographies in play alongside a sense of the emerging and dominant characteristics of different, and possibly new kinds of, biographies and subject positions.

While modernity has bred new forms of translocality, hybridised identities and subjectivities, my analytical attention has also focused on how some of my participants are fixed in place by both circumstances – material, economic, familial, cultural – and neoliberal discourses. More specifically, I have attempted to show how these young men are not receptors of a free-floating global youth culture. Instead, they engage in processes of confrontation and meditation and experience things in uneven and fragmented ways, where they draw upon an egalitarian habitus that reaffirms and fixes certain identities. An egalitarian habitus operates in a very different way outside the classroom where gender identity, specifically a heteronomativity, comes to the forefront and where they subjugate forms of non-normative masculinity. Through the use of visual images, we see how 'othering' becomes a structuring practice, where the participants engage with 'intra-habitus tensions' or 'general incongruences between dispositions' and are, therefore, pushed to reflexively secure their own sense of identity (Mouzelis, 2007).

In understanding what we can learn from white working-class boys' educational experiences, the data show how the habitus of white working-class boys is divided against itself (Reay, 2002: 223), or, more specifically, how the egalitarian habitus is pushed and pulled, shaped through its capacity to rebuff the neoliberal rhetoric. To view habitus as overtly unconscious and pre-reflexive (Sweetman, 2003; Adams, 2006) underestimates the actors' rationality and reflexivity (Sayer, 2005: 16). In understanding what the boys' perception of their experience with the daily processes of schooling tells us about white working-class educational 'failure', we see these school sites as places where the boys value averageness, ordinariness or 'middling' and ultimately where they want to 'fit in' rather than 'stand out'. We see how they are wary of the corrupting force of power and resist having power over others. In my analysis of neoliberalism and identity, I have considered how the field structures the habitus and also how the habitus, as a logic of practice, contributes to making the field meaningful. Through exploring the identity work of these young men, using the method of habitus, we see how social identities influence learner identities and how aspiration is constituted through embodiment and agency, a compilation of collective and individual trajectories, an intricate interplay between past and present.

Though the habitus is durable and therefore difficult to alter, Bourdieu (2002) recognises it can be changed and, if this is so, we must consider why and how it resists change, and the various ways it comes to be reaffirmed. While the school inculcates a habitus that reinforces its institutional habitus, my data support the creative capacity of the habitus to function as a counter-habitus to the institutional habitus. In *Distinction* (1984: 674), Bourdieu writes:

> The dialectic of downclassing and upclassing which underlies a whole set of social processes presupposes and entails that all the groups concerned run in the same direction, toward the same objectives, the same properties, those which are designated by the leading group and which, by definition, are unavailable to the groups following, since, whatever these properties may be intrinsically, they are modified and qualified by their distinctive rarity and will no longer be what they are once they are multiplied and made available to groups lower down. Thus, by an apparent paradox, the maintenance of order, that is, of the whole set of gaps, differences, 'differentials,' ranks, precedences, priorities, exclusions, distinctions, ordinal properties, and thus of the relations of order which give a social formation its structure, is provided by an unceasing change in substantial (i.e., non-relational) properties.

While Bourdieu's argument centres on social processes that entail 'that all the groups concerned run in the same direction, toward the same objectives, the same properties', the data from this research strongly suggests these boys are capable, through symbolic violence, of distancing themselves from the dominant neoliberal ideology of aspiration and middle-class ideals. Furthermore, it is through this process that they are inadvertently maintaining the social order, what Bourdieu describes as 'gaps, differences, "differentials," ranks, precedences, priorities, exclusions, distinctions, ordinal properties' and preserving middle- and upper-class advantageous positions.

When there is disjuncture between habitus and field, where 'dispositions encounter conditions (including fields) different from those in which they were constructed and assembled' (Bourdieu, 2002: 31), the egalitarian habitus allows for the boys to 'opt out' of the pursuit of symbolically legitimated goods. They distance themselves from a dominant ideology that privileges certain capitals they do not feel they possess. The habitus, in order to accrue value, is (sub)consciously steering the boys away from the dominant ideals in order to protect/maintain their pride and dignity and, by extension, their working-class identity. While the boys momentarily adopt the neoliberal discourse in their subjectivities, their egalitarian habitus, as a counter-habitus, represents a set of strategies or agentic practices to generate value.

Bourdieu argues reflexivity to be a 'critical theory based on a phenomenological questioning of knowledge creation; whether, how, and to what extent a research process allows the subject of knowledge to grasp the object of his or her study in essence' (Grenfell, 2008: 200). Acting as a methodological tool to help him defend his own intellectual positionality (Yang, 2013: 9), reflexivity considers the social and intellectual unconscious embedded in analytical operations surrounding research and, in Bourdieu's eyes, serves as a buttress to epistemological security (Bourdieu and Wacquant, 1992: 37). For Bourdieu, reflexivity means that all 'knowledge producers should strive to recognize their own objective position within the intellectual and academic field' (Grenfell, 2008: 201). Throughout my research I made attempts to analyse my unconscious, embedded social position and how it impacted upon my mode of analysis, developing what Bourdieu and Accadro (1993: 608) call the 'sociological "feel" or "eye"' that 'allows one to perceive and monitor on the spot, as the interview is actually taking place, the effects on the social structure within which it is occurring'. Being relatively close in age, yet of a different nationality, placed me in an interesting research position. Research into identity work contains quandaries regarding reflexivity, particularly 'how to maintain a reflexive and critical lens on identities and identifications within any one of the influential contexts for identity making without losing sight of the impact of other, even broader contexts such as the policy field, the nation state and even the global arena' (Reay, 2010: 281). This research has made attempts to weigh nuanced identity work against larger educational policy shifts where, as a reflexive ethnographer, there is always a balancing act to keep the focus equally distributed between researcher and participants.

Implications for policy and practice

In Humphries' (1981) historical analysis of the working-class experience with education between 1889 and 1939, he shows how working-class youth were characterised by 'types of intellect and character, ranging from those capable of "abstract thought" to those who could not progress beyond "concrete thought"' (p. 19). Historically, working-class boys were characterised as psychologically deficient, prone to delinquency and resistance. While there have been some moderate advances, unfortunately today we have politicians such as Peter Brand, of the Social Mobility and Child Poverty Commission, arguing how working-class children must be taught to think and act like their middle-class counterparts (Graham, 2014). According to Brand, the real leverage of change for children from poor homes to get ahead in life is in changing their deportment (the way they eat, dress) and how they conduct personal relationships. This pejorative view of working-class class culture consciously ignores wider structural issues that contribute to why many white working-class underperform academically.

During the course of the research, it was difficult to see what the implications were for policy and practice. As a former educator in this part of South London, much of the research process was about disassociating myself from that role and embracing the role of school-based ethnographer. Another reason for my resistance to making recommendations for policy and practice is my general refusal to view the white working-class boy underperformance/poverty of aspiration phenomenon as 'a problem to be solved', where it is clearly an effect of much larger, more complex issues in the UK. Unfortunately, the recent Parliamentary Inquiry into the *Underachievement of White Working Class Children* (Select Committee on Education, 2014) staunchly refused to acknowledge how contextual the issue of white working-class underachievement is. The report argued for 'revolutionary' solutions such as longer school days to improve test scores, incentives to get better teachers into disadvantaged schools, and free schools targeted specifically at the white working-class population. Unfortunately, these are nothing more than tweaks parading as magic-bullet solutions.

The UK's education system, in which pupils' performance has an extraordinarily strong positive association with social class, is mired by persistent issues such as a lack of progress and innovation, deficit thinking concerning students' ability, a fetish for continual change, inadequate teacher training, etc. (MacBeath, 2009). Students who have no control over the quality of education they receive are often the primary individuals held accountable. This is especially true of the white working class, the majority of whom attend failing schools. While *London Challenge* and *Teach First* initiatives have been implemented, there is nothing in London similar to the Knowledge is Power Program (KIPP) model that enacts an aggressive 'no excuses' ethos toward raising aspiration and in which school culture is taken very seriously. Furthermore, it was clear in the meetings and dialogues I had with leadership teams that the standard tropes in school improvement literature were viewed with suspicion. School improvement, founded upon a strategic and cohesive approach, was viewed as some nebulous black box. I was consistently surprised by how my research sites continued to use the same methods (punishments such as detention, missing break time, etc.), even though such punitive measures were completely ineffective. The majority of references made to raising attainment by obdurate school leaders was always coupled with increasing the level of punishment, rather than capitalising on a multitude of other strategies to engage students and raise aspirations.

The education institutions in this study were very reactive environments with few proactive and positive strategies in place, creating challenging working atmospheres for all involved. As a result, deficient Dickensian teaching and learning models and pernicious complacency – 'what will be, will be' – are pervasive in many schools throughout the UK, including the ones in this study. This mind set contributes to poor classroom climate and rampant behaviour issues in UK schools[1] (Haydn, 2014) and the lowering of aspirations by teachers for their white working-class students, who are marked in popular discourses as 'unteachable' (Archer *et al.*, 2010: 89). Simultaneously, this mind set is also furthered by a morose pop culture fascination with social class, education and behaviour as seen in the popularity of recent television shows such as Channel 4's *Educating Essex* and *Mr Drew's School for Boys*, as well as the BBC3 documentary series *Tough Young Teachers*, which followed exceedingly posh *Teach First* educators into deprived schooling environments.

Infused with a neoliberal prerogative, the classroom cultures observed in this study were largely fixated on learning skills equated with access to high-status or high-income employment. Furthermore, this prerogative is compounded by a repetitive, reductive, and restrictive National Curriculum that is rarely engaging. Furedi (2009), one of the loudest critics of the bleak state of contemporary UK education, maintains 'The purpose of education is to help young people develop their capacity for thinking, knowing, reflecting, imagining, observing, judging, questioning' (p. 56). Throughout my data collection, in each school site I saw very few examples of any critical thinking in action. At no point in the study did I feel student voice was recognised, and such silence only leads to further misrepresentations (Hattam and Smyth, 2003). I was witness to teachers' consistent rejection of students' tastes and appreciations, which reinforced the boundaries between students' social and learner identities. Frequently, it struck me how perceptive the boys were in evaluating the quality of the educators, knowing which teachers cared about their progress and which teachers did not. Following Archer *et al.*'s (2010) findings, my participants valued respect and reciprocity, and they were drawn to teachers who were fair and measured. The majority of the boys were aware the quality of the schooling was substandard, and this contributed to arguments put forth that schooling would not be integral to their trajectory.

Given how raising white working-class aspiration is very much on the government radar, it is interesting to note that none of the institutions who participated in the study had any form of aspiration programme, much less a targeted approach toward the white working class (Gillborn and Kirton, 2000; Keddie, 2013a, 2013b). Additionally, the careers counselling was so slight it might as well been non-existent, and these schools also lacked a strong well-being focus, which has been documented to increase engagement, aspiration and achievement (Wrench *et al.*, 2012). Unfortunately, vocational training, which the boys valued and had the potential to become a highly profitable venture in South London (where they could make considerably more money than their teachers), was not valorised by the school.

To understand the work of teachers in these South London education environments, we have to first understand how ability was constructed through the schools' ideological structures, or what Carter (2012) refers to as 'soft structures'. Or, more specifically, how ability becomes fixed as part of people's identities. As Gillborn and Youdell (2000: 15) argue, 'The view of "ability" that currently dominates policy and practice is especially dangerous. The assumption that "ability" is a fixed, generalized and measurable potential paves the way for the operationalization of deeply racist and class-biased stereotypes'. The notion of ability – ascribed through frequent references to students as 'bright', 'thick', 'lovely', 'feral', 'fucked up', 'a dream' – is hugely important to understanding how pedagogy is shaped. These labels serve to validate a system of 'symbolic violence' which constructs daily practices that prevent children from learning (Epp and Watkinson, 1996: 1). Through the use of labels, students become further imprisoned in a vicious cycle of deprivation, educational underachievement and failure; furthermore, it allows educators to divorce themselves from their chief responsibility: to educate. Learning in environments that 'ration education' (Gillborn and Youdell, 2000), the boys and their classmates were often subject to the 'soft bigotry of low expectations' (Dumenden, 2013).

To be clear, I do not want to blame teachers (many of whom were excellent and worked incredibly long hours) as they have little, if any, control over their professional lives (MacBeath, 2009). Students and educators are subject to complex pedagogic negotiations where they 'develop modes of institutional habitus distinctive to schools as places in their lives' (Zipin, 2009: 326). The data strongly suggest the pressure imposed on schools ultimately becomes pressure for students; these are residual impacts of the neoliberal order. National, local, school and teacher pressure trickles down to the students, inculcating a pedagogy of limited, score-based understanding of student learning and student success. As with Gillborn and Youdell's (2000) work, most of the teachers were aware of the troublesome and ethically compromising nature of their actions and how they were constructing opportunities and life chances for their students, yet they were required to work within severe constraints.

The data reminds us that education 'involves a complex interplay of multiple realities in which some realities get valued and others do not' (Hattam and Smyth, 2003: 387). Studies focused on re-engaging students in their learning have found proven success with a funds of knowledge [FoK] approach where education is able to exceed the 'rote-like instruction ... children commonly encounter in schools' (Moll et al., 1992: 132) and offers opportunities to transforming students' diverse knowledges into pedagogical assets (Moll and Gonzalez, 1997: 89). A FoK approach, which works as a scaffold for a 'curricula of engagement', typically asks students to bring cultural artefacts from outside of school that have 'rich identity resonances, and to talk/'teach' about their social-cultural meanings' (Zipin, 2009: 328–329). FoK offers space to recognise students' lifeworlds, their 'virtual schoolbag' where learners 'carry' cultural knowledge and dispositions from lifeworlds into the school-world (Thomson, 2002). A meaningful curriculum, as opposed to a reductive one, would have had the capacity to invert longstanding cultural deficit views (Comber and Kamler, 2005; Mills, 2008; Wrench et al., 2012) that depict non-elite communities 'as places from which children must be saved or rescued, rather than places that, in addition to problems (as in all communities), contain valuable knowledge and experiences that can foster ... educational development' (Moll and Gonzalez, 1997: 98). The boys certainly would have benefited from a curriculum where their own working-class culture, rich in docklands history, was recognised with a sense of meaning, by 'recognising a diversity of cultural knowledge embodied by learners' (Zipin *et al.*, 2012: 181). If the boys were to view their cultures and immediate lifeworlds as valued by educators, this would have opened up spaces for important dialogues concerning aspirations, motivations and engagement.

Recommendations for future research

This research is a partial story of how some working-class boys are engaging with their school experience and also how they see school (and education) playing a role in their lives. I did attend parents' evenings at each school site, where I spoke with parents in a casual manner, but ultimately the study would have benefited from me distancing myself from the institution and engaging more with their community and family lives. The parents I encountered did not enjoy 'the taken-for-granted knowledge and ability to understand and navigate the education system that characterises many middle-class families' engagement with education' (Archer *et al.*, 2010: 31); nor were programmes in operation to facilitate such knowledge. The majority of the boys came from families who did not possess the various forms of cultural capital that would positively shape their experience with education (Appendix B, C). The study would have benefited from me interviewing families in order to understand how the egalitarian habitus, averageness, ordinariness and 'middling' were fostered in the home. An ethnography that brings together the home life of the boys with their experiences at school would better explore some of the processes I have attempted to highlight.

In terms of curriculum, the boys would have benefited through a broadening of the curriculum at GCSE level, where many were pushed out of language-intensive subjects (e.g. history,[2] social sciences, citizenship) that would have fostered a more reflexive approach, as well as an awareness of how inequality is constructed in contemporary society. Referencing Bourdieu, Mills (2008: 82) writes, 'Many marginalised students, for example, take things for granted, rather than recognising that there are ways that their situation could be transformed'. I do believe the institution should be contending with the sensitive dynamics of social class and that students should be encouraged to analyse social class in their society, as opposed to taking their so-called realities for 'granted'. Within the exploration of society, the focus must not only be on the existing knowledges of working-class young people, but also on pedagogies that emphasise a collectivist approach to the learner, as opposed to a neoliberal competitive one (Perry and Francis, 2010).

Unfortunately, there has been little educational research in working-class boys' identity work surrounding learning practices where boys actively engage. Within music education, it has been well documented that boys, particularly working-class boys, tend to opt out and view music education as a 'feminised' subject, when actually music arguably 'provides an ideal medium through which dominant forms of masculinity can be problematised' (McGregor and Mills, 2006: 222). In a study I conducted with Pete Dale, we showed how white working-class boys developed new skills and embraced learning in areas they were passionate about, specifically in DJ-ing and MC-ing (Stahl and Dale, 2012, 2013). Through these new skills, our participants inverted both the 'bad boy', anti-school, masculine identity and the 'apathetic', lazy, non-worker in favour of teaching one another and enjoying a challenge. There is a need for schools and youth centres to be more proactive in designing courses, programmes and teaching approaches that challenge the 'dominant culture of aggressive, heterosexual manliness that thrives in many areas today' (Salisbury and Jackson, 1996: 15), and that embrace new literacies to supply a space to interrogate such conceptions of gender identity. Within the literature on anti-school cultures among school-boys, it has been argued that it is important for educators to equip these learners with the necessary capacities to interrogate gender binaries and reflect on how they construct their masculinities (Mills, 2001; McGregor and Mills, 2006). We have seen how boys change their masculine identity when the learning is of interest to them; through alterations in their masculine identity formation, the boys in the study came to see themselves as 'successful' and adept learners.

Conclusion

While these working-class boys were located in South London, many of the issues that were addressed – specifically identity work in response to neoliberal ideology, inequality and gender identity – were not particular to the UK. The neoliberal processes in educational contexts are global and, when scrutinised in relation to learner identities, it is essential to see how students agentically respond by constructing counter-narratives to feel value. As they make sense of their restricted opportunities and the cards they have been dealt, these young men articulate they are content with being 'ordinary' or 'average' (Stahl, 2013, 2014). Success in school is 'not simply a matter of academic ability but assumes a reservoir of expertise necessary to understand and play the system' (MacBeath, 2009: 82). In the interactions between the habitus and the economic, social, cultural and symbolic capital, it is clear the value afforded to different forms of capital is largely dependent upon the extent to which capitals are recognised as symbolically legitimate (Skeggs, 2004a). Understanding how the boys view their capitals and their social class is essential to understanding their paradoxical responses. Their reflexivity as to their place on the hierarchy had an influence on whether they 'bought in' or 'bought out' of education, though this is pushed and pulled along a continuum. In terms of 'fixed' and 'fluid' identity shifts, I feel the boys that were able to engage in their education had elements of fluidity, where they could assume different dispositions within the schooling environment from those adopted beyond the school environment.

The boys knew the value of education, but the majority of the participants saw education as a risk rather than a certainty, whereas their educators saw education as the certainty and low-skilled employment as the risk. As Reay (2002, 2004) and Skeggs (2004a) have argued, shame and the fear of shame haunts working-class relationships to education; in the study of white working-class boys in an era of high neoliberalism, I would argue shame and fear are intertwined, but there also exist two opposing manifestations. First, the boys clearly have a fear of academic failure and, given their deprived school contexts, their fear is a very rationale one. Second, grounded in their social class identity, they also have a fear of academic success.

My final thoughts are with the participants. Over the course of my research, I met, got to know and worked with individuals who both surprised and inspired me. In conclusion, I feel there are two anecdotes that occurred during the course of the research that serve as illustrations of the social disparity that framed the research. First, early in my teaching experience, I taught in a traditionally white working-class school overlooking Canary Wharf (the financial district of London), so everyday I saw the juxtaposition of abject poverty against extreme wealth, which was incredibly striking and also disheartening. Through conversations with my students regarding the skyscrapers, I came to understand the processes associated with dis-identifying with a lifestyle infused with wealth and competitiveness. Second, when transcribing the data for this study in the Faculty of Education at Cambridge, I recalled the words of George and Thomas, two self-described 'cheeky chappies', who always had the cheerful capacity to tune out any schooling pressures and who were truly 'happy with less'. When I finished one transcription I got up to get some coffee and overheard two staff members discussing two recent undergraduate suicide attempts. Obviously Cambridge is an intensely competitive environment, but I have often thought of this moment of contrasts between individuals of little economic means who are content and individuals who are exceedingly unhappy, burdened by the weight of privilege.

Notes

1   In 2010–2011 there were 330,000 pupil exclusions in the UK, which conflicts with the generally positive picture presented by the Steer Report (2009) and recent Ofsted judgements on the proportion of schools that were deemed to be less than satisfactory in terms of pupil behaviour (cf. Haydn, 2014 for a more detailed analysis of the debate) (Department for Education, 2012).

2   In London Academy, history was required for study from Years 7–9 (Key Stage 3) and was generally an hour per week in Years 7 and 8 and two per week in Year 9. It was then optional at GCSE.

References

Adams, M. (2006) Hybridizing habitus and reflexivity: Towards an understanding of contemporary identity. *Sociology*, 40(3), 511–528.

Archer, L., Hollingworth, S. and Mendick, H. (2010) *Urban youth and schooling: The experiences and identities of educationally 'at risk' young people*. Berkshire: Open University Press.

Bourdieu, P. (1984) *Distinction: A social critique of the judgement of taste*. Oxon: Routledge.

Bourdieu, P. (2002) Habitus. In J. Hillier and E. Rooksby (eds), *Habitus: A Sense of Place* (pp. 27–34). Aldershot: Ashgate.

Bourdieu, P. and Accadro, A. (1993) *The weight of the world: Social suffering in contemporary society*. Stanford University Press.

Bourdieu, P. and Wacquant, L. (1992) *An invitation to reflexive sociology*. Cambridge: Polity Press.

Carter, P. (2012) *Stubborn roots: Race, culture, and inequality in U.S. and South African schools*. Oxford: Oxford University Press.

Comber, B. and Kamler, B. (eds) (2005) *Turn-around pedagogies: Literacy interventions for at-risk students*. Sydney: PETA.

Department for Education (2012) *Permanent and fixed period exclusions from schools in England 2010/11*. London: Author. Online at: www.education.gov.uk/rsgateway/DB/SFR/s001080/index.shtml

Dumenden, I. (2013) The soft bigotry of low expectations: The refugee student and mainstream schooling. (Unpublished Doctoral Dissertation). La Trobe University, Melbourne. Online at: http://hdl.handle.net/1959.9/200217

Epp, J. R. and Watkinson, A. M. (1996) *Systemic violence: How schools hurt children*. London: Falmer.

Furedi, F. (2009) *Wasted: Why education isn't educating*. London: Continuum International Publishing Group.

Gillborn, D. and Kirton, A. (2000) White heat: Racism, under-achievement, and white working-class boys. *Inclusion and Special Educational Needs*, 4(4), 271–288.

Gillborn, D. and Youdell, D. (2000) *Rationing education: Policy, practice, reform and equity*. Buckingham: Open University Press.

Graham, G. (2014) Working class children must learn to be middle class to get on in life, government advisor says. *The Telegraph*. 3 March. Online at: www.telegraph.co.uk/education/10671048/Working-class-children-must-learn-to-be-middle-class-to-get-on-in-life-government-advisor-says.html

Grenfell, M. (2008) *Pierre Bourdieu: Key concepts*. Durham: Acumen.

Hattam, R. and Smyth, J. (2003) 'Not everyone has a perfect life': Becoming somebody without school. *Pedagogy, Culture and Society*, 11(3), 379–398.

Haydn, T. (2014) To what extent is behaviour a problem in English schools? Exploring the scale and prevalence of deficits in classroom climate. *Review of Education. DOI: 10.1002/rev3.3025*

Humphries, S. (1981) *Hooligans or rebels? An oral history of working-class childhood and youth 1889–1939*. Oxford: Basil Blackwell Publisher Limited.

Keddie, A. (2013a) 'There isn't kind of a White History Month or anything like that for them': Equity, schooling and the problematics of group identity politics. *International Journal of Inclusive Education*, 1–14.

Keddie, A. (2013b) 'We haven't done enough for white working-class children': Issues of distributive justice and ethnic identity politics. *Race Ethnicity and Education*, 1–20.

MacBeath, J. (2009) Border crossings. *Improving Schools*, 12(1), 81–92.

McDowell, L. (2000) 'It's that Linda again': Ethical, practical and political issues involved in longitudinal research with young men. *Ethics, Place and Environment*, 4(2), 87–100.

McGregor, G. and Mills, M. (2006) Boys and music education: RMXing the curriculum. *Pedagogy, Culture and Society*, 14(2), 221–233.

McLeod, J. (2002). Working out intimacy: Young people and friendship in an age of reflexivity. *Discourse: Studies in the Cultural Politics of Education*, 23(3), 211–226.

Mills, C. (2008) Reproduction and transformation of inequalities in schooling: The transformative potential of the theoretical constructs of Bourdieu. *British Journal of Sociology of Education*, 29(1), 79–89.

Mills, M. (2001) Violence and the signifiers of masculinity. In D. Epstein and M. Mac an Ghaill (eds), *Challenging violence in schools: An issue of masculinities* (pp. 19–51). Buckingham: Open University Press.

Moll, L. and Gonzalez, N. (1997) Teachers as social scientists: Learning about culture from household research. In P. M. Hall (ed.), *Race, ethnicity and multiculturalism: Missouri symposium on research and educational policy*, 1, 89–144. New York: Garland.

Moll, L., Amanti, C., Neffe, C. and Gonzalez, N. (1992) Funds of knowledge for teaching: Using a qualitative approach to connect homes and classrooms. *Theory into Practice*, 32(2), 132–141.

Mouzelis, N. (2007) Habitus and reflexivity: Restructuring Bourdieu's theory of practice. *Sociological Research Online*, 12(6). Online at: www.socresonline.org.uk/12/6/9.html

Perry, E. and Francis, B. (2010) The social gap class for educational achievement: A review of the literature. In *RSA Projects* (pp. 1–21). London: RSA.

Phoenix, A. (2004) Neoliberalism and masculinity: Racialization and the contradictions of schooling for 11-to-14-year-olds. *Youth Society*, 36(2), 227–246.

Reay, D. (2002) Shaun's story: Troubling discourses on white working-class masculinities. *Gender and Education*, 14(3), 221–234.

Reay, D. (2004) Gendering Bourdieu's concepts of capitals? Emotional capital, women and social class. *Theory Culture Society*, 20(6), 57–74.

Reay, D. (2010) Identity-making in schools and classrooms. In M. Wetherall and C. Talpade Mohanty (eds), *The Sage handbook of identities* (pp. 277–294). Los Angeles: Sage Publications.

Salisbury, J. and Jackson, D. (1996) *Challenging macho values: Practical ways of working with adolescent boys*. London: The Falmer Press.

Sayer, A. (2005) *The moral significance of class*. Cambridge: Cambridge University Press.

Select Committee on Education (2014) *Underachievement in Education by White Working Class Children*. 1st Report. Session 2013–2014. UK Parliament. House of Commons. Online at: www.publications.parliament.uk/pa/cm201415/cmselect/cmeduc/142/14202.htm

Skeggs, B. (2004a) *Class, self, culture*. London: Routledge.

Skeggs, B. (2004b) Exchange, value and affect: Bourdieu and 'the self'. *Sociological Review*, 75–95.

Stahl, G. (2013) Habitus disjunctures, reflexivity, and white working-class boys' conceptions of status in learner and social identities. *Sociological Research Online*, 18(3). Online at: www.socresonline.org.uk/18/3/2.html

Stahl, G. (2014) The affront of the aspiration agenda: White working-class male narratives of 'ordinariness' in neoliberal times. *Masculinities and Social Change*, 3(2), 88–118.

Stahl, G. and Dale, P. (2012) Creating positive spaces of learning: DJers and MCers identity work with new literacies. *The Educational Forum*, 76(4), 510–523,

Stahl, G. and Dale, P. (2013) Success on the decks: Working-class boys, education and turning the tables on perceptions of failure. *Gender and Education*, 25(2), 1–16.

Sweetman, P. (2003) Twenty-first century dis-ease? Habitual reflexivity or the reflexive habitus. *The Sociological Review*, 51(4), 528–549.

Thomson, P. (2002) *Schooling the rustbelt kids: Making the difference in changing times*. Crows Nest, Australia: Allen & Unwin.

Woods, P. (1986) *Inside schools: Ethnography in educational research*. New York: Routledge.

Wrench, A., Hammond, C., McCallum, F. and Price, D. (2012) Inspire to aspire: Raising aspirational outcomes through a student well-being curricular focus. *International Journal of Inclusive Education*, 17(9), 1–16.

Yang, Y. (2013) Bourdieu, practice and change: Beyond the criticism of determinism. *Educational Philosophy and Theory*, 45, 1–19.

Zipin, L. (2009) Dark funds of knowledge, deep funds of pedagogy: Exploring boundaries between lifeworlds and schools. *Discourse: Studies in the Cultural Politics of Education*, 30(3), 317–331.

Zipin, L., Sellar, S. and Hattam, R. (2012) Countering and exceeding 'capital': A 'funds of knowledge' approach to re-imagining community. *Discourse: Studies in the Cultural Politics of Education*, 33(2), 179–192.

Appendices

Appendix A

Table A1 Thematic organisation of interviews and focus groups

Stage and theme(s)	Methods	Tools	Various topics and aim
(Preliminary observation phase)			
1 Life history approach	Semi-structured interview	Pictures of occupational masculinities	Family, national identity To understand students life experiences
2 Schooling experience	Semi-structured interview	Music: Eminem's *The Way I Am*	School experience, respect in school, parent involvement, bullying, teachers, etc.
3 Masculinity perceptions	Focus groups and/or semi-structured interview	Pictures of working-class masculinities	Primary socialisation, employment and masculinity, style/dress To capitalise on 'student voice' and enable boys to rationalise and explain engagement with learning and attitudes toward schooling
4 Social class and education	Semi-structured interview	Pictures of masculinity variations	To gain knowledge of social class positioning, 'lived' social class experiences
5 Power and aggression	Semi-structured interview	Pictures of media masculinities and kinesthetic activity	Positions of power/autonomy, sexuality/homophobia, priorities To understand the boys' conception of power in their lives
6 Racism, police, dilemma	Focus groups and/or semi-structured interview	Film: *Football Factory*	Racism, police, response to film To understand how they perceive elements of social control
7 Influences	Semi-structured interview	Worksheet and drawing activity	Conceptions of admired students, conceptions of each other, individual questions based on interviews 1–6 To facilitate dialogue on points of confusion in previous interviews

Appendix B

Table B1 Labelling and setting in schools and household structure

	Year	Talented and gifted	Science sets	Maths sets	English sets	FSM (free school meal) status	Household structure (M = Mother, F = Father, B = Brother, S = Sister)
London Academy							
Thomas	11	N	4 BTEC	3	2	N	M, F
Billy	11	N	4 BTEC	4	4	Y	M, B
Terry	11	N	4 BTEC	3	3	Y	
Luke	11	N	2 GCSE	3	2	Y	M, B
Phillip	11	N	4 BTEC	2	3	N	M, F
Mitchell	11	N	2 GCSE	4	3	Y	M, S, B, B, B
Alen	11	N	3 GCSE	3	2	Y	M, F, S
Frankie	11	N	3 GCSE	3	3	N	M, F, B
George	10	N	2 GCSE	2	2	N	M, F, S
Harry	10	N	1 GCSE	1	1	N	M, S, S, S
Keith	10	Y	3 BTEC	1	2	N	M, F, B
Connor	10	N	4 BTEC	3	4	N	M, F, S, B, B
Liam	10	N	4 BTEC	4	4	N	M, F, S, B
Lewis	10	Y	4 BTEC	1	1	N	M, S
Ryan	10	N	4 BTEC	4	4	Y	M, F, B
World School							
Amin	10	N	middle	middle	middle	Y	M, F
Calum	10	N	middle	bottom	Top	Y	M, F, S
Ronnie	10	N	Top	middle	middle	Y	M
Ben	10	N	Top	bottom	Top	N	M, F, S, S
PRU							
Greg	11	N/A	N/A	N/A	N/A	N/A	M, F, B, B, S
Alfie	11	N/A	N/A	N/A	N/A	N/A	M, F, S
Dan	11	N/A	N/A	N/A	N/A	N/A	
Jake	11	N/A	N/A	N/A	N/A	N/A	

Appendix C

Table C1 Free school meal (FSM) status and parental occupation

	Year	FSM status	Mother's level of education	Mother's occupation	Father's level of education	Father's occupation
London Academy						
Thomas	11	N	A-levels	NHS secretary	Drop-out	Salesman
Billy	11	Y	Unknown	Long-term disability	N/A	N/A
Terry	11	Y	Unknown	Full-time mother	Plumbing qualification	Plumber
Luke	11	Y	Unknown	Teaching assistant	Unknown	Self-employed
Phillip	11	N	No GCSEs	Cleaner	City and Guilds training course	Carpenter
Mitchell	11	Y	GCSE	Baker	Drop-out	Lorry driver
Alen	11	Y	University	Unemployed	Unknown	Unemployed
Frankie	11	N	Unknown	Teaching assistant	Unknown	Printer delivery
George	10	N	Unknown	Music studio manager	Unknown	London Underground operator
Harry	10	N	College	Teaching assistant	College	Council worker
Keith	10	N	College	Secretary	Military training	Draughtsman
Connor	10	N	Unknown	Admin	Unknown	Lorry driver
Liam	10	N	Unknown	Full-time mother	Unknown	Scaffolder
Lewis	10	N	Unknown	Childminder	Unknown	Disc jockey
Ryan	10	Y	Unknown	Teaching assistant	Unknown	Lift engineer
World School						
Amin	10	Y	College	Unemployed	Electrician qualification	Unemployed
Calum	10	Y	None	Unemployed	None	Supervisor
Ronnie	10	Y	None	Launderette worker	City and Guilds training course	Redundant
Ben	10	N	Unknown	Full-time mother	Plumbing qualification	Plumber
Pupil Referral Unit (PRU)						
Greg	11	N/A	Unknown	Unknown	Unknown	Unknown
Alfie	11	N/A	Expelled from school	Unemployed	O-Levels	Unemployed
Dan	11	N/A	O-Levels	School office secretary	Unknown	Lorry driver
Jake	11	N/A	N/A	N/A	N/A	N/A

Index